Walt Disney World® with Disabilities

Unofficial in-depth planning guide for fun, comfort & safety

Includes tips & info you won't find anywhere else!

By

Stephen Ashley

Walt Disney World® with Disabilities
Unofficial in-depth planning guide for fun, comfort & safety
By Stephen Ashley

Visit us on the Web at http://www.Diz-Abled.com
Email us at info@Diz-Abled.com

Disclaimer

We are not affiliated, associated, authorized, endorsed by, or in any way officially connected with The Walt Disney Company, Disney Enterprises, Inc., or any of its subsidiaries or its affiliates. The official Disney web site is available at www.disney.com. All Disney parks, attractions, lands, shows, event names, etc. are registered trademarks of The Walt Disney Company.

Walt Disney World® is a registered trademark of The Walt Disney Company. This book refers to various Disney copyrighted trademarks, characters, marks and registered marks owned by the Walt Disney Company, Disney Enterprises, Inc., and other trademark owners. The use in this book of trademarked names and images is strictly for editorial purposes, and no commercial claim to their use, or suggestion of sponsorship or endorsement, is made by the authors or publisher. Those words or terms that the authors and publisher have reason to believe are trademarks are designated as such by the use of initial capitalization, where appropriate. However no attempt has been made to identify or designate all words or terms to which trademark or other proprietary rights may exist. Nothing contained herein is intended to express a judgment on, or affect the validity of legal status of, any word or term as a trademark, service mark, or other proprietary mark.

While all attempts have been made to verify information provided in this publication, neither the author nor the publisher assumes any responsibility for errors, omissions, or contrary interpretation of the subject matter herein. This publication is not intended for use as a source of legal, medical advice or any other type of professional advice. The information contained herein may be subject to change at any time. The purchaser of this publication assumes responsibility for the use of these materials and information.

Please call your destination in advance to receive the most up-to-date information. Though we have researched and done our best to be accurate in every way, we do not guarantee accuracy. The author and publisher assume no responsibility or liability whatsoever on the behalf of any purchaser or reader of these materials. Any perceived slights of specific people or organizations are unintentional. Any stated opinions are the authors' alone, unless otherwise noted, and do not represent The Walt Disney Company or anyone else.

This book provides information on our experiences and that of others. We are not medical doctors and therefore cannot make recommendations that are health-related. We are not responsible for anyone's experiences at Disney World or Disneyland. We are not making any promises or endorsing or condemning any products, businesses, rides, hotels or entertainment. This book is intended to provide meaningful assistance to persons with disabilities, however the reader should verify for himself/herself their ability to engage in various activities with their particular condition prior to undertaking any activity.

We will name conditions that could be of concern on each ride. These conditions are not a complete list. By reading this book you agree that we are in no way responsible for your choice to participate or not to participate in any mentioned activity, and/or for anything resulting from that choice. There may be other conditions that we do not mention where caution should be used, or where you should avoid a ride, entertainment or exhibit. We do not claim that these are complete lists. Disney World may make changes to the attractions, rides, restaurants and stores. We do not guarantee that this book contains the latest information. Everything in this book is subject to change, and there may be things that are not covered here. Call in advance of your trip to get updates on anything that could be relevant to you.

If you have health issues, before going to Disney please consult with your doctor or licensed healthcare professional to determine what is safe for you. Do not make choices based on the authority of the material in this book. Everyone is different. What has been safe for us and others mentioned in this book may not have the same effect on you. What feels acceptable to us may feel different to you.

This book contains links to various sites. We are not responsible for the content, software, or the privacy practices of such websites. We are not responsible for the products, claims, information or the links to other sites on these sites. The Linked Sites are provided for your convenience only, and you access them at your own risk.

This book has coupons and also mentions a variety of companies. We are not responsible for the products, claims, information or service of those companies. We are not endorsing any companies, services or products. The coupons and information on these companies are for your convenience only and you contact and use them at your own risk.

The information and opinions expressed in this book cites our personal experience. Wherever personal opinions and testimonials are expressed, be aware that your experiences will not necessarily be the same.

This book is not tailored to address compliance by The Walt Disney Company, Disney Enterprises, Inc., or any of its subsidiaries or its affiliates, with the Americans With disabilities Act (ADA) statute requirements and accordingly does not address the same. This book makes no comments as to the compliance of Disney World to the American With Disabilities Act.

Use of this book signifies your agreement to the above terms.

ISBN 13: 978-0-615-16760-2

Welcome!
Inside your guide you will find:

✓ The most in-depth and full descriptions you'll find in any book of the physical "feel" and emotional experiences of Disney World attractions to help you decide if an attraction is right for you.

✓ Warnings & alerts you won't see elsewhere about things that can impact people with disabilities. One popular attraction, for example, unexpectedly pokes you in the back. We tell you how folks with back pain can prepare and enjoy the attraction anyway, while avoiding this jab to the back.

✓ Extensive tips on how to participate in attractions with greater comfort even if you have disabilities and concerns.

✓ In-depth information & alerts for various fears, anxieties and emotional concerns including claustrophobia, fear of the dark and discomfort with violence.

✓ Warnings, tips and support information for people dealing with a variety of issues including:

- Pain
- Back & neck problems
- Mobility issues
- Heart conditions
- Vertigo & dizziness
- Diabetes
- Dietary issues
- Hearing impairment
- Visual impairment
- Fears, phobias and mental health issues
- Chronic Fatigue Syndrome
- Temperomandibular Joint Disorder (TMJ)
- Fibromyalgia
- Allergies & chemical sensitivities (including fragrances, pesticides & mold)
- High blood pressure
- Joint & muscle pain
- Motion sickness
- Epilepsy
- Weakness
- Oxygen use
- Overstimulation & hyperactivity

✓ Tons of tips for dealing with disabilities in the parks, attractions, transportation and resorts—many of which you won't see anywhere else!

✓ Extensive information about wheelchair use at Disney World with resource information.

✓ Information on taking and using medicines and medical equipment in the parks.

✓ Extensive information on diet issues in the parks, resorts and entertainment area restaurants, with contact numbers around Disney World for help with your specific dietary needs.

✓ Allergy information including what rides have fragrances and smoke pumped in.

✓ Advice on how to have your specific needs met in the Disney resorts and parks.

*This guide is not intended to cover all possible conditions or sensitivities. You are urged to use your own judgment and discretion.

Walt Disney World® with Disabilities

Unofficial in-depth planning guide for fun, comfort & safety

Dear Reader,

Walt Disney World is an awesome place where staff works hard to see to the comfort and safety of their guests, especially their disabled guests. Still, for years we went to Disney World without the benefit of in-depth information from anyone who really understood firsthand the challenges we faced. The available pamphlets and books never touched on all kinds of things we really needed to know (and eventually learned) in order to plan with confidence for a safe, comfortable and relaxing vacation.

Over the years we encountered many issues and situations that caused physical pain, discomfort or stress. After several years of research and experience, Disney has become smooth sailing and a joyful getaway for us, and we want to share what we've learned with you! We bring you all the extensive insights, tips and information we've gathered that have given us the edge when we travel to Disney World.

Our goal is to help you enjoy all the wonders and fun Disney has to offer without stressing or worrying about what you will encounter. We also hope to help you come very prepared so that your time will be spent having a carefree vacation, as opposed to researching, seeking help, recovering after doing something you shouldn't have or missing things you wished you had tried.

Disney World, even with disabilities, can be a blast! Enjoy the book and, most of all, enjoy your trip!

Stephen

P.S. Come join us on our website! We have big plans to fill it with new and important information for you. We'll continually post updates to our book, and we'll offer a forum where you'll be able to connect with other diz-abled people to share information and tips. We'll check in regularly to answer your questions. The site will include photos, videos of rides and of the resorts, and information on the other Disney theme areas such as Downtown Disney.

Visit us at:

www.Diz-Abled.com

We look forward to meeting you there!

TABLE OF CONTENTS

Introduction

We are true Disney fans. We've been going to Disney World for over 30 years, with much more frequency since we moved to Florida over 17 years ago. I'll never forget the thrill of going through the Disney gates in our car that first time.

We've gone so consistently over the years that our friends and family tease us good-heartedly about it. Actually, it's been our place to rest, relax, escape and enjoy. With the disabling health problems Sarah has had to deal with, we have found it to be the easiest and most pleasant place to vacation. In general, we find Disney to be a company that has made it their business to make those with health issues and disabilities feel at home.

On Disney property, Sarah is able to travel almost anywhere in a wheelchair, be made comfortable in her room, take care of her medical needs, enjoy the entertainment and eat within her dietary limitations. In the beginning years there was a lot of trial and error in the parks and resorts because of her health challenges. Over the years we've learned the ropes, which has made it easier and easier for us to relax and enjoy ourselves.

My own issues were not as severe as Sarah's, but we've had to take into account my back, neck and dietary issues related to blood sugar. For Sarah, over time we have had to deal with a whole host of issues including joint and muscle pain, neck and back problems, chronic fatigue, muscle weakness, vertigo, blood pressure and heart issues, fibromyalgia, dietary needs, allergies and chemical sensitivities, severe TMJ, sudden infections, dealing with the heat and the need to stay out of the sun, wheelchair use, mobility issues, sleep disorders, a torn ligament in the ankle, and even claustrophobia, which she developed after being trapped in an elevator.

Despite all these problems we have been able to really enjoy Disney. We realized that we had a lot of information and tips that would be useful to others that we have not seen in any other book. We gradually learned all the ins and outs of enjoying Disney World despite disabilities.

As we tried to prepare for upcoming trips in the past, we found very few resources for those with disabilities. We found those that did exist to be vague and incomplete. Also, the majority of what we saw out there was written by people who did not have the disabilities and issues they were writing about. While we did find some useful information, we felt that it didn't come close to helping us discern what rides to go on, what to avoid and how to have the best trip possible.

In the beginning we had to grill cast members (this is what Disney calls its employees) and research each attraction in the park as we went along. That was time-consuming and at times frustrating. The cast members do try to be helpful in any way they can. However, since they did not have the disability issues I was asking about, they simply were not aware of things that Sarah or I would have noticed in an attraction. If there still wasn't enough information to decide if Sarah could handle an attraction, I tried it for her. I was nominated guinea pig or test dummy! Even then, it wasn't until Sarah got on herself that we knew whether it was going to be okay or not. That feeling of not quite knowing made for some tension that detracted from the fun in the beginning years.

There was a learning curve, and even some experiences that turned out to be painful for Sarah. Over the years it's become so much easier for us to go and enjoy Disney now that we know what to expect. We want to give you the benefit of what we've found so that you will enjoy the daylights out of your trip! We'll give you in-depth information, tips and tactics from our personal experiences. We'll also include feedback and information we've gathered from other disabled Disney travelers with a variety of disabilities including various phobias.

There are a few rides that we have not able to experience first-hand, such as some children's rides or a few of the physically roughest attractions. For these attractions we will include information that we've gathered from extensive research. This includes reports from Disney guests with disabilities.

Our goal is to help you plan a great vacation even while dealing with disabilities. Going to Disney should be fun and relaxing, and we'd like to help you have that experience. We'll go as in-depth as possible discussing the feel of the attractions and the issues related to them. We will share tips for enjoying the parks in depth. We will also touch on the restaurants within the parks, and give some general tips for the Disney resorts.

We want to give you a sense of just how harsh or gentle various attractions are. This is challenging to accomplish because perceptions can be so different from one person to the other. Also, within a particular ailment, there can be a vast range of severity and symptoms. We will mention our personal experiences, and we will also share the opinions of other people with disabilities and special needs.

Remember that everyone is different, so what might feel one way to you may feel like something different to us or to others. For example, you may have different pain thresholds, tolerance for height and motion, sensation experiences and perceptions. Ultimately we recommend that you observe and obey the warnings that Disney posts, and if you're still uncertain after seeking the advice of Disney cast members, have someone you trust try the attraction, or skip it altogether. You're better safe than sorry!

Some of the people mentioned in this book participated in attractions despite the fact that Walt Disney World warns against it for people with their conditions. We are not recommending that you do this. The warnings and recommendations given by Walt Disney World should always be taken as the final word. We are simply sharing experiences. Please always consult your doctor about how to stay safe with your condition, and observe and obey all of the Walt Disney World warnings.

We realize we can't address every issue for every disability that anyone may have, but we will do our best to address the most common concerns, and to give you the resources to get any other answers you may personally need. We can give you plenty of relevant information—some of which you won't see anywhere else—to help you make your plans and choices.

Also keep in mind that Disney regularly makes changes in the parks and throughout the Disney World property. For example, they open and close attractions, alter and update attractions, open and close restaurants, change menus in restaurants, add or remove shows and entertainment and alter the stores. Of course, this means that everything in this book is subject to change, and that there may be things that are not covered here. Call in advance of your trip to get updates on anything that could be relevant to you. The Disney staff is more than willing to help!

Although this book contains a wealth of information that you will not see elsewhere, there are some good books out there with general planning information that can be helpful. Our favorite is *The Unofficial Guide to Walt Disney World®*, which we suggest as a useful adjunct to this book. Also, pick up the disability guidebooks that Disney offers to see their specific recommendations and restrictions for attractions.

We hope to expand this book over time to include even more tips for all of the individual resorts, other Disney entertainment and off-site attractions, and we would love your input. We would also love to hear your opinions, corrections or suggestions for improving future versions of this book. Please note that by emailing us, you are agreeing to allow us to reprint your email or a portion of it in our books. We can keep it anonymous if you prefer. Please feel free to email us at:

info@Diz-Abled.com

Finally we wish to give thanks to God for enabling us to write this book, and for all of the many wonderful blessings He gives us! Having Him in our lives is amazing and wonderful beyond what I can even express. We hope this book is a blessing to you as it has been for us.

Walt Disney World Overview

To put things in perspective, Disney World is twice the size of Manhattan. It's a city with a culture all its own. You can take your vacation there with a wide variety of experiences and never leave the grounds. Walt Disney World is spread over 43 square miles with beautifully planned and maintained grounds. Overall, we find it to be beautiful, clean, well run and pleasant.

Stepping on Disney World property is kind of like leaving reality and entering into a different, more ideal world. Everything revolves around your good time (along with your safety). We find most of the Disney staffers to be cheerful, polite and extremely helpful. This makes the experience even more restful and pleasant.

Keep in mind, though, that the cast members (Disney's term for staff members) are human beings. There has been the occasional cast member we felt could have done better or behaved more politely. Despite the extensive Disney training they receive, every so often we've had a less-than-ideal encounter. This can usually be remedied by asking for a manager if necessary, or moving on to someone or somewhere else in Disney World for better service and support.

There are four main parks at Disney World, and we will cover these in this book. At the end of the book we will offer some pointers for making the most of and enjoying the resorts. You will find some important tips in this book that you will not see anywhere else!

Here are some of the basics needed to navigate Disney World.

Transportation

© Disney

Monorail in front of Disney's Polynesian Resort

Monorail – The monorail in itself is really a pleasant ride, and we find it worth taking just for the experience. There are two loops for the monorail from the Transportation and Ticket Center. The first loop goes to the Epcot Center and back, and the other one has multiple stops: the Magic Kingdom, the Grand Floridian Resort, the Polynesian Resort and the Contemporary Resort. (This is the really interesting stop that actually goes inside and through the lobby of the resort.)

You can change monorail trains at the Transportation and Ticket Center to travel between Epcot and the Magic Kingdom. If you are in a wheelchair or ECV (electric convenience vehicle or scooter), a cast member will show you where to board the special monorail car designed for wheelchairs. When the monorail comes to a stop, a cast member will put a portable ramp down so you can ride into the train car. They will direct you, if you need help, to move your chair into the correct position. You can then stay in your wheelchair or transfer to a monorail seat. If you stay in your wheelchair or ECV, you will have a horizontal grab bar so that you can steady yourself. Be sure to lock your wheelchair in place.

The cars are spacious, and there are large windows on both sides. The seats are hard benches with high backs. The ramps up to the monorail, and down as you depart, are wide but quite steep. Non-electric wheelchair users will find this extremely challenging.

The motion of the monorail is fairly smooth, but there is a gentle and consistent jerking. Sarah has problems with any kind of motion that jostles her jaw because of TMJ. She is able to manage the monorail without too much difficulty, but by the time we reach our destination it becomes uncomfortable to her jaw, and she's happy to get off. Most folks will not even be aware of this motion or feel that it is uncomfortable at all.

Buses – Disney has an excellent bus system. Each hotel has bus stops with continuous bus transportation to all of the Disney parks and hot spots.

Most Disney buses are equipped for at least two non-folding wheelchair passengers. When we go to the bus stop, we get to the front of the crowd by the curb so that the bus driver can spot us as upon arriving. This may feel like cutting in front of others, but the bus driver must board wheelchair passengers first, before letting the rest of the riders on. We have not had any complaints from non-wheelchair riders, but we have gotten an occasional funny look. Yet this is the procedure for wheelchairs, and so we don't let it get to us!

Once we are situated in front of the crowd, the bus driver usually notices us, but we also wave at them as they do occasionally miss us. Also, depending where you are boarding, there could be a number of buses stopping that go to different destinations. It may be necessary to let the bus driver know you want to board their particular bus.

Once they see you, the bus driver must situate the bus so that they can let down a ramp from the back/side entrance of the bus. You may have to back up to let the ramp unfold out of the bus and onto the ground. The bus driver will instruct you how to proceed from there.

Please keep in mind that some motorized chairs and ECVs are just too wide or too long for the standard bus lift of 32" x 48". Your chair must fit into the lift without it being forced. If you are using an oversized chair that will be too large for the buses, consider renting an accessible van for the trip.

Some buses require you to back in with an ECV or wheelchair. Some allow you to board facing forward. If you are backing in, you will need to be able to turn your head and look behind you. Sarah is unable to turn her head because of neck pain, so she gets off the chair and I back it in for her. If this isn't a possibility, the bus driver will usually coach you back, telling you which way to steer.

Once on the bus, the bus driver will direct you to park your chair. If the parking is not perfect, some of the drivers will actually lift the chair into a better position. However, some of the drivers can't or won't do that. They might also take the control bar and navigate the chair into place. They then tie down the chair with some straps.

Once it's parked, they prefer that you do not stay in your wheelchair. ECVs and wheelchairs are just not as stable and secure as a bus seat. However, staying in your wheelchair is technically allowed. You can also choose to transfer to a seat nearby. The bus seats are usually hard bench seats with high backs.

The best things about the buses are that they are free and they allow you the freedom of going just about anywhere on Disney property with a wheelchair. Also, despite the occasional sour personality, the bus drivers tend to be really helpful and friendly.

The downside of the buses is that they can get very crowded, especially at the beginning and end of park hours. Depending on your destination and start point, you may need to have patience through several stops as people get on and off. There will often be guests standing in the aisle, and that can uncomfortable for those with claustrophobia or allergies. Also, when the bus approaches or other buses leave the area you are waiting in, there can be a lot of gas fumes.

Boats – I read a statistic that Disney has the seventh largest boat fleet in the world. I haven't verified this, but I do believe it's possible. Several of the resorts and parks have boat services. A few of the resorts have boats that go to a park, Downtown Disney, Boardwalk, and other resorts. The destinations are limited, so check with your resort to see if they offer boat service and where they go. There is also boat service inside Epcot that takes you across the lagoon.

Many boats are wheelchair accessible. We very much enjoy the open-sided boats, and whenever possible, we choose them over buses. The boats are a pleasant way to enjoy the nature of Disney and some great views while getting to your destination.

Some boats are enclosed with a large seating area inside and a small outside seating area in the back. We find these boats uncomfortable and only take them if necessary. Unless it's a very cool day, the outdoor seating area in the back of the boat can be uncomfortably hot. Depending on the sun's position, it can beat down on you for your entire trip. We also find that there are heavy gas fumes in this outside area. The indoor area is usually not well cooled and there is no hope of a breeze. Frankly it's miserable in warmer weather, but hey—you're in Florida!

In any case, you may find yourself onboard one of these boats at some point during your visit to Disney. Once aboard, you may be asked to navigate into the indoor area, or you may be asked to park in the outdoor section in the back of the boat. If we have to park outside in the back, we leave the chair and try to find seats in the indoor section. Although it's not well cooled inside, it's cooler than outdoors in the full sun, with fewer gas fumes as you move further toward the front of the boat. Those who are sensitive may wish to bring a cloth to breathe through.

To board, we usually try to get in front of the crowd so the boat driver can see us. This is not always possible with the boat queue lines, but when it is, it allows the driver to board us first.

Boarding is accomplished with the boat driver placing a ramp from the dock to the boat. On some boats you will just drive right in and go straight to your spot. Others require some maneuvering. The boat cast member will direct you.

> *Tip:* Several times we've had a boat driver tell us we did not need the ramp, even as the boat was bobbing and the dock was several inches higher or lower than the boat! Sarah was very adamant that the ramp was necessary, and they always gave in. I suspect they were tired of carrying the heavy ramp. It's a good idea to insist on the ramp for safety and to avoid jolts.

At times Sarah has had trouble backing the chair out of the boat, as she was unable to turn her head to see behind her. Usually I do it for her. If you must do it yourself and find it difficult, remember to take your time and ask the cast member for assistance. They can coach you on how to steer. Don't get stressed. The other guests will wait.

We recently heard that the newer ECVs that you rent from Disney are unable to board some of the boats in the parks because of their design. Apparently these vehicles are lower to the ground for the sake of stability.

Crowd Size

We generally hate big crowds, so we try our best to visit during the slower times. Crowds make it more difficult to navigate an ECV, the lines and waits are much longer and it's just less peaceful for us. We realize that crowds may not bother some folks. For others, schedules may only permit traveling to Disney during peak periods. We feel it's still worth going even if you're going in a peak crowd time.

Although Disney has some recognizable peaks and valleys in park attendance, we have found it to be less predictable of late. We've gone when it was supposed to be very quiet and found it mobbed. Sometimes Disney will run special programs so that a typically slow time will become busier. Still, Disney is Disney (deep, huh?), and we manage to have a great time even with crowds.

You can be pretty certain that most of the summer when kids are off from school will be very crowded. Long weekends as well as holidays can also be mobbed.

> *Tip:* There is a website (www.touringplans.com) that predicts crowds in each park for each day of the year! They use a lot of different variables, which they explain on their site. It's definitely worth taking a look. Choose the link on the left-hand menu that says "Crowd Calendar."

Tip: We've recently heard about a site that's getting good reviews: www.tourguidemike.com. When you join, they will actually plot an itinerary for you based on crowd data for the dates of your trip. We hear that they do an amazing job at helping Disney guests avoid any long waits, even during peak crowd periods. The site was created by Mike Hewell, who has been a VIP tour guide for about 10 years and is the owner of Michael's VIPs. The price for this service is currently $21.95.

Again, during the busiest times you can expect longer lines and waits everywhere. This means that you will be participating in fewer attractions on any given day, so you need to factor this into your planning. Decide which attractions are an absolute must, and go for those first.

Wheelchairs & ECVs

The "ECVs" we refer to in this book include the electric scooters that are available for rent in the Disney World parks, as well as any other electric wheelchair or scooter that you own or rent from an outside vendor.

"Wheelchairs" mentioned in this book are the non-electric standard wheelchairs that require "people power." These are far less expensive than ECVs, which at the time of this writing run about $30 a day from private companies and $35 at the Disney parks.

Aside from cost, the electric vehicles make for a far better experience for everyone, provided the rider is able to drive them. When you are navigating a huge park, having to push a wheelchair everywhere can be exhausting. The freedom the electric scooter gives the driver and the potential pusher is itself a huge perk.

You must be 18 to rent an ECV, although we hear that some outside companies may bend that rule for experienced ECV users. For those with pain or fatigue who are younger than 18 or unable to drive a scooter, using a manual wheelchair can be better than walking.

Should I rent a wheelchair rather than walk the park? Don't rule it out too quickly! Even if you don't require a wheelchair in your daily life, you may want to consider using one at Disney World. If you are dealing with any kind of pain, weakness, heart problems or fatigue, the chair can make your visit a far better experience.

The parks are huge, and the walking alone is extensive. Then there's the standing and waiting in lines. On a busy park day you can stand in one line for as much as an hour or even 1 ½ hours for a single attraction. You will be on your feet the majority of the day, either walking or standing. If that sounds strenuous or difficult to you, we strongly suggest you get an ECV.

For years we never even considered the idea of getting a wheelchair for Sarah. Although she had back and joint pain along with chronic fatigue, the idea never occurred to us. I also suspect she didn't want to see herself as disabled, and didn't want to succumb to a wheelchair. At the parks we just got a GAC (Guest Assistance Card), which helped in various ways, such as allowing us to wait out of the sun. Sarah would sit on the ground as we waited in lines. By the end the day she would have excruciating back, neck, foot, knee and joint pain, exhaustion and a migraine.

On one of our trips, she came to Orlando with a torn ligament in her ankle. Rather than cancel the trip we ordered an ECV. At the end of the first day, we realized that her conditions were far less flared up than they normally would be. Now she gets a scooter every time. Her Disney trips are much less painful and exhausting, and far more fun. The scooter has given her freedom, mobility, less pain and has helped her conserve her energy. As for me, I wait for her trips to the ladies room, so I can sit in her seat!

The ECV also made things easier in other ways. Sarah's illnesses are not apparent when you look at her. When she was in a wheelchair, it took far less effort and explaining to engage the cooperation of the cast members for assistance with issues like needing to wait out of the sun.

If you know you need a wheelchair or ECV and have one that you can from home, definitely do so. If you're not certain about needing one, we suggest you err on the side of caution and rent an ECV.

When we come to Disney World, Sarah now rents an ECV for the entire stay from an outside company. Not only is the scooter valuable at the parks, but it also helps at the huge, sprawling Disney resorts and entertainment areas such as Downtown Disney. At this writing, renting from an outside vendor is usually less expensive than renting at the park. Since you cannot reserve a chair from the parks in advance, there is a chance that they'll be sold out once you get there. By reserving a chair from an outside company before your trip, you're assured that you'll have an ECV.

Disney is very wheelchair friendly. However, the newer the park and resort, the better the wheelchair accessibility. Magic Kingdom is the oldest park and was built before the current-day focus on wheelchair accessibility. They have some walkways and bathrooms that are quite tight and a bit challenging for maneuvering wheelchairs. Also, far fewer attractions in this park can be experienced in your wheelchair than in the newer parks.

That said, we feel that Disney goes all out to make things as accessible as possible for those in wheelchairs. For example, almost all the Disney transportation is set up to take wheelchairs and ECVs. It gives visitors freedom that they might not have on foot.

ECVs usually have steering like that of a bicycle. The speed is controlled by applying pressure with the hand to a lever. These vehicles can go pretty fast and take some getting used to. Be sure to start slow and practice for a few minutes before heading out into the crowds.

> *Tip:* Lower your speed dial when maneuvering around people or getting on and off rides and transportation. If you keep your speed dial at its maximum, the chairs will often jerk forward and go faster than you planned, even if you are hardly applying any pressure to your speed control. You run the risk of hitting people, walls and other objects. Keep your speed dial low and then you can always move it up when you are free and clear of obstacles.

> *Tip:* Sarah has had weakness and pain in her hands and wrists. She has found the control levers on the ECVs in the park to be a bit more tight and uncomfortable to control than the scooters she gets from an outside company (Care Medical—see below). In a pinch she can manage the ECV, but the one she rents from an outside company is more comfortable for her. People without hand and wrist pain and with normal hand strength won't notice the difference.

The Disney ECV seats have a vinyl covering and are fairly firm. The seat backs are pretty straight. There is a basket that can be a great relief, as you won't have to carry anything. If your chair is vinyl, be sure to bring something to cover the seat in the hot weather, as these seats can get very hot and sticky.

Care Medical has scooters that are fabric covered. They may feel more comfortable to some people than the vinyl, as they are softer and feel more "cushiony" on the seat and back. The downside to this chair is that if it rains, the fabric can get soaked. These scooters also have baskets.

> *Tip:* We always take two large garbage bags with us to the park to cover the seat and the seat back, should it rain. If you don't have garbage bags with you, you can use two poncho raincoats that you can buy inexpensively almost anywhere on Disney property. Just make sure that the ponchos don't hang over and get caught under the tires. You can have the poncho cover the handlebars as well. You may also want to take along a shower cap to cover the control unit on the handlebars.

> *Tip:* With any rental company, ask for the newest scooter available. We have found that older scooters tend to have more problems and are less comfortable. The cushioning on the newer ones is not as worn in and is more comfortable. There can also be newer features that make the chair easier to adjust and use.

There are other companies with similar chairs that please many people. We will list some of them in the following section.

Wheelchair Facts & More Tips

Most of the Disney resorts have a very limited number of manual wheelchairs that you can use for the length of your stay. They are available only on a first-come, first-served basis. There is no charge, but you must put a deposit of $250 on your credit card. If someone takes your chair or you lose it, they will keep your deposit money. We have heard that these chairs are not always in good condition.

You can rent a manual wheelchair at each park, or an ECV if you are 18 or older. There is no way to reserve these in advance. There is a limited number of ECVs inside each park. They are rented on a first-come, first-served basis. The earlier you go to the park and get your ECV, the better your chance of getting one. We have gone mid-day during slow seasons and have been able to rent an ECV, but they can go early during busy times. It's always more likely that there will be manual wheelchairs available.

Problems with your chair: If you are renting an ECV in the park, check it over well when you take possession of it. Ride it in all directions, check the tires and check the power reading to make certain it has been fully charged. If there is anything at all that doesn't seem right, request a different ECV. If the chair breaks and the ECVs have all been sold out at the park, you may not be able to get a replacement. At times if the park is out of replacement ECVs, they may be able to get you one from another park. However, that can take quite a while, so it's a good idea to start out with a fully functioning ECV.

If your chair does have a problem, take it to one of the chair rental or repair centers in the park. We list the locations of these centers for each park in the individual park chapters. If you are unable to get your chair to the repair center, you can let a nearby cast member know. They can call for help.

Keep in mind that Disney will not service wheelchairs that are not their own. If you have a problem with your wheelchair or ECV, even if you are in a park, you will need to call your wheelchair rental company. Be sure you have the name and number of the rental company with you at all times. If your chair has a problem, you will need to call them for service. Sarah has had a flat tire and even lost her key once. (They charged us a service fee for that one.) The outside company can usually come right into the park to help you.

Park hopping with a Disney rental: If you are park hopping (going from one park to another), you must leave your ECV at the park you are leaving. Then you can pick up an ECV at the next park, as long as there is one available. Keep in mind that the next park could be all out of ECVs (a good reason to rent from an outside company). If you plan to pick up another ECV at the next park, you must turn in your ECV at the park you are leaving. They will keep your deposit. Make sure you keep your receipt with you, and bring it to the rental location in the next park to get a new chair.

When you return the chair at the end of your day, Disney will refund your deposit. Also, if you will be leaving a park but returning to that same park that day, they will hold the same ECV for you. Just bring it to a rental location and let them know you will be returning.

There are a limited number of oversized wheelchairs for rent at each of the parks.

Help in and out of wheelchairs: Throughout Disney World and at the attractions, cast members are not allowed to lift guests as they transfer in or out of a wheelchair. They cannot physically lift you to transfer into an attraction seat. However, they can help steady you or the ride vehicle when you transfer, and they can push the wheelchair onto a ride. They can also move your wheelchair or ECV to park it or to bring it to you after the ride is over.

Leaving your chair: When you leave your ECV for any reason, be sure to take your ECV key with you. Also, don't leave anything of value in the ECV, but do leave something that will help you know it's your ECV. There can be many look-alike ECVs. You can leave anything that doesn't have value, such as an empty water bottle or a piece of paper with your name on it. You can also tie a ribbon or string on it to make it easier to identify.

> *Tip:* For many of the attractions at Disney, wheelchair users will be required to go through the regular queues. At times these can be narrow, with barely enough room to maneuver around the corners. In the beginning of her wheelchair use, Sarah and I felt a lot of pressure to have her move quickly so as not to hold up the people behind us. It felt very stressful. Now we have learned to take whatever time is necessary, and for Sarah to do her best without worrying. Although we are always conscious of being polite and considerate, if anyone is annoyed with us, we've decided not to let it get to us.

> *Tip:* If you expect that you will ever need to go in and out of non-automatic doors in your wheelchair or scooter, and you will not always have another person there to hold the door, you need a door stop. Many of the room doors at the Disney resorts don't stay open themselves. Other Disney locations such as Downtown Disney stores have doors that are not electric and won't stay open on their own.

> When we arrive, we call housekeeping and let them know we need something to prop the doors open with. They usually bring over a small wooden door stop that we can tote in the chair basket wherever we go. Since Sarah is mobile, she can drop the door stop to the floor, position it with her foot, and let herself through the door. She does have to bend to pick it up when she's done, which can be a challenge. If you are not able to set up the door jam yourself, you will need to ask for help from folks passing by.

For those who can transfer from a wheelchair or ECV to an attraction seat, it is often a good choice. Sarah finds it easier than having to load the wheelchair on to the attraction vehicle, and at times the regular seating locations are better. For some attractions we have had to wait for some time to get a wheelchair accessible vehicle.

Additionally, for some attractions you cannot experience all of the special effects from a wheelchair. Of course, that can be desirable sometimes.

Usually you can park your chair right in the boarding area. For many attractions you can take it right up to the ride car and transfer. Either way, you can either retrieve your chair yourself after the attraction is done, or you can have a cast member deliver it to the disembarking area or right to you for transfer at the end of the ride. Just let a cast member in the boarding area know if you need this service.

> *Tip:* Be sure to recharge your chair at the end of each day. To be on the safe side, when we go out and about with the wheelchair, we always take the charger that comes with the chair. The newer chargers look like a plain electrical cord. One side plugs into the chair and the other into any normal outlet. It is possible you may get a larger one, but most of them can travel with you in your chair basket.

> If your chair meter starts to look low, you can plug in anywhere you will be hanging out for a while, such as in a restaurant. It may mean transferring to a seat in the restaurant so your chair can be placed near an electrical outlet. Ask a cast member for help in finding an appropriate outlet.

> The only time we've had to do this was when Sarah had forgotten to charge her scooter the night before. We charged it at breakfast and never had a problem. A normally functioning chair should easily take you through a full day and evening at a park, with some charge left over. If that's not happening, call your ECV rental company to exchange your batteries or your ECV.

Be sure to turn the power off on your chair whenever you are not moving for any length of time. This should extend the charge in your battery.

Non-Disney Wheelchair Rental Companies

We always rent from a non-Disney, off-site rental company for the length of our stay. Disney does not offer length of stay rentals, but they will suggest you use an outside company. There are several choices within the Orlando area. Some of these companies are full-service medical supply providers and can rent wheelchairs, ECVs and other medical equipment. The following list includes the company we use, as well as those we have heard about from others. Please note we are not endorsing or recommending any of these companies. This list is provided for your convenience.

Care Medical
www.caremedicalequipment.com
This company can also provide oxygen with a prescription.
Phone (407) 856-2273
Toll free in the U.S and Canada (800) 741-2282

Walker Mobility
www.walkermobility.com
Toll free (888) 726-6837

Scootaround Mobility Solutions
www.scootaround.com
(204) 982-0657
Toll free (888) 441-7575

Wheelchair accessible vans: Many people just use Disney transportation to get around. If you wish to have your own transportation, many wheelchairs can be taken apart and stored in your car trunk. Check with your chair provider. If you need an ECV that can be broken down and stored in a car, be sure to let your wheelchair company know. For many chairs, the heaviest piece will be approximately 40 pounds. That can be quite heavy for some people to manage.

Another option is to ask bell service at your resort to call for a van cab with a wheelchair ramp. It should cost approximately what a regular cab will cost. If you wish to go somewhere that the Disney transportation doesn't service, this is a great alternative. For example, you may wish to go from your resort to another resort for dining.

You can also rent a van that makes it easy to get the whole chair into the car without any dismantling or strength required. Of course, that makes it easy to get everywhere! Here are a couple of locations that do rent out these vehicles:

Wheelchair Getaways
www.wheelchairgetaways.com/florida-orlando.html
(407) 281-8369
Toll free (800) 242-4990

Discount Mobility USA
www.discountmobilityusa.com/van_fleet.html
(407) 438-8010
Toll free (800) 308-2503

If you will be driving, be sure to bring your handicapped driving permit with you so you can use the handicapped parking and get complementary valet parking at the resorts that offer it.

Oxygen Use

If you need oxygen for your flight, you will have to contact your airline to make arrangements.

If you will be using oxygen during your stay and will need supplies and refills, contact your current oxygen supply company and/or your social worker to request a Disney-area company. They can locate a company that would be appropriate for you, and they can pass on all of your insurance information in advance. Since oxygen refills require a prescription, they should be able to share that with the Orlando-area company as well. It's a good idea to bring a copy of your prescription just in case you have an unexpected need during your trip. Be sure to find out which company will be supplying you, and call in advance to confirm the date, location and the items to be delivered.

You can usually arrange for delivery to your hotel, and we have even heard of people being met with their delivery at the airport.

Keep in mind that if you are renting an ECV, you will wish to request one that has a place to hold your oxygen bottle. The Disney parks do not have ECVs with this feature.

Once in the park, you can keep a spare tank at the First Aid Station. They do have oxygen at the parks; however, we don't recommend relying on that. It's important to plan in advance to have the appropriate amount that you need with you.

Disney Dining

The cost of dining within any theme park is generally higher than in the "real world." Disney is no exception. However, we've decided that it's well worth the expense just to enjoy the themes, and in some restaurants the food is really very good. Many of the full-service restaurants are events in themselves. We enjoy the ambiance so much that we consider dining at Disney to be a big part of the fun.

The fast food you'll get in the over-the-counter restaurants, such as burgers and fries, doesn't quite have the flavor of the big fast-food chains. Still, it fills you up and it's adequate for fuel.

As far as dress code goes, even in the upper-scale restaurants your normal park attire is usually fine. We'll note any exceptions.

Full-service & made-to-order restaurants*:* There is a huge variety of dining options throughout the parks, resorts and the Disney grounds. You can make reservations up to 180 days in advance for most of the restaurants even if you won't be staying at a Disney resort. Reservations are necessary for most full-service restaurants, but you can take your chances and try to get in when you get there. We've found that sometimes it works and sometimes not. We've actually gotten in many times on the fly without reservations by just going to the restaurant when it fits into our schedule. However, there have been times when we just couldn't get in that way and had to resort to over-the-counter food.

Advance Reservations *(previously called Priority Seating reservations):* You can make dining reservations several ways. Call:

> ➤ Disney Dining directly at (407) WDW-DINE, or (407) 939-3463.
> ➤ Central Reservations Office, where you call to book your resort. That number is (407) 934-7649.
> ➤ Toll free numbers include:
> (877) 939-3732   In the United States only. Press option 3.
> (800) 828-0228   Press option 3.
> ➤ Spanish toll-free number: (800) 459-5432.

You can also make reservations from your hotel by calling Disney Dining from your room. There is an area within each park where you can call and make dining reservations. Ask a cast member to direct you to the call location when you enter the park. You can also go right to the restaurant to make a reservation. In addition to park dining, Disney Dining Reservations will take care of you for most restaurants on Disney property, including those found in Downtown Disney and the Boardwalk.

For the majority of the restaurants at Disney, the reservations you make are called "Advance Seating" or, formerly, "Priority Seating" reservations. They do not work like regular restaurant reservations. They do not reserve you a table at the exact time of your reservation. What they do is:

- Guarantee you a seat.
- Guarantee that you will be seated ahead of walk-ins.

- Give you the first seat available.

When you are given your reservation, you receive a confirmation number. Your name is placed on the schedule. We always write it down and take it with us; however, we've never needed it to date. We always take it, though, just in case of a mix-up; we have heard of others who have needed it on rare occasions.

It's a good idea to arrive 15-20 minutes before your reservation if you hope to be seated around your reservation time. Keep in mind that at times it could take even longer to be seated. Occasionally we've been escorted right in. In our experience the wait is not usually more than 10-20 minutes, but there have been several exceptions. In fact, we've waited as long as an hour at Ohana's in the Polynesian Resort. If you want a particular seating area such as a window seat, you may wish to arrive even earlier.

When you arrive at the restaurant, check in with the hostess. If they can seat you immediately, they will. Of course, those ahead of you with reservations will be seated first. If there is no seating available when you check in, you will be asked to wait for the next available table. There is usually some kind of wait area with seating. Some of these areas serve drinks and appetizers.

If a restaurant is completely booked with advance reservations, they will not take walk-ins.

There are times when we have not been able to make it to our reservation. There is no penalty or problem with that for most restaurants. Disney expects some no-shows and works it into their system. If you can, call and cancel so someone else can take your place. If not, don't worry. However, there are a few restaurants where you actually pay in advance. Canceling or not showing up can mean a cancellation or penalty fee, or even the entire amount being charged to your credit card. There are very few restaurants that do this, and your reservations agent will tell you at the time of booking.

> *Tip:* If you call for a reservation and can't get in, or can't get a time you prefer, try calling back again. Often we will take a less desirable reservation, but we may call daily to check back for an opening. People cancel and change their reservations all the time. We often end up with just what we wanted.

If you are in a wheelchair, have a service animal, have allergies or special food requirements or if you have any other special need, be sure to let them know when you make your reservation. Many of the full-service restaurants will go out of their way to meet your needs. If you wish, you can call the restaurant in advance and speak with a chef. Just call the main park number and ask to be connected to the restaurant. When you're connected, ask to speak to a chef. We find that most chefs are accessible, friendly and helpful.

The main number for all the parks is (407) 824-2222.

See the section on allergies & special diets for more information on dining in the full-service restaurants.

Fast-food & over-the-counter restaurants: Most of the fast-food and over-the-counter restaurants, particularly in the parks, don't have any leeway to take special requests for dietary needs. Sometimes they can make substitutions, such as replacing something with fruit. You may also be able to have something left off of the meal. For example, vegetarians may be able to get a chicken salad without the chicken at some locations. If you have a special request and a cast member says it can't be done, try asking for a manager. Sometimes they are willing and able to go further for you than one of their underlings!

Many of the fast-food and over-the-counter restaurants have special foods already available such as gluten-free, no sugar added, sugar-free, low-fat, low-carb and low-sodium. Many of the restaurants offer at least one vegetarian or vegan dish. Some of them have kosher meals as well. You'll find a fresh fruit cart in each of the theme parks.

Most of these restaurants will be able to give you a listing of the ingredients in their food options if you request it.

The menus do change periodically, so to find out exactly which over-the-counter locations can meet your specific dietary needs, you can call the dining headquarters at each Disney park. They will have the latest information and can help you plan. Call:

Animal Kingdom	(407) 938-3288
Epcot	(407) 560-7292
Magic Kingdom	(407) 824-5967
Hollywood Studios (MGM)	(407) 560-7830

Most of the over-the-counter restaurants can show you a notebook that lists the ingredients of the foods they serve. If the server isn't aware of the book, ask for a manager to assist you.

Wheelchairs in the restaurants: All Disney restaurants allow you to stay seated in your wheelchair or ECV. Since Sarah can walk, she usually parks and leaves the ECV wherever the cast member at the restaurant directs her. It's more comfortable for her to sit in most restaurant seats than reaching from the ECV to a table. Some restaurants are much tighter than others, so it would be more challenging to stay in a wheelchair, or even to ride to your table. We'll make note of restaurants where it is tough to maneuver a wheelchair. That said, if you need to stay in your wheelchair the cast members can usually assist you by opening up a path. They can move chairs and even ask other guests to move if necessary.

Most—but not all—of the over-the-counter restaurants in the parks and resorts are a challenge for wheelchair guests to order from. If you are on your own, you may need to ask for assistance. To find a wheelchair-accessible line, look for the wheelchair symbol, or ask a cast member. Most of the time if there are multiple queues, it's the queue on the end that is wheelchair accessible. Not all over-the-counter restaurants have an ordering line that is accessible.

Even if you do go through an accessible line, it may still be challenging to take your tray back to your seat. Just ask the nearest cast member to help you. The cashiers also can help you, or they can call someone else to assist you. If the line is not accessible, they will order for you. They will also carry your tray for you. If the first person you ask is not helpful (that is rare, but it's happened), ask someone else. Normally, Sarah will just approach the menu boards to choose what she wants. She goes to find a table, and I order and carry the food for both of us.

Resort food courts: Most of the resort food courts have the ability to accommodate various special dietary needs to some extent. This depends on the resort and the food court. It's a good idea to drop in to the food court after arriving. Just ask a cast member there, and they'll let you know if they can help with your particular needs.

There is the occasional cast member in the food court who is not familiar with what special dietary accommodations they can make. Occasionally you find someone who doesn't have great language skills or who is fairly new and inexperienced. Just ask someone else, or ask for a manager. You may wish to speak with a chef.

Try to go at an off time to talk with the food court personnel. The food court can get really packed with people, and it would be very difficult for cast members to help you during the rush.

Snacking: If you are on a special diet, you may wish to bring some snacks with you on your trip. We usually eat a low-carb diet for blood sugar and health reasons, so we bring low-carb bagels, protein bars and other low-carb snacks. We bring the bagels to breakfast at the resort (remember to bring baggies to transport your snacks and foods). We order coffee and a side of eggs, and we're good to go. We take our other snacks to the parks and also eat them when we're in the room. This helps us resist temptation when we pass by some of the sugary, carb-rich and very appealing snacks that you see all over Disney! All four parks have fruit stands. This can help visitors eat healthier.

> *Tip:* The Disney resort food courts offer you the purchase of a special mug, which is refillable at that resort only, for your length of stay. Depending on your length of stay, how much you drink, and how much you will be at your resort, it can save you a bunch of bucks! You can have all the refills you want of soda, coffee, tea and hot chocolate. Most of the resorts will only allow refills at their food court location. Some do allow refills at other locations in the resort, such as the pool snack bar. Ask the cashier at your resort food court where they allow guests to refill the mugs.

Allergies & special diets: The full-service, made-to-order restaurants in the parks and in the Disney resorts and grounds will prepare foods based on your dietary needs including those for allergies and diabetic requirements. Even at buffets such as the Cape May restaurant, Sarah has been able to have special dishes prepared for her.

When you call Disney Dining to make your reservation, be sure to make your special needs known. It's best if you call at least 72 hours in advance to let them know. When you check in at the restaurant, remind the hostess that you called in advance and have special needs. Let your wait staff know once you are seated. If you are dining without an advance reservation, they still may be able and willing to accommodate you, but it's not a sure thing. Let the hostess know that you have special needs, and they can let you know if the chefs can accommodate you.

Often the chef will come out to talk with you. In our experience they will graciously bend over backwards to make you a nice meal you can enjoy, within your dietary limitations. This is true even for the buffets. For example, when we ate at the Cape May Café Clam Bake Dinner Buffet, the chef came and gave Sarah a tour of the buffet foods being served to everyone. They discussed the ingredients, and together they decided what she could eat on the buffet and what she couldn't. He then came up with special dishes that would meet her particular needs. She was able to have a great meal that she enjoyed immensely. He was enthusiastic and pleasant, which made the experience very positive. We find this to be the attitude of most of the chefs we've encountered.

We have heard occasional accounts where people were not so well taken care of in a Disney World restaurant, but most experiences we hear of are glowingly positive. Still, if you have a particular allergy or health concern, don't be shy about going as far as you need to in order to be certain that your food is safe for you.

If you wish, you can actually call the restaurant directly by calling the main parks number and asking for the restaurant. They should be able to email you their menu. You can also request to speak with a chef. The number is (407) 824-2222. We have heard that many of the chefs will even purchase special items for you to meet your dietary needs. Just be sure to contact them far enough in advance to give them time to plan and acquire the right foods.

Many of the full-service restaurants can provide kosher meals if you order them at least 72 hours in advance. Let the cast member know when you make your reservation. You will be required to give a credit card to make the order.

Keep in mind the possibility of cross-contamination when you eat out. If you have a very severe allergy, you may need to avoid buffets and stick to having things prepared for you specially. Even if buffet foods are prepared separately, you never know if a guest has switched a serving utensil. Also, though an ingredient may not be listed in the food you're ordering, if it's used for other foods in the restaurant there may be some exposure during the preparation.

One item of note is that, over the next year, Disney will be removing all added trans fats as well as partially hydrogenated oils from food served in parks and resorts.

Restaurant menus & reviews: For pretty much every major Disney restaurant, we have found that there are usually folks who love it and those who hate it. Wherever it's appropriate, we will try to give an overview.

Tip: For samples of menus and pricing at Disney World restaurants, go online to:

http://allearsnet.com/menu/menus.htm#epc

This will give you an idea of each restaurant's offerings, though the menus may not be the most current. If you need specific information because of dietary issues, you may wish to call the restaurants directly.

Tip: With so many restaurants on Disney property it's usually possible to stick to most special diets. If you feel it's not possible to eat within your diet limitations there, you may wish to consider getting a hotel room with a kitchen. The Disney Vacation Club resorts as well as the Wilderness Cabins have kitchens. This will enable you to prepare your own meals, which you can bring to the parks with you.

Tip: Some folks may prefer or need to bring their own food to the Disney restaurants. If one person in your party will be bringing food, it's usually no problem to do so, as long as someone else in your party is ordering from the restaurant. Bringing all of your own food is fine in any resort food court.

In-room Refrigerators: All of the Disney resorts, except the value resorts, have a small refrigerator in each room. In the value resorts you can request that a refrigerator be placed in your room. Currently the cost is $10 plus tax a night; however, it is free if you need it for medical purposes. Just let them know when you make your reservation. By the way, the majority of the refrigerators are those small dorm room types. They do not have a freezer section. If you need ice, the resorts all have ice machines.

On a couple of visits we've had refrigerators that were not very cold. If you call maintenance or the front desk, they can send someone to adjust your refrigerator.

Smoking Laws

Florida law prohibits smoking in most indoor public places. This includes all enclosed restaurants and most other indoor public locations. Smoking is allowed outside, even in a restaurant seating area. It's also allowed in hotel bars that are not in hotel lobbies or restaurants. There are outdoor places that are designated spots for smoking at the resorts and parks. As non-smokers we tend to avoid these areas or walk by as fast as humanly possible. Even outdoors when there's no one there, an intense smoke smell lingers in some of these locations.

Almost all indoor locations at Disney are non-smoking. If smoke is an issue for you, avoid Jellyrolls (a piano club with dueling pianos and a sing-along), and the bar at ESPN Club. We've eaten in the restaurant at the ESPN Club, and we didn't smell any smoke in the dining area.

Smokers can pick up a Guide Map upon entering the park. All of the designated smoking areas will be shown. These are the only areas where you can smoke.

As of June 1, 2007 smoking will be banned in all Disney-owned hotel rooms. Even patios and balconies will be non-smoking areas. There will be designated smoking zones on the grounds. Keep in mind that some of the hotels on Disney property not owned by Disney will continue to allow smoking.

Allergies & Chemical Sensitivities at Disney

Plants: Of course there are flowers in bloom all year long in Florida. Though summer has a lot in bloom, we find fall, winter and spring are particularly full of flowers. The heat of the summer can actually be too strong for some plants, so there tends to be less variety. In the cooler months there are many more varieties that can thrive. There are many beautiful gardens all over the Disney grounds. This includes the parks, where flowers can be decorative as well as part of the theme.

In the warmer months the heat and humidity may add to the impact of allergens in the air. The moisture combined with the heat can create more molds in the environment. The cooler, dryer air that is more typical in winter can be easier to breathe and far more comfortable for many people. We generally do not go to Disney in the summer months because it's just too harsh for Sarah. She has a much easier time breathing the outdoor air in the cooler months.

Special room requests: For detailed information on chemical or dust sensitivities when dealing with the resorts, see the resort chapter.

Pesticides: Disney does use pesticides in the resorts and parks, though you seldom see it being applied. Remember that this is Florida and bugs can be a problem. It's a fact of life for Florida living. They apply pesticides on the grounds as well as in the rooms. They do use a program called "Integrated Pest Management."

From what I understand, this program tries to minimize the amount of pesticide that's actually in the air. For example, they typically use gel pesticides in the resort rooms instead of sprays. We are told that the gels have less of an impact on the air than the sprays. However, if a spray is needed in a room, they will use it.

You can request that no pesticides be used in your room before checking in. Let them know when you make your reservation. Also call the hotel directly the day before and even on the day of your check-in. They will usually try to accommodate you, but occasionally our requests have not been granted. On occasion, we have opted to change rooms when something was wrong with the pre-assigned room. This means that any preparation the resort did in advance was not done for the newly assigned room. That said, we have never been able to smell pesticides in our room.

To avoid the use of pesticides and other sprays, we have often declined to have our room cleaned by housekeeping once we have checked in. We notify housekeeping that we don't want service, put up our "Do Not Disturb" sign during the day, and call for anything we need such as towels and extra glasses to be delivered to us.

See the resort section of this book for further information.

Bees & bugs*:* Although we seldom see any on the Disney grounds, they are there all year round. Florida also has fire ants, which have a very irritating bite and may cause an allergic reaction. We have seldom seen any on the grounds because Disney is aggressive about getting rid of pests. Still, we have learned as Florida residents to avoid going barefoot outside as a precaution. Sarah travels with allergy medication and cortisone in her purse. She also brings antihistamine liquid for the skin, which she keeps in the room. Those who need it should carry an epinephrine kit in case of difficulty.

By the way, there are a lot of lizards in Florida. They are usually very small and Sarah actually finds them to be cute. Most people do. They are a fact of life here, and they are frightened of people. If they think you are approaching them they will run for the hills.

Perfumes*:* We do not usually find a lot of perfume or colognes permeating the air on Disney transportation or while attending the parks. Most people go very casual at Disney, but you may get a whiff of sunscreen or the occasional person who can't do without perfume or cologne. On occasion Sarah has had a challenge on the bus transportation when it was crowded and close. At times it's too crowded to change seats. You may consider bringing a cloth to cover your nose if you are sensitive.

Keep in mind that some attractions do use fragrance to enhance the experience. We will let you know about these particular attractions.

Dining*:* See extensive information on food allergies in the dining section.

Concerning allergies in the parks, see the parks section of this book.

Service Animals

Throughout much of Disney you can have your animal accompany you as long as it's on a leash or harness. Of course there are many attractions where an animal's presence is not feasible.

There are many attractions allowing service animals that will include sights, sounds and even smells that your animal has never experienced before. You are the best judge of what your animal can handle calmly. If you are uncertain after reading this book, just talk to a cast member at the attraction entrance to discuss your concerns. They should be able to address your specific questions and help you decide if your animal can cope with the attraction.

If you can't take your animal into an attraction you wish to participate in, you must leave him/her with someone from your party. The cast members cannot take charge of your animal. In addition to being leashed or harnessed at all times, service animals cannot be left unattended.

There are areas that are designated for animals to relax or relieve themselves. Many cast members can point you to the nearest one; however, we've heard that some cast members are just not familiar with the locations. It's best to go prepared. We'll list the locations of rest stops for each park at the beginning of each of the park chapters. Of course things can change quickly at Disney, so it's a good idea to check with Guest Relations when you enter the park for the most current locations. If you know where a designated location is and can ask for it specifically, the cast members can help you get there.

Be sure to bring your animal anything it might need for the day including food, treats, regular medications, and a water bowl. You will be required to clean up after your animal. Be sure to bring plastic bags to the park for this purpose. We have heard that it's difficult to find plastic bags in the park.

Keep in mind that the walkways and pavement in Florida can get burning hot, especially in the summer months. Please plan for this if this is a concern for your animal. There are options available for keeping paws cooler on the pavement, including paw wax. During warm weather you may want to wet your animal down once in a while.

Also, the intense stimulation of the parks can be exhausting for some animals. Crowds, heat, multi-sensory rides and a very strange environment can impact your service animal. Be sure to allow for this by giving your animal appropriate breaks and knowing when to quit for the day.

The parks can be tiring for anyone! If you need to rest, you can take your animal into the First Aid Station with you.

For each attraction look in the "Extra Info" area at the end of the attraction description. We'll let you know if service animals are not allowed. If it's not mentioned, then service animals should be allowed. Of course, it's important to read each attraction description in detail to determine whether your animal will be comfortable with the experience.

Medication

If you will require medication during your trip we can make a few general recommendations. First, we always suggest that you bring more than you need for your trip. This protects you if you should lose a dose, or if for some reason your trip is extended.

If you're flying it's a good idea to keep your medication in your carry-on, or in your purse or pocket. In fact, we'll often split the pills and put half in a carry-on bag and half in Sarah's purse.

Most Disney hotel rooms have a refrigerator. If yours does not, you can order one at no charge if it's being used for medical reasons. Check with the cast member when you make your reservations.

We often leave our medications that don't require refrigeration in the small room safe. Perhaps this is overkill, but we prefer to be on the safe side. We've never had a single item taken from our room in the Disney resorts, but we just wouldn't want to have to deal with replacing our medications if they went missing.

If you need your medication cooled during your park visits, you can either bring a small, soft cooler into the park, or leave your medication at First Aid. They can refrigerate it for you.

Florida Weather

There are certain things you can count on in Florida. The summer will be very, very hot and it will rain nearly every afternoon. Usually this rain is a temporary event, lasting 20 minutes to a couple of hours. Occasionally we get unrelenting rain.

Hurricane season begins in June and lasts until the end of November. For many years it was rare to get any foul weather in Florida. Then we had a couple of really bad seasons. Even though there are lots of professionals out there making educated predictions, it's completely unpredictable. You can watch the tropical weather before your trip, but some hurricanes come up quickly and without much warning. You can see the Orlando weather here: **www.weather.com**.

When we have been in Orlando with possible hurricanes approaching, we found the local news to be lacking. For excellent news you can go online at **www.sun-sentinel.com**. This is the website for a South Florida paper but we find they do an excellent job of plotting hurricane paths. You can see any approaching hurricanes charted with predicted probable paths.

The winters are usually much drier, with occasional rains. In winter you can't really predict temperature well in advance. There are times I've needed a good winter coat while at Disney, and at other times shorts and tee shirts were appropriate. Nights are significantly cooler than days during fall, winter and spring. The weather can change by 20 degrees or more during the course of a day and evening.

One thing is for sure: All year round be sure to bring sunglasses, lots of sunscreen and a good shade hat. (Disney sells a lot of nice hats for that purpose.) Drink a lot of water when it's warm! Keep in mind that even in cooler weather or during cloudy times, the Florida sun can cause bad sunburn. A good way to ruin your trip is to go unprotected.

You may wish to bring compact umbrellas, as they are quite expensive on Disney grounds. Disney sells rain tunics at a very reasonable price almost everywhere on the grounds. You may wish to check the weather before you go. You can see the predicted weather 10 days in advance, along with averages for rain and temperature at **www.weather.com**. Keep in mind that the forecasts can change daily, so it's a good idea to check just before you leave for your trip and even during your trip.

Because temperatures vary in the fall, winter and spring, you may need to pack both cool and hot weather clothing. Sarah dresses warmly in the morning and brings shorts and a tank top in a beach bag if the day is going to be warm enough to warrant a change. She changes in the restroom as the day heats up. In the evening she goes back to her warmer clothing.

As for the parks, some attractions have queue waiting areas where the general public will have air conditioning, or at least wait out of the sun. Many attractions have queues that are in direct sun. Even so, there may be special shaded or air-conditioned wait areas for those with GACs (Guest Assistance Cards) or in wheelchairs who request it. See the information on GACs if you feel you need this option.

Keep in mind that on those occasional cold winter days, Disney does not provide heat in the waiting areas for the attractions. The need for heating is so rare in Florida that they just don't include it.

Local Hospitals

A hospital close to Disney property is the Florida Hospital Celebration Health. Celebration is a nice little town just outside of the Disney property that was created by Disney.

The hospital phone number is (407) 303-4000.

Some people feel that the best nearby hospital for children and women's issues is the Arnold Palmer Hospital for Children and Women. This is approximately 20 miles from Disney on the Downtown Orlando Regional Health Care campus. Their phone number is (407) 841-5111.

Dialysis: One of the closer dialysis centers is Celebration Dialysis. Their phone number is (407) 566-1780. Another center is Orlando Dialysis at (800) 424-6589.

The Parks

For each park we will offer tips for gaining the most enjoyment with the least discomfort. We'll discuss the park in general as well as the individual rides, attractions and restaurants.

Keep in mind that these parks are huge. If you will be on foot (as opposed to riding a wheelchair), be certain to wear your best walking shoes! There is much to do, and most of it is worth doing. Although we think Disney usually has great "people moving" strategies, it's difficult to see everything in any of the parks in one day. We recommend that you have a basic plan before going to the park, but be ready to be flexible if needed.

As a part of our planning process, we pick our priority attractions. When we check into our hotel at Disney we request a map of each park. You can also have them sent to you when you make your reservation, or call (407) 939-7630. We mark our priority attractions on the map and create a general plan of approach. Again, we suggest you be flexible once you get there, and just enjoy yourself!

If you have health issues, I suggest you be sure not to overdo it. Most people have an intense drive to get everything in, especially if they won't be coming back for some time. We've found when we've tried to get everything in within one day it became a highly stressful experience. It also negatively impacted Sarah's health. It can wreck a potentially great time. We find that we have a much better time when we take our time, relax and enjoy the experience at our own pace.

There is a reality of waiting in Disney lines. During peak times you can wait as much as 90 minutes to get into an attraction. During slower times you may be able to get into that same attraction in 5 minutes, or even right away. If you are attending during a slow season, you can cover much more ground in a day than if it's a crowded time. Whenever it's convenient to your plan, use the FASTPASS discussed later in this chapter to avoid waiting as long in lines.

You can view projected crowd sizes at the Disney theme parks at www.touringplans.com. (Choose the "Crowd Calendar" link on the left-hand menu.) You can also join www.tourguidemike.com to purchase a personalized itinerary that is designed to help you avoid long lines.

The Unofficial Guide to Walt Disney World® is a book that gives various strategies for touring the park in a logical way in order to reduce wait times. It takes into consideration the locations of the attractions and the best and worst times for crowds. It also makes recommendations on the best use of

FASTPASS. Of course, for some people with disabilities it will be necessary to make some changes to their suggestions. We recommend that book as a companion to this one in your planning.

Many Disney travel books suggest that you arrive before the park opens and, once you're let in, head to the most popular rides first. This is a good idea if you are comfortable getting up early in the morning. We are not early risers, and it exhausts Sarah to get up before she is naturally ready to wake up. We just get there when we get there, even if it means a longer wait. We make use of other strategies to minimize wait times, which we will discuss as we go.

Extra Magic Hours

If you are staying in a Disney hotel, you get a perk. Disney allows early entry and late exit at one park for each day. Since the park is only opened to Disney resort guests during that time period, it's far less crowded than during normal hours. You can check the Disney site for these special park hours (www.disneyworld.com) for Disney hotel guests, or you can call Disney at 407-939-7630.

Keep in mind that on the days that a particular park has an early open or late close, it tends to be more crowded throughout that day during regular hours.

Park Ticket Strategies

There are a variety of options for buying park tickets. They span from buying a single park ticket for a single day, to multi-day passes with the "Park Hopper" option. Park hopping allows you entrance to all four parks in a day. You can also add on the "Water Park Fun and More" option, which can include visits to Typhoon Lagoon, Blizzard Beach, Pleasure Island, Disney's Wide World of Sports Complex and DisneyQuest. DisneyQuest is an indoor, interactive theme park. You can also buy admission to any of these places individually.

Multi-day tickets normally expire 14 days after the first ticket is used. The "No Expiration" option will allow you to come back and use your unused tickets any time. This is great if you think you will return to Disney World in the future. This gives you some freedom to take rest days away from the parks as you need them, without feeling you're wasting money on unused tickets.

The "Park Hopper" option can be helpful in several ways. First, we prefer to avoid crowds in the parks as much as possible. It makes for a calmer experience and reduces wait times for the attractions. People with mobility issues will find it easier to move around the parks when they're less crowded. The "Park Hopper" option can be used to avoid the most crowded times in the parks.

For example, if you are staying in a Disney resort, park hopping can be helpful when used with the extra magic hours described in the previous section. During those extra hours the park will be far less crowded than during regular hours, because only Disney resort guests are allowed to be there. However, keep in mind that those parks tend to be more crowded than normal during regular park hours. This is because, in addition to the regular crowds, many resort guests take advantage of the extra magic hours. If you have a park hopper pass, we recommend visiting the park during expanded hours and then moving on to another less crowded park for the rest of that day.

Another benefit of having the "Park Hopper" option is that it can take some time pressure off of you. If you don't finish seeing everything at one park, you can spend part of another day there finishing up. You can then move on to another park when you're done. For example, suppose you didn't have time to experience several attractions at Epcot on your first day. With a multi-day "Park Hopper" pass, you can return to Epcot another day, and after you're done with the remaining attractions, you can head over to Hollywood Studios (MGM) or any of the other parks.

Park hopping can be convenient for other reasons as well. One day we were in Animal Kingdom. An intense thunderstorm was approaching. Since much of Animal Kingdom is outdoors, as are many of the queue lines, we find that it's not the best park to be in during a lightning storm. We left Animal Kingdom and, using our "Park Hopper" passes, moved on to Hollywood Studios. Hollywood Studios has a lot of indoor attractions with indoor queues, so we were able to enjoy our day despite the storm.

Theme Park Parking

The parking lots are vast with a free tram that comes and picks up guests throughout the lot sections. If you can walk a short distance and manage the tram ride, you can park in the main lot and take the tram in. If you have a handicapped parking sign, display it. Tell the cast members directing traffic that you need to park towards the front where the trams pick you up. This will shorten your walk. If you don't request this you could end up quite a distance away from the tram pick-up point. Trams will drop you off fairly close to the gate. However, for some folks with walking difficulties this may still be a significant walk.

The tram is an open-sided vehicle with overhead covering. It has hard bench seats with backs. You must be able to hold yourself up in the seat. The tram can make some sharp turns and there are no seat belts. Sarah actually finds it a bit challenging to hold on, but you can hold on to the bars or the seat in front of you for support. If you have a hard time holding yourself upright during sharp turns, you may wish to avoid the tram, or make sure you are seated in the middle of the seat so that you don't fall out.

At times we have noticed we could smell exhaust fumes while riding in the tram. Bring a cloth to cover your nose if you are sensitive.

Handicapped parking: If you wish to park in the handicapped section, clearly display your handicapped sign as you come into the parking lot. Flash it to the parking attendants, and they will direct you to the right path. The handicapped sections are fairly close to the park entrance, but it is still a significant walking distance for some folks.

There are usually courtesy wheelchairs at no cost available in the handicapped parking areas that you can use to get into the park and to the wheelchair rental location. They will not allow you to ride around the park in these, though. These chairs have blue seats, backrests and blue flags. If there are none in view you can have someone in your party go to the gate and request one from a cast member. Your party member can then take the wheelchair back to you.

During busy times the handicapped parking section can fill up quickly, so try to get there early if you require a handicapped space. Handicapped parking is available only to those with legal permits.

Entering the Park

To avoid long lines it's best to get your park tickets in advance. You can do this either by phone or at your hotel guest services window. If you are buying your tickets at the park and you use a wheelchair, you will still need to wait in the queue. You will need to enter through a wheelchair access gate. Anyone carrying a bag of any kind will then need to go through security gates to have their bags checked and possibly searched. If you are going to rent an ECV (electric convenience vehicle or scooter) at the park, you will usually need to get there early to secure one.

Many books about the Disney parks will tell you to get to the park early and run to the rides that get the most crowds. You can take this route—you can even grab a FASTPASS at one ride and move on to the next most crowded ride. This is usually advantageous.

Personally, we prefer to avoid the large lines and crowds that are there waiting for the gates to open. We've been there many times, so we don't have that huge urgency that comes with the first few visits. We prefer to take our time. We often get to the park around 10:00 or 11:00 AM. We usually don't have much of a wait getting in then, but there's no guarantee that later entry will mean smaller lines.

Getting & Using a Wheelchair

Inside each park are wheelchair rental locations. There is always one near the main entrance. There may be additional locations. There are also wheelchair repair centers. We will share the location of these centers for each park within the park chapters.

If you are renting a wheelchair at the park, you will want to get there as early as possible. These can sell out pretty quickly, especially during busy seasons. ECVs sell out much more quickly than manual wheelchairs.

Rides & attractions with wheelchairs: For some rides, Disney requires guests using ECVs to transfer into a manual wheelchair before entering the waiting queue. ECVs, in this case, refers to the scooter-style vehicles, not electric wheelchairs or manual wheelchairs. The cast members at the attraction will provide you with a standard manual wheelchair. They cannot push you through the queue, but they can push your wheelchair to a ride vehicle.

When a wheelchair or ECV user is transferred directly from their chair into a ride car, the Disney cast members will have the chair moved to the disembarking area. If you can walk, this is usually fine. The chair is usually pretty nearby in a convenient spot. If you are unable to step off the ride car and walk to your chair or you can't stand and wait for someone to get it for you after disembarking from the ride car, tell the cast member when boarding the ride. They will bring your wheelchair or ECV right to you so that you can transfer from the ride car into your chair.

At times you may park and leave your wheelchair or ECV. We have never had a problem with theft or heard of anyone who has. Be sure to take your ECV key with you to be on the safe side. For both wheelchairs and ECVs, be sure to leave something on the chair or in the basket that will help you recognize it. Just don't leave anything valuable behind.

Wheelchair Etiquette: Riding in a wheelchair is actually a big responsibility. Especially the ECVs! They are actually pretty heavy and can travel quite fast. You can really do damage if you hit someone. Even rolling over a foot or hitting someone while moving slowly can really hurt or injure someone.

If you are driving an ECV and are inexperienced, take a few minutes to practice with it before you head into the park. By applying pressure to the squeeze handles you can make your chair go forward or backward. The more pressure you apply, the faster you go. Also, there is usually a setting dial you can adjust that increases or limits the power and speed. When you are in a crowded area, it's a good idea to put your speed dial at a low setting level. It's very difficult to control an ECV at a low speed when you have the power settings on high. When the speed is set to a high level, even if you are just gently applying pressure to the squeeze handles, the ECV can leap and take off.

Keeping the power setting on low in crowds and on low when you restart the chair after stopping is a good rule of thumb. When you are traveling in a fairly clear area you can increase your speed. Just be aware that others on foot may not be watching for you. People will often suddenly pass right in front without looking. They can be really distracted by all the attractions, so it's up to you to be very careful. Sometimes people on foot can be oblivious to the wheelchair. Politely alert people as you are passing by. Unfortunately, Sarah has run over or knocked into her fair share of people. She's become a much more careful ECV driver over time.

With any type of wheelchair, keep in mind that you're taking up a lot more space then you would if you were standing and walking. Because it may take some time to get used to this, stay vigilant when you first start so that you don't roll over a foot or worse.

It's easy for an ECV user to get distracted by all the wonderful sights. You can quickly lose track of the people around you. If you know you are looking at your surroundings, try slowing down so that you don't crash into someone by mistake. Look around you every few seconds.

If it takes some time to maneuver your chair, such as in a tight queue, don't worry. The people behind you will usually wait with patience and grace. Just do your best, be polite and don't get nervous. If the occasional person behind you does act impolitely, don't let it ruin your mood. You're there for vacation fun, so don't let it ruin your mood. For the most part we have found that guests are kind, patient and pleasant.

> *Tip:* Turn your wheelchair off when you are not moving. This will save your power.

Lockers

Near the entrance of each park you will find lockers that you can rent. For us these lockers are inconvenient. They are usually far from wherever you are in the park. However, for some folks the extra walking is worth not having to lug things around. Remember that if you have medical equipment or medication that needs storing you can leave it with First Aid.

If you rent a locker and move on to another park on the same day, you can get a locker at the new park at no extra cost if there is one available. Just be sure to save your receipt from your first locker.

Guide Map and Time Guide

These are available at the ticket booth, Guest Relations and most stores and food carts. The time guide will give you all the current information on show times, character appearances, early or late closings of attractions and parade times. The Guide Map is an up-to-date map to help you get around the park. Also, when you enter each park look for the special board somewhere near the entrance that tells you approximate wait times at major rides and attractions, any attraction closings and special events.

Guest Services - Guest Relations Area

These offices are always located near the entrance of the park. They provide various services, such as upgrading your park tickets, getting you priority seating for dining, providing park guide maps and entertainment schedules, helping with disability issues, supplying a small booklet for guests with disabilities, renting some special devices for the handicapped and dealing with any of your general questions. If you are using a wheelchair or ECV they can give you a book that will tell you how to enter each attraction.

If anyone in your party gets separated, Guest Relations can help. You can leave a message with them, and when someone from your party comes in and inquires, they can relay that message. For example, you can leave a message saying that you will be waiting in the waiting area at 50's Prime Time Café. You can sit down and have a cool drink while waiting for your party. Guest Relations will let them know where you're waiting.

Guest Assistance Cards (GAC)

This card can help you access various forms of help around the park. You can get these at Guest Services. If you will be using a wheelchair or ECV, you don't usually need this card. I have heard of some folks getting a GAC even with a wheelchair for things like needing to stay out of the sun. However I have found that the cast members will generally honor a request like this if you are in a wheelchair without a GAC. If a cast member questions you and asks for a GAC, you can try telling them you were told you didn't need it if you were in a wheelchair. If you have an unusual need, you may wish to get a GAC even if you are in a wheelchair.

If you will be parking your chair at times and walking into an attraction queue, but you still need assistance, then you may want to get a GAC. If you have a disability that is not visible or obvious, you may want a GAC. The GAC tells the cast members what your needs are and can make for a much easier experience. Without a GAC or a wheelchair you will not be allowed in the special wait areas, entrances or handicapped seating areas.

Issues that GACs can be extremely helpful for include invisible ailments like autism, ADD/ADHD, heat and sun problems, claustrophobia and crowd phobias. Wherever possible, the cast members will take you to an alternative queue or wait area that can make things much easier. Those with other issues such as visual or hearing problems can benefit from a GAC. For example, you may be able to be seated toward the front of shows.

What the GAC *won't* usually do is get you to the front of the line; however, this does sometimes happen. The GAC can get you various forms of assistance, which may differ from attraction to attraction. Just approach a cast member at the entrance, show your GAC and make your needs known.

Occasionally, we've gotten a cast member who just wouldn't help. You can try asking for a manager, which may get you better results.

Some forms of help a GAC can get you include:

➢ The ability to use your stroller as you would a wheelchair, taking it through the wheelchair entrances and paths.

➢ Use of the special entrances, exits and waiting areas as needed.

➢ Allowing you to sit in front seating areas of shows if you have visual impairments.

➢ Allowing you to wait in a shaded or air-conditioned area if the waiting area is too hot or sunny.

➢ The ability to approach a cast member with your specific and unique needs. They will then usually try to help if your request is possible at that attraction.

If your disability is not visible, you will have a much easier time getting a GAC if you supply some kind of proof of your issue. Years ago it was easy to get a GAC. We noticed over time that the Guest Relations staff were getting less willing to hand out the card. Sarah's physical issues were not visible, and so after meeting some frustrating resistance we finally started bringing written evidence. We've brought doctor's notes that were written for other purposes, and on another occasion a copy of a legal document confirming Sarah's disability. Though this is not required, it made things go smoother.

You may wish to have a doctor's note written stating the nature of the problem and the need for special assistance. If you prefer, the note does not have to reveal the actual diagnosis, but it should mention the special needs you may have.

Be sure to bring the person who needs the GAC into Guest Services with you. We have heard that there have been people who have tried to fake the need for a GAC. Guest Relations tries to be certain that the person the GAC is being requested for is really there at the park. They also want to be sure that there is true need for a GAC, before issuing it. It can help the process go more easily if the Guest Relations cast member can see the actual person requesting the GAC.

Here's an example of a note that your doctor might write:

To Whom It May Concern:

I am writing concerning _____ who has been diagnosed with _____. These problems cause an inability to [stand, sit or walk for extended periods of time, stand in crowds (whatever your issues are)...] This will definitely impact his/her ability to wait in lines. Additionally, he/she should also be out of the sun and in a cooler environment as often as possible. Please offer any assistance you can.

Sincerely,

Your Doctor's Name

On occasion we have encountered a cast member at Guest Relations who did not know about the GAC. Don't argue or bother explaining. There's a whole park out there waiting for you, and it's not worth the time. You don't need to spend time demanding your rights or correcting someone. Once in a while some cast members may be fairly new, inexperienced and/or not thoroughly trained. Just nicely request a manager, who is likely to be knowledgeable and able to help you.

On occasion at the attractions you may encounter a cast member who does not understand what to do with GAC holders, or who does not handle your issues with the sensitivity required. If this occurs, just politely ask for a manager. Don't let it get to you! You're there to have a blast, and sometimes people lack experience, maturity or judgment.

One GAC is fine for all four parks on the date(s) specified on the GAC. You can obtain a single GAC out for the entire length of your stay.

Rides & Attractions With Disabilities

How do I know what attractions to avoid and what to try? What if you've read the descriptions of the attractions, and you're still uncertain about experiencing some rides with your particular condition?

One way to handle this is to have someone in your party who understands your situation try the ride out first. Some rides actually have single rider lines with much shorter waits!

Another option is to talk with the cast members at the attraction. Make certain they've actually been on the ride, and ask them about it. Let them know your specific concerns and get their opinions.

If you're still uncertain, we really believe the old adage is appropriate here: If in doubt, do without! There's so much to do at Disney that you will still have plenty to try. It's not worth the risk of injury and a ruined vacation.

Queues & Entrances

For many attractions, guests with disabilities are sent through the lines or queues with everyone else. Some of the rides and attractions do have separate entrances or allow you to bypass the queue or certain parts of the attraction. At times being in a wheelchair has cut down our wait time considerably. For some attractions we've actually had to wait longer. For many attractions, we probably waited about the same as everyone else. To reduce wait times, FASTPASS is usually the quickest way to go (see the FASTPASS section).

We have found that when entering an attraction there is usually a cast member who will direct you to the correct waiting spot or queue path for a wheelchair. For this reason we do not highlight every attraction's wheelchair entrance, as it's usually evident or simple to ascertain. For those that may pose more of a challenge, we will share the details. There is also a booklet that you can get at Guest Relations that lists all special entrances.

Some of the queues are indoors with air conditioning. Some are outdoors with full sun, partial shading or full shade. We will try to make note of the queue conditions. Most queues do not have any seating whatsoever. On occasion you will find a rail to lean on or the occasional prop such as a rock to sit on. Before Sarah began using an ECV, she would just sit on the floor in front of me. I'd stand behind her to keep people from stepping on her.

There's a book that may be helpful for those queues that are particularly long or boring. It's called *The Disney Queue Line Survival Guidebook* by Kimberly Button. It has activities, puzzles and trivia questions related to the attraction, as well as tips for avoiding long lines. This may be an effective way of keeping kids occupied and entertained. You can buy it on the web at www.disneysurvivalguide.com.

FASTPASS

This is a free tool, available to all guests, which can help you avoid long waits. Many rides allow you to take a FASTPASS ticket, and to come back to the ride during a pre-assigned time period with much less of a wait. You are allowed to go through a different queue at any time during your designated time slot. Sometimes you can even get right in with no wait!

To get a FASTPASS for a particular attraction, you need to locate the FASTPASS machine. Ask a cast member if you don't see it. Slide your park entrance card into the special FASTPASS machine, and it will issue you a ticket with a designated time period printed on it. Come back to the attraction any time within that period and enter at the FASTPASS queue entrance. For example, your FASTPASS could tell you to come back between 4:06 PM and 6:20 PM. You would come back to the FASTPASS return area at any point within that window of time. If you arrive before 4:06 you will be required to wait.

Keep in mind that you can only have one FASTPASS at a time. You will not be able to get another FASTPASS until the time period of the older one has begun. If you change your mind about a FASTPASS that you already have for one attraction and want to get one for a different attraction, you can see a cast member and request a cancellation of the old FASTPASS. Then you can get a new one for another attraction.

A lot of extra walking may be required to get a FASTPASS and then go somewhere else while you wait for your designated FASTPASS time period. One option is to send someone from your party to get the FASTPASS tickets (make sure they take everyone's park entrance tickets with them). They can then come back to your party and continue on to other attractions. Another option is to hang around the area of the attraction for which you've obtained the FASTPASS. Keep in mind that at times a FASTPASS time period may be several hours away.

"Switching Off" on Rides

Some attractions offer this option. This is for guests who have a person in their party who can't go on a ride and can't be left unattended. It's also for guests with service animals when the animal can't go on the ride. Your entire party can go through the ride queue (attraction waiting line) together with the person and/or animal who won't be riding. While one or more of your party stays with the non-riders, the others can go on the ride. Then you switch so that the person who already went on the ride stays with the non-rider, and the ones who haven't yet ridden can go on the ride. See a Cast Member at the attraction entrance for details on how to proceed in that particular attraction.

Boarding Rides & Help from Cast Members

When you approach an attraction, there are usually cast members at the entrance. If you are in a wheelchair or have a GAC, they will direct you toward the correct entrance. They can also explain the boarding procedures to you. Many times you will be directed to the exit to board. Let the cast member know at that time if you have any special circumstances that need to be taken into account when boarding the attraction. For example, even if you are not in a wheelchair but need extra time to board, let the cast member know.

If you have a special need, you may need to go into the wheelchair entrance. Don't just enter the regular queue, as they may not be able to accommodate you from there.

If you have any questions about whether you should participate in an attraction, you can discuss it with the cast member at the entrance. They can answer your questions and help you decide. Verify that they've been on the ride. Usually they have tried it many times, but we once ran into a cast member who had never experienced the ride. His recommendations were really different than the next cast member we asked who had been on the ride many times. If the cast member has not been on the ride, ask for someone who has.

Some of the rides have a sample ride car for viewing or practicing in. The cast member can show you the ride car and explain it to you. Many times it's possible to go all the way through the queue and check things out without committing to going on the ride. Some of the queues are events in themselves and worth walking through. Sarah was able to go all the way through the queue for the Mission Space non-spinning ride. A cast member escorted her out of the exit designed for those who decide to back out at the last minute.

There are some rides that allow you to go through the queue and board the ride car in a standard wheelchair but not an ECV. An electric wheelchair may be okay as well, though they may ask you to transfer into a standard wheelchair, which the cast members will provide. After the ride, either they will allow you to go back for your ECV using their wheelchair, or they will bring your ECV to you. Let them know if you need them to bring you your wheelchair. Some of them do it all the time, but on some rides it's not standard practice.

To transfer from your wheelchair or ECV into a ride car, cast members are not allowed to lift you. They are allowed to help steady you, push your wheelchair up to the ride car so that you can transfer, steady the ride car, and get your wheelchair to you after the ride is done.

There are some rides where you have to walk or ride your wheelchair onto a moving walkway to board the ride. They move at the same speed as the ride car. On many of these rides they can either slow down the walkway or stop it completely. Let the cast member know that you need this. There are some that can't be slowed or stopped and the cast member will let you know if this is the case. We'll try to make note which attractions have moving walkways, and which can or can't be stopped or slowed.

How Many People Can Accompany Wheelchair or GAC Users?

When you are going through the GAC or wheelchair queues or being seated in a wheelchair area, the number of people you will be allowed to take with you will vary. Officially you are allowed to take 5 people with you in the wheelchair queue. Depending on the attraction, the cast member may direct you to take somewhere between three and six people in addition to the person in the wheelchair.

The number of people who can stay with the wheelchair rider during the attraction can change because of the nature or set-up of the attraction. It can be as few as 1 companion, and we've heard of families of up to 12 being allowed to accompany a person in a wheelchair. If you can't be seated together, we have been told that they will try to place you close together if that is possible. It is really dependant on the ride and the cast member you encounter.

Special Devices & Assists

The following is a list of items and services that are available within the parks. Most of these are for people with hearing disabilities. Folks with hearing disabilities seem to really get a lot of benefit from the devices. Some of these are accessed at the Guest Services area and you take them with you through the park. Others are available at the attractions. They are as follows:

- Enhanced Handheld Assistive Device: This is the newest device created by Disney engineers. It's about the size of a PDA and combines handheld captioning and closed captioning. By September, 2007 it will also provide amplified audio for assistive listening. Eventually the device will also provide descriptive audio for people who are blind or have low vision. This device provides wireless technology and can take appropriate pre-programmed actions based on what attraction you are in. It is available at Guest Relations in the four main parks and is free of charge.

- Reflective Captioning: This uses an LED display to project captions onto an acrylic panel in front of the Guest. This is something you can request at the attraction. Contact a cast member at the attraction if you wish to use this.

- Assistive Listening Devices: This amplifies the audio and is available at Guest Relations. A $25 deposit is refunded to you as long as you return it on the same day. This is lightweight and primarily for those with mild to moderate hearing loss.

- Handheld Captioning: This is a portable captioning system that uses a wireless handheld receiver to display text. The captioning appears whenever it's available at attractions. Receivers are available at Guest Relations. You have to leave a $100 refundable deposit. Be certain to return the captioning device on the same day to get your deposit refunded. We hear that it can be a bit heavy and uncomfortable to carry around all day. We also hear that some folks find the type to be a bit small to read and that it's not adjustable.

- Translation Device: You can rent this at Guest Relations locations, also with a refundable deposit.

- Video Caption-ready Monitors: You'll find these at many of the attractions. These are monitors that are designated with a "CC" symbol. They are activated by a remote control unit, which you get at Guest Relations. You have to leave a refundable deposit of $25. You only get your money back if the unit is returned on the same day.

- Sign Language: Disney provides sign language interpreters for many of its attractions. They often offer the service on particular pre-scheduled days. See more on this in the hearing impairment section in this chapter.

- Portable Restraints: At some of the more physically challenging rides you can get a portable shoulder restraint, which can add support to the upper body. Just ask a cast member for one.

Hearing Impairments

In addition to most of the devices and assists in the previous list, pay phones are available throughout Disney World that are equipped with amplified handsets. There are also pay phones with a Text Typewriter. To find the locations, check the park guide map or the Guidebook for Guests with Disabilities. You can get both of these at Guest Relations.

It can be a good idea to get a GAC so that you have a better chance of sitting up front in the attractions and shows.

Sign language: Interpretation is available on a rotating basis at the parks with a minimum of seven days' notice. This is a free service. As of this writing, this is the schedule:

Animal Kingdom	Saturdays
Epcot	Tuesdays, Fridays
Magic Kingdom	Mondays, Thursdays
Hollywood Studios (MGM)	Sundays, Wednesdays

This schedule may have changed, so it's best to call and confirm. In fact, it's a good idea to go to Guest Relations when you arrive at the park and ask them to give you the most up-to-date schedule for the duration of your visit.

Try to arrive at your attraction or show early, and ask a cast member to seat you in the area reserved for those utilizing the sign language interpreter.

In addition to the parks, sign language interpretation can be requested for other special events and shows. This includes the "Hoop-Dee-Doo Revue", "Disney's Spirit of Aloha" dinner shows and some Pleasure Island shows. You must contact Disney a minimum of 14 days in advance for these shows.

For assistance with sign language and hearing impairment issues, call (407) 824-4321 [voice] and choose option 0 to speak with a representative, or (407) 827-5141 [TTY]. Ask to speak with the Deaf Services Coordinator. I would highly recommend calling at least two weeks in advance of your trip to make any arrangements necessary and to determine probable schedules.

The number of the Services for Guests with Disabilities (in case you need further assistance) is (407) 824-5217.

Cast members at most attractions have access to Guest Assistance Packets for hearing impaired guests. They contain dialogue or a script of the show, flashlights, pen and a pad of paper. This is available at most performance and attraction entrances. Ask the cast member at the entrance. The cast members who know sign language wear a language pin that identifies them.

Noise sensitivity: There are many attractions that can get very loud. We have tried to note where that is an issue within the ride descriptions. There are a couple options available to help people who are extremely sensitive to still enjoy those attractions.

A simple solution is to bring along earplugs. There are some soft foam earplugs that you can get in most pharmacies. Sarah and I have found them to be very comfortable. They block out enough noise so that it's tolerable, but not so much that you can't hear anything.

For those who are willing to spend the money, Bose makes noise-canceling headsets. Some people find these very helpful.

Visual Impairments

Although we do not have firsthand experience with this, we will share information based on our research. We have heard that it is possible for people who are visually impaired to really enjoy Disney. Many of the attractions are multi-sensory, engaging smell, sound, touch and motion. There are features that are designed specifically for sight-impaired guests. Animal Kingdom has something called manipulatives. These are hands-on features around the animal enclosures. They are designed for the sight impaired so that you can touch and feel items that teach you about the animals in that location.

Some sight-impaired people enjoy the intense physical sensations of thrill rides. There are attractions that actually put visitors in the dark in order to engage the other senses, such as Sounds Dangerous Starring Drew Carey at Hollywood Studios (MGM).

We have heard that it would be difficult for a sight-impaired person to move through the parks alone, even with the tools Disney supplies. In part that's due to the crowds, and also the fact that the parks are huge and fairly complicated in their design. Especially for those whose visual impairment is not readily noticeable, it may make it easier for you to use a white mobility cane. This will let others know that you have an issue, and it will be a cue to cast members that you have a disability. It may make it easier to get assistance, and there will be less explanation necessary. It may also make it easier to navigate through crowds. If people can see that you have a visual impairment they may be less inclined to knock into you!

Upon arriving at the park, you may wish to get a GAC or Guest Assistance Card, described in this chapter. Guest Relations will provide this. For some attractions, this will allow you to enter through a different queue. Some of these queues are shorter and less difficult to navigate. You may be able to obtain more assistance from cast members, and you may be allowed more time to board a ride vehicle. There may even be a shorter wait time in some of these special queues. Once you arrive at an attraction there should be a cast member near the main entrance. You can ask them to direct you to the handicapped entrance.

During live shows, some sight-impaired people prefer to be close to the action in order to experience the full force of the show. With a GAC you can request to be towards the front. You'll usually be able to have your request met, but it may depend on crowd levels, how far in advance of show time you arrive, and other variables. If you can arrive early you can request to be seated before the general crowd is let in. This can help you to avoid the throngs of people pushing in to get a good seat. Again, for many shows you will be allowed to do this, but for some shows there is no pre-seating allowed. It can't hurt to ask, though—and it may depend on the cast member on duty.

Disney supplies the following support tools:

- Braille Guides: You can get these at all four of the parks in the Guest Relations area. They give a general overview of the specific park you are visiting. You must return the book on the same day you use it in order to get your refundable $25 deposit back.

- Stationary Braille Maps: All four parks and Downtown Disney offer stationary Braille Maps that represent the orientation of those locations. These maps use large print with a clear Braille overlay. There are also some raised graphics that highlight key landmarks and attractions. You will find them at or near the Guest Relations Lobby in each location. They are also located near the Tip Boards at all four Parks. You'll find them in Downtown Disney at Downtown Disney Marketplace, Pleasure Island and the West Side.

- Audiotape Guides: At each park Guest Relations offers cassette tapes that will give you a sense of direction and descriptions of the attractions. You must return the tapes and tape player on the same day you use them in order to get your refundable $25 deposit back. The headset that comes with this may have a short cord. You may wish to bring your own headset with a longer cord so that it's easier to use as you walk through the park.

  There are two versions of these audiotapes. One gives a general layout orientation, an overview of services you can receive and brief description of the attractions. The other gives a very detailed tour of the park by giving you a route to take, including distances between attractions and important stopping locations. We have heard that it may be difficult to listen while walking through the park. It may be easier to obtain your tape, sit down, and listen before proceeding.

Attraction Length of Time

We will give you the length of time that each attraction runs. Sometimes this can help you make a decision as to whether you should participate or not. Please be aware that the length of the attraction times that we give you is approximate.

Single Rider Queues

Sometimes on certain rides a single rider queue will open up. If you don't mind being split up during the ride, these lines usually have a far shorter wait time. This is also great to use if only one member of your party wants to try an attraction.

Ride Failure Issues

In all our years of visiting Disney, on only two occasions did we experience a ride stopping in the middle, and stalling for maybe 15-20 minutes. It was a bit disconcerting, but eventually problems were resolved. Please note that if an evacuation is necessary—we've never experienced that and it doesn't happen often—you will be required to walk and climb stairs. If you are unable to do that and you need assistance to evacuate, you will need to wait for as long as it takes for the Disney cast members to assist you off the attraction. We are told they have contingency plans for these situations.

At times rides also stop briefly so that a guest can transfer from their wheelchair to the ride car. Another reason a ride might stop is that someone may have stepped out of the ride car. We have been told that the rides have floor sensors so that if someone gets out of a ride car in the middle of a ride, the ride will stop automatically, for safety reasons. The Disney cast members will then investigate before starting the ride again.

> *Tip:* Some of the rides are pitch black at times. If you have a fear of the dark, you may wish to bring along a small pen light in case your ride stalls in a dark area.

Dealing With Fears

Fear with attractions: For each of the attractions we provide as detailed a description as we can. We'll try to mention the possible triggers for fear. Of course everyone is different, so if you have a concern that is not addressed here, discuss it with the cast member at the attraction.

Keep in mind that the parks are meant to be fun. Allowing sensitive people, including young children, to be scared out of their wits can ruin a vacation and even worse. It's just not worth it when there's so much fun to be had in the Disney parks.

There are some things you can do that may minimize fears concerning attractions. For example, you can share details of what will happen in advance so there are no surprises. If you take the surprise out and talk about the fact that it's all make believe, you may be able to dispel fears. Of course, very young children and people with certain conditions may still not be able to grasp the difference between reality and make believe. I strongly advise against forcing these people or even allowing them to engage in an attraction that can cause fear.

One other thing you might do to research the issue and even minimize fears is to observe and/or talk to people exiting an attraction. See what children and/or adults say about the scariness of the attraction. Look around at the faces and reactions of the people as they exit. Do you see kids crying or even adults looking stressed? Take that to heart and consider skipping the attraction. If they're happy and excited, this can calm your child's fears or those of a sensitive adult. Remember, fun is the goal here. If there's any question or doubt, it's best to move on and enjoy something else!

I remember on our honeymoon in Bermuda there was a sign at the beach warning of Man-of-War fish. I was ready to ignore the signs and go in the water until I saw a large, muscular man come out of the water sobbing hysterically. He had been stung, and it was painful. I decided to heed the warnings and not go in. Smart, huh? Let others test the waters for you, and play it safe!

Other fears: If you have problems with crowds, you may wish to get a GAC. This will enable you to use an alternative entrance for some of the attractions. It might cut down on some of the crowded situations. For some attractions, if you ask a cast member, they might be able to provide you with an alternative place to wait if you have a GAC.

If an attraction has FASTPASS, this can often be your best bet for avoiding crowds. However you may still be required to wait in a queue even with a FASTPASS. It's just likely to be a much shorter wait, and possibly less crowded.

Timing your trip to coincide with the least crowded times at the parks would be best for someone with discomfort in crowds.

> *Ride Tip:* For those who have a fear of the dark, you may wish to bring a tiny flashlight, like the ones that can fit on a key ring. On many rides, there are moments of darkness. For some folks just being able to see a small light, or even just knowing that they have that light, may be all they need to ward off the fear.

Dealing With Fatigue

To avoid fatigue or if you deal with weakness, we have found that it's best to take a leisurely pace through the parks. It's so tempting to try to experience every last attraction within the time limitations of a vacation. However, long ago we realized that this just made us feel pressured and frustrated. In the end, instead of relaxing, Sarah was exhausted, stressed and weakened. We recommend that you create a list of priorities in advance, and then in a relaxed way, go for it. Determine that if you can't get to everything, it's okay. The objective is to have fun and relax!

Park hopper tickets can help take the pressure off by eliminating the need to finish everything in one day. Standard tickets allow admission to only one park in a single day. Park hoppers allow you to go to more than one park in a single day. The benefit of a park hopper ticket is that you can come back on another day and fit in anything you missed, or do something again you particularly liked. Then you can move on to another park on that same day.

Resting in your resort room: If you suffer from fatigue and need to rest, you may prefer to go back to your hotel room in the afternoon and return to the park later. If you know that you will be going to a particular park more often than the others, you may wish to stay at a Disney resort right near that park to cut down on travel time.

We tried going back to our room for a rest once using Disney transportation. We found that it took too much time for us to wait for a bus, travel back to our room and then rest. By the time Sarah got back to the room she was too exhausted to go back out again. Even if you are staying on Disney grounds, using the public transportation can be quite time consuming. If you plan to take afternoon breaks by going back to your resort for a rest, you may wish to have your own vehicle to cut down significantly on travel time. If we are using Disney transportation we find that we would rather stay at the park and just leave earlier when Sarah has reached her physical limit.

Resting in the parks: Another thing Sarah has done to rest is to find a fairly secluded spot either on a bench, grass or pavement. She then lies down and actually takes a nap. I generally sit near her to keep an eye on her. Additionally, the first aid stations do have cots, and people with health issues who need to lie down can go there to nap. The cots are separated only by curtains, so the area is not soundproof.

> *Shopping Tip:* If you are staying in a Disney hotel you can have your packages sent to your room as long as you're not leaving the next day. This is a fantastic convenience for us, and it frees us up to enjoy the park without the burden of carrying packages around. We love to shop at the Disney parks, and we frequently take advantage of this. You can also do the same at Downtown Disney.

ECVs & fatigue: If you tire easily, please consider renting an ECV even if you don't normally need one. The idea of being in a wheelchair was disturbing to Sarah, but once she did, it was such a relief that she has done it every time since. In addition to helping with pain, it makes the long distances and lines at Disney more manageable. A wheelchair can help you conserve energy and strength.

Crowd & weather strategies: We avoid summer altogether, as it's just way too hot and exhausting. The crowds can be brutal in the summer as well, because kids are out of school. Additionally, we do tend to avoid the parks at all the peak crowd times. When it's very crowded, we feel it's more stressful, exhausting and physically more demanding in part because of the longer wait times for attractions. We try to time our visits to the lower attendance times. You can view projected crowd sizes at www.touringplans.com. (Choose the "Crowd Calendar" link on the left-hand menu.)

Other strategies: To allow Sarah's body to rest, we seldom go to the parks two days in a row. Instead we go every other day. On the off days, we simply relax by the pool and dine out in the evening. This pace allows Sarah to physically recover from the stimulation of the park days. With this in mind we usually plan our longer Disney stays around the spring and fall when the weather is warm enough for pool use, but cool enough so that we don't experience sun and heat exhaustion.

If you have kids, especially if they are overactive, you may choose to allow your kids to blow off some energy while you get to sit and relax. Bring the kids to one of the play areas in the parks, or go back to your hotel and let them swim.

Overstimulation Issues

Some people have difficulty with the massive stimulation involved with being in the parks. There are thousands of people, new sights and sounds everywhere you look, exciting rides and attractions, and even live actors walking the streets performing.

You may wish to get to the park really early before the biggest queue lines start. Consider spending part of the day in the park and part of the day in a calm, quiet setting. You can always go back to the park in the evening when activity dies down a bit.

Some folks choose to take their break in their hotel room. Another possibility is to visit one of your resort's quiet pools. Many of the resorts have smaller pools scattered around the grounds. These usually don't have extra amenities like water slides, lifeguards or towels. However, as a result, there are often far fewer people at these pools and they can offer a nice, quiet place to relax.

You also may want to consider using things like earplugs or earphones with calming music to reduce the effect of sound stimulation in the parks.

Another way to avoid overstimulation is to take some time to just relax in a sit-down restaurant or in one of the pleasant outdoor sitting areas around the parks.

When entering an attraction, let a cast member know if you have a seating preference that may help you avoid overstimulation. There may also be quieter, less crowded places to wait at an attraction if you have a GAC. Ask the cast member at the attraction entrance. If you do run into any problems in the park, most of the cast members will be able to help you. If you encounter one who can't or won't, just ask politely for a manager. There is the occasional newer cast member who hasn't had the full Disney training yet.

One other thing you may want to consider is the location of your hotel room. You may wish to request a room in a quiet location. The amount of activity around your room can vary drastically depending on room placement.

Diabetics

There is a website that has tips for dealing with type 1 diabetes at Disney (http://allearsnet.com/pl/diabetes.htm).

If you use insulin, you can have it refrigerated at the First Aid station. However, you may find it inconvenient to have to keep going back to that location. Instead, you may wish to bring a small cool pack so that you can carry your insulin with you.

See the various food sections in the previous chapter for ways to meet your dietary needs at Disney properties.

> *Tip:* Remember that if you're walking the parks, your insulin requirements may go down from the exercise.

Restroom Issues

If you need to use the restroom frequently, don't worry! Disney has placed many bathrooms all over the parks in convenient locations. There are rarely lines. Almost all are wheelchair accessible, and there are many companion restrooms as well. We will note the locations for these in each park.

Most, if not all, of the full-service restaurants have restrooms, though the rare restroom is not wheelchair accessible. Some over-the-counter restaurants do have restrooms inside, and those that don't usually have one nearby.

> *Tip:* If you have bladder or stomach issues, be sure to use the restroom before getting into a ride queue. Once you're in line you won't have an opportunity to leave.

> *Tip:* At the parks, there are no bathrooms by the bus stops, monorail or boat docks. Be sure to use the restroom before you leave the park. There are usually no restrooms at the resort boat docks.

> *Tip:* Believe it or not, there is a website with photos of the bathrooms at Disney World! Here is the link: www.cassworld.ca/photosbathrooms.htm

Epilepsy

We recognize that there may be different seizure triggers for different people. Please be aware that we can't guarantee we've mentioned them all. Honestly, it's possible that we just didn't notice a possible trigger. This can even include flashing and strobe lights. More importantly, Disney's Guests with Disabilities (407-824-5217) says that the attractions are changed so often that they are not able to keep up-to-date information for guests with epilepsy or seizure disorders. Even Guest Relations will not have information that's up-to-date. They recommend that you ask a cast member at each attraction.

When you are reading our attraction warnings and details, please be aware that things can change daily at Disney. Do not use this book as the final decision-making tool, but as a starting point for your research once you are at Disney. Even if we don't mention your triggers with an attraction description, they might still exist. If we observed the triggers and mentioned them, it's also possible they've been removed or the attraction has changed.

While we feel it's a good idea to check with a cast member at each attraction, be sure they've been in the attraction for the full ride or show very recently. If not, ask to speak with someone who has. Even if they have experienced the attraction recently, keep in mind that they may not have noticed your potential triggers because it may not be something they would ordinarily notice or think about. Finally, if there's any uncertainty, have another member of your party try the attraction first.

It's also important to consult your doctor before going to Disney World to see if he or she can provide any information on how to avoid a seizure with your particular condition.

Here are some general suggestions that may help:

- When you enter the park go to Guest Relations to get a Guest Assistance Card (GAC). This can help you in a variety of ways. For example, some attractions have indoor air-conditioned areas where you can wait out of the sun. Even in the winter the sun can be intense. For some attractions a GAC will allow you to skip part of an attraction that may have triggers, such as the pre-show in the Haunted Mansion, which has a lot of flashing lights simulating lightning. A GAC can also give you seating options. For example, you may wish to sit near an exit in a theater so that you can leave if you need to.

- Be sure to read the next section in this book on medication. It's also a good idea to carry more medication than you need with you in the parks. You wouldn't be the first person to drop a pill and lose it. It's best to be prepared with extra.

- It's our understanding that changing your sleep/wake cycles or medication times can make some people more vulnerable to seizures. Do your best to get plenty of rest. If you can even keep the hours you normally keep at home, this might help your body cope with the other changes. This would include going to bed as the same time that you're used to, and taking your medications at the same time you ordinarily take them.

- Some people find it helpful to bring something to the parks with which you can cover your eyes. It is possible that you may encounter something unexpected, such as flashing lights. Many pharmacies sell sleep masks that effectively block light, and some people use a sweater, scarf or bandana. This might be helpful when you're caught off-guard, or you can be prepared when you are expecting something.

- It's a good idea to take rest breaks if you feel you need it. It's tempting to push yourself because there's just so much fun to be had at Disney. However, if you take that rest you'll be able to enjoy far more of Disney than if you overdo it and have a seizure. First Aid is a cool place where you can have a bed to rest in. The other option is to go back to your hotel room and rest. Staying on Disney property makes this more convenient.

- Be sure to keep hydrated. We hear that dehydration can make some people more vulnerable to seizures. It's so easy to get dehydrated in the Florida sun, particularly with all the walking involved at Disney. This can happen even in the winter and on cloudy days. You can buy bottled water at almost any vending station at Disney. Most of the restrooms have water fountains as well. You may wish to take breaks inside air-conditioned areas such as restaurants. Many of the full-service restaurants have a waiting area you may be able to rest in.

- If you do have a seizure, have someone in your party alert a cast member. They can call the Disney World Emergency Medical Service.

- If you are traveling alone, or even if you will be with others, it's a good idea to have medical identification with you identifying you as having epilepsy. MedicAlert jewelry is a good example of this type of identification. It's also a good idea to keep a list of your medications and dosages with you, as well as any emergency contacts. Place it somewhere that it can be found easily.

- If over-exertion is a trigger, consider getting a wheelchair or ECV. For many people this can cut down dramatically on physical and mental fatigue. However there is another side to this. Using an ECV does require a lot of concentration, especially if the parks are crowded. Some people feel this is more draining than walking, so your choice must be based on your condition. Also, if you do not have warning before a seizure, an ECV would not be a good idea. These vehicles are heavy and are capable of moving fast. It would be possible to have a serious accident if you lost control.

VIP Tours

VIP Tours may be helpful for people with disabilities and impairments. This service lends extra support, some perks and guidance by a trained guide. VIP Tours are available for up to 10 people in your group. They provide special seating at many of the stage performances, parades and big fireworks shows. Tour guides also get you priority seating at full-service restaurants. Mainly, they can help you plan your day. They know where everything is, when each ride tends to be busy or empty, and the quickest paths between attractions. They can even get you situated in one attraction or show and go get you a FASTPASS for another attraction.

VIP tours are pretty expensive, but for some it may be worth it. Some guides will be willing to help push a wheelchair throughout the park, but this is at their discretion. Some may not be willing or able. You pay by the hour with a minimum of 5 hours, and this is in addition to the normal park entrance fee. Depending on the season and whether you are staying on or off Disney property, the fee is currently running $95 - $125 per hour. To book a VIP tour call 407-560-4033.

First Aid Stations

First Aid Stations are clearly marked on the map that you get when you enter the park. In addition to the basics you would expect at a first aid station, such as bandages and aspirin, they can help you with other needs. For example, you will find a nurse there who can help you with all of you non-emergency needs. They can also hold and refrigerate medication. First Aid can hold medical equipment and health supplies for you.

They also have private areas where you can take your treatment or rest. Every First Aid Station has cubicles separated by privacy curtains. These areas have cots, a bedside table and a chair. Each First Aid Station also has rooms like doctors' examination rooms, with exam tables that can be made lower or higher. The exam rooms have a sink and an actual door that you can shut.
We have heard that older guests (larger children, teens or adults) who need diaper changing can do this in the First Aid Station. People with fatigue, pain or other issues can lie down on a cot and rest. Keep in mind that the cot rooms are not soundproof, so they are not be perfectly quiet.

If you have a special need, you may wish to call in advance and confirm that they can help you. For all emergencies in the parks or resorts, alert a cast member and/or call 911 on your cell phone.

The main number to the parks is (407) 824-2222. The operator will try to answer any of your questions, but they may not know how First Aid deals with your specific needs. They can call and check it out for you while you are on hold, or they can transfer your call to a First Aid Station in one of the parks. If you wish to talk with First Aid directly, request a transfer to the First Aid Station in the park in which you will need assistance. You will find that some of the operators are more helpful than others. If you get someone who is not so helpful, call again until you can get the information you need.

How Long Will I Spend in Each Park?

The parks are large, with much to cover. If you are there during a busy period, you will spend a significant amount of time waiting in lines, even with the use of FASTPASSES. When are the busy periods? This used to be quite predictable, but there are times we've gone there expecting quiet and found massive, overwhelming crowds. That said, you can be pretty certain that the entire summer and holidays will be very crowded.

> *Tip:* There is a website (www.touringplans.com) that predicts crowds in each park for each day of the year! They use a lot of different variables to make their predictions, which they explain on their site. It's definitely worth taking a look. (Choose the "Crowd Calendar" link on the left-hand menu.)

Regardless of the time you go, you can count on some waiting and a huge amount of walking. If you have limited time, the stress of trying to get everything in can cancel out the fun of the parks! One thing you can do is to prioritize the rides you most want to experience. Then determine the order of the attractions you wish to follow in advance. Since everyone will have different preferences, it wouldn't be practical for us to outline a plan for you. However, you can make your own by taking a map of the park, circling the attractions you want to try and then plotting your own course. You can view and print out detailed maps of each park on line at *www.disneyworld.com*. Choose the park you wish to see, and then choose the tab that says "map". You can choose the "printable version" option.

You can also request that Disney send you maps of all the parks in advance by calling (407) 939-7630. This is really the best option, as their maps are extremely detailed, easy to read and easy to carry with you in the park. You can also call the parks themselves at (407) 824-2222. *The Unofficial Guide to Walt Disney World®,* which we recommend as a companion to our book, also has detailed maps.

Park hopper tickets can help take the pressure off by eliminating the need to finish everything in one day. Park Hopper tickets allow you to visit more than one park in a day. The benefit of a park hopper ticket is that you can come back on another day and fit in anything you missed, or do something again you particularly liked. Then you can move on to another park.

Communication with Your Party in the Parks

If you think you might separate from anyone in your group, you may want to bring walkie-talkies, cell phones or both. We do find that we have a more consistent signal with a walkie-talkie. We get a lot of dropped calls on cell phones within the park.

Walkie-talkies are fairly inexpensive. You can expect that there will be other Disney guests communicating on the same channel as you, but it's not usually a problem. Just don't say anything you wouldn't want the rest of the park to hear!

Sarah and I find that walkie-talkies are really helpful. There are several attractions I can go on that she can't. She may go off and shop or rest while I go on a ride. With the walkie-talkies I can alert her when I'm done so we can meet, or I can let her know if a queue is taking a long time.

Warnings for Attractions

At the beginning of each attraction's description we share some general information about problems that may be of concern. Please keep in mind that these lists are not all inclusive, and each person must decide for themselves if their particular condition could be made worse by a ride. Also, you should take notice of the signs that Disney posts at each attraction to view their warnings. We recommend taking them seriously. We do our best to describe each attraction and its particular issues, but if in doubt either skip the ride or consult with a Disney cast member at that attraction.

For each attraction we've included a section labeled "Quick Notes." These sections provide you with very brief descriptions of the attractions at a glance. This can come in handy when you're in the parks. Please keep in mind that the information is not all-inclusive. It's simply a quick review of some of the highlights, for your convenience. If you are interested in trying a ride or an attraction, we urge you to carefully read the full description before doing so.

Motion sickness: Some people who do not regularly experience motion sickness may still experience this on some attractions. Even if you've never had this problem, it might be worth considering the motion sickness warnings.

Riding with others: Some of the high-velocity rides where you ride in a seat with another person can present various challenges. When I was young I went on a ride with a much bigger kid. The ride was a spinning attraction, and the other rider absolutely crushed me. I could barely breathe. If you are going on a ride that spins or takes corners at a high velocity, ask the cast member at the attraction if there is a "safe side" to sit on. If not, request to sit by yourself.

More Allergy Issues in Disney Parks

Many attractions have various effects including smoke, fog and fragrance. We will mention those in the ride descriptions.

Concerning the smoke and fog we could not get a complete answer about the various rides and how the fog and smoke is created. We do know that on some of the attractions they create the effect with dry ice. However we can't be certain that this is all they use on all of the attractions. The best information we could get from several Disney cast members is that Disney is very conscious of folks with allergies and tries to avoid using things that will bother them. Additionally, they said that they stick to non-toxics.

Many of the indoor attractions have some kind of a smell. For many attractions this is very subtle. However, it can still be quite noticeable to those with sensitivities. We have found this to be more prevalent in Magic Kingdom, where many of the attractions are the oldest in Disney World. Also, when there is an effect that creates moisture in an attraction, you may experience a musty smell. We find that when there is a combination of moisture and a dark environment, especially on an older attraction, there is usually musty air. Most people will not notice it at all, but we wanted to include this information for those who are extremely sensitive.

> *Tip:* If you are very sensitive, it may help to bring a washcloth to breathe through. If you're concerned that something in an attraction may set off allergies, a cloth may help get you past the offending effect.

> *Tip:* The large fireworks displays do create a lot of smoke; however they are set off high in the air. Most of the time the smoke does not hit street level unless the wind is just right. To avoid possibility of smoke, it's best to determine which way the wind is blowing and view the show upwind.

> *Tip:* We have heard that at times the smoke at the Epcot night-time show IllumiNations can drift over the wheelchair viewing section. Once you're in the wheelchair section it can be difficult to leave until the show is over. If smoke is a concern, you may prefer to view the show from a regular viewing section so that you can move if the smoke drifts your way. There are many places where a wheelchair can be parked right up front for viewing the show, which would be far easier to move out of than the wheelchair section.

Parades

We really enjoy all the Disney parades. Sarah says the "cuteness rating" is off the charts. Adults and children alike will be drawn in. Crowds start assembling early on the parade paths.

Check with Guest Relations to determine the special locations for wheelchairs and those with GACs. You can also refer to the Disney park guide maps. They will show you the parade routes, and these special wheelchair locations are marked with little wheelchair symbols.

These roped-off areas often start filling up early. They usually provide great viewing of the parades. Another benefit is that the cast members usually keep the area in order. For example, they will ask someone to move if they are blocking the view of a person in a wheelchair. Keep in mind that once a wheelchair is in the roped-off area, it will be difficult and at times impossible to leave until the parade is over. Also, the wheelchairs can be packed in pretty tightly. This may put you very close to a stranger.

If the area is not very crowded, they will sometimes allow more than one person to accompany a wheelchair guest. If the special area gets crowded they will ask people not in wheelchairs to leave the roped-off area, allowing only one person to stay and accompany the guest in a wheelchair. If there is room, you can have up to six people with you. If you must separate because it gets crowded, be sure to determine where to meet after the parade.

Guests in wheelchairs can view the parade from the regular viewing areas, but they must stay on the sidewalk. (Wheelchairs cannot park on the street.) Unfortunately, that may mean people standing in front of you.

People start staking their claim on a patch of land very early—I've heard folks say they get there as early as two hours before the kick-off. We have on occasion gotten into the wheelchair viewing area as little as 10 minutes before the start of the parade. It all depends on crowd conditions. The parade routes can get extremely crowded. On a sunny day you may wish to find a spot with some shade. This may mean arriving early to grab a premium shade spot.

> *Tip:* During parade time some of the very long lines at the most popular rides may diminish. This can be a good time to go on busy attractions to reduce your wait times, though there's no guarantee.

Tours

Disney offers many fascinating behind-the-scenes tours of the parks. People in ECVs and wheelchairs can usually participate. Just be sure to let the reservation agent know that you or a member of your party is in a wheelchair when you call in. Also let them know of other disabilities or special needs that are relevant. Call (407) WDW-TOUR.

Disney's Hollywood Studios – Formerly MGM Studios

MGM is one of our favorite Disney Parks. There is so much to do there that's physically comfortable and fun. Although there are some top-of-the-line thrill rides, there are also many good shows, rides and attractions that are physically manageable to those who can't do the rougher rides. The focus at this park is on television and movies, and of course it helps that Sarah and I are huge movie fans!

As of January 2008, MGM Studios will be called Disney's Hollywood Studios. This is to reflect the shift in focus from the golden age of movies to contemporary Hollywood. This new title allows for the current trend of expansion in the park that includes not only movies, but music, television and theater. Newer attractions such as Rock 'n' Roller Coaster Starring Aerosmith, and Lights, Motors, Action! Extreme Stunt Show are all about today's Hollywood culture.

The park is large, but not the largest at Disney World. With 154 acres, there is still quite a lot of walking involved. It is possible to experience the park in one day, especially during slow attendance times. However, we feel that the park is best enjoyed without the stress and pressure of trying to get it all done quickly. One solution for people with time limitations is a park hopper ticket. It allows you to go to multiple parks in any one day. You can come back on a second day and fit in anything you missed, or do something again that you particularly liked. Then you can move on to another park.

Most of the streets at Hollywood Studios have smooth pavement and are comfortable for wheelchair driving. There is the occasional textured area that gives a rougher ride, but only on a small portion of the streets and sidewalks. Most wheelchair ramps are easily spotted, though a few are hard to spot. Just keep looking, as pretty much everywhere is accessible.

Hollywood Studios is actually used for some real production work. Occasionally, you will see something in the process of being filmed. We have only seen this on rare occasions, and there was never much going on that was really interesting to see. That said, you never know what might happen while you are there!

Park Facts for Disability Issues

You can stay in your wheelchair or ECV during these attractions:

- ABC Sound Studio
- American Film Institute Showcase
- Beauty and the Beast
- Backlot Tour
- Fantasmic!
- Honey, I Shrunk the Kids
- Indiana Jones Epic Stunt Spectacular
- Lights, Motors, Action! Extreme Stunt Show
- Muppet Vision 3-D
- Playhouse Disney - Live On Stage!
- Voyage of the Little Mermaid
- Walt Disney: One Man's Dream

These attractions require you to transfer into a wheelchair (available at no charge at the attraction) if you are in a motorized vehicle or ECV:

- The Great Movie Ride
- The Magic of Disney Animation (You may be allowed to stay in your ECV, depending on the cast members.)

These attractions require you to transfer from your wheelchair to the attraction seat:

- Rock 'n Roller Coaster
- Star Tours
- The Twilight Zone Tower of Terror

Wheelchair rentals:

➢ The rental location for ECVs, strollers and wheelchairs is at Oscar's Super Service inside the Main Entrance to the right. It looks like an old-fashioned gas station.

Wheelchair service locations:

➢ Tatooine Traders at the Star Tours attraction
➢ The Writer's Stop, which is a tiny snack, coffee and souvenir shop

Companion restrooms: Most, if not all, of the restrooms throughout Disney have bathrooms allowing access by guests in wheelchairs. You can find companion-assisted bathrooms at the First Aid Station, as well as at these locations:

- Fantasmic! within the amphitheater area
- Next to what formally was Soundstage 3 Who Wants to Be a Millionaire. This attraction was

closed and will eventually be replaced; it may be labeled differently at some point. It's on the right side of this building.

- Across from Star Tours
- Across from the Twilight Zone Tower of Terror
- By Rock 'n Roller Coaster
- At the Lights, Motors, Action! Extreme Stunt Show Theater just to the right of the main entrance

Attractions with FASTPASS:

- Indiana Jones
- Star Tours
- Voyage of The Little Mermaid
- Rock 'n Roller Coaster
- Twilight Zone Tower of Terror

Service Animal rest stops:

- The Studio Kennel's main entrance
- By Star Tours at the backstage gate
- To the left of the Courthouse (Washington Square) backstage
- Near Who Wants to be a Millionaire by the backstage gate. This attraction is closed and may have a different name by the time you visit.
- Backstage, close to the restrooms by the Animation Courtyard
- Backstage behind the Theater of the Stars

Braille map: You will find it inside the park by Guest Relations on the left side.

First Aid Station: You will find this next to Guest Relations just beyond the Main Entrance.

Disney's Hollywood Studios Attractions

Hollywood Boulevard – The main street

When you enter the park, you will encounter a street lined with many unique shops. (We are suckers for the Disney merchandise, especially the Hollywood Studios stuff!) Wheelchairs can maneuver through most of the aisles in the shops, though there are some areas where racks are too close together. Many of the shops open into the next shop from inside, which makes access easier. There are ramps periodically going from the sidewalks to the street areas.

Sometimes you will find street performers here, and they're worth watching. They will interact with the guests, which makes for some lively fun!

Thrill Rides

We'll start with the most physically challenging rides!

Rock 'n Roller Coaster Starring Aerosmith

Cautions: Heart problems, blood pressure issues, back or neck problems, motion sickness, difficulty keeping yourself upright under force, pain issues of any kind, headaches, vertigo, fear of heights, fear of dark, flash of light with picture taking

Quick Notes: High speed, intense G-force pressure, inversions, sharp drops and twists in darkness

© Disney

Rock 'n Roller Coaster® Starring Aerosmith

This is a high-powered roller-coaster ride with three upside-down loops, themed around the band Aerosmith. The story for this ride is that you are going to a backstage party across town and you have to use the LA freeway system. According to Disney, this ride goes from 0-60 mph in 2.8 seconds, which they say has the force of a supersonic F-14. To compare, the space shuttle gives astronauts about a "three G" experience, and this ride gives guests a "five G" experience. This can be a lot of pressure on the body. It has high-speed loops and turns, three inversions, sharp drops and twists.

We have heard that shorter people can experience extreme discomfort around the head from the restraints. If you have tried Space Mountain and been able to handle it, that is not a guarantee that you will be okay with this attraction. This is far more forceful and physically challenging.

The ride car has two car seats per row. The seats are padded. They have harnesses that drop down over your head and over your shoulders. Additionally, the seats are pretty low and you need to get in and out of a low position. There seems to be enough room in the seats for most people of size to feel comfortable. You have 30 seconds to board. They cannot slow down the boarding area for you. There is a practice car that you can use to rehearse, if you feel you need it. Ask a cast member to help you with this.

The Aerosmith music is very loud, as you can imagine. It's piped in through the headrests so it's close to your ears. Here's the kicker: The ride is in the dark with occasional black-lit road signs. You can't see what's coming to brace yourself. This can be completely disorienting and adds to the physical demand and roughness.

There is a bright flashing of light when your picture is taken during the ride.

There is a shaded outdoor queue, and a standing pre-show movie with Aerosmith. There are usually big crowds here, as this is a popular ride. If you wish to change your mind and leave before getting on the ride, or if you just want to go in the queue to see the pre-show, there is an exit before boarding the ride. Let a cast member know you wish to leave after the pre-show instead of going on the ride. The exit lets you out at the gift shop. You can wait in there for your party to exit the ride.

There are so many physical demands here that we feel only the very healthy, strong and daredevil-inclined should try this. However, there are roller coaster loving folks who use a wheelchair but can handle roller coasters. You must have strength to keep yourself in place at strange angles and high speeds, and not be vulnerable to a worsening of your condition from the force, speed and angles. Also, you must be able to handle the strain on the shoulders from the restraints when you are inverted.

If you wish to enjoy the queue and the pre-show without going on the ride, or you just make a last minute decision not to try it, there's an exit right after the pre-show and before boarding. Let a cast member know and they'll escort you out.

For strong roller coaster fanatics, this attraction gets high praises! It's dark like Space Mountain, but it's smoother, faster, and has a lot more thrill motion to it, such as the inversions.

Extra info:

- Time: Approximately 1 ½ minutes
- If you're in an ECV you will be transferred to a wheelchair, and then transferred from the wheelchair to the ride.
- For obvious reasons, service animals are not allowed on this ride.
- Be careful with any jewelry that could easily come off.
- The height requirement is 48" (122 cm) or taller.

Star Tours - The Ultimate Star Wars Thrill Ride
Cautions: Heart problems, back or neck problems, motion sickness, pain issues, problems with strobe lights, headaches. Motionless option may be available, which negates most of these issues.
Quick Notes: Turbulent simulator ride with dives, hairpin turns, bucking

Themed after Star Wars, this ride simulates a harrowing flight through Star Wars-style space. You are put in an "intergalactic simulator," which has the atmosphere of a spacecraft. It's a moderate-sized theater, which we feel is spacious enough not to feel closed-in or claustrophobic to most people. Forty people enter at a time. The front window is actually a movie screen through which you see the action as if you were looking through the window. The sound is quite loud, to add to the effect.

This ride is extremely turbulent. You are jostled and bucked around, as the simulator moves like a spaceship. It's amazing how the movie combined with the motion makes you feel like you are in a spacecraft moving at high speeds. Just imagine the types of moves seen in the Star Wars movies to know what's being recreated with this ride. It includes motion such as dive-bombing, quick turns and flying through turbulence. The attraction doesn't seem to be designed to scare. It's more of a thrill/action ride.

I tested this out for Sarah. She's a big sci-fi fan and wanted to try this ride if it was at all physically possible for her. I determined that it was too turbulent for her back and neck. We've spoken to other people with less severe back problems who felt that this ride did not cause them problems. If there's any question at all, we suggest that you skip this ride.

I actually left this ride very nauseated, and we hear that this is not uncommon. With all of the dives, hairpin turns and other effects, it was tough on my stomach. I couldn't shake the motion sickness for the entire day. On a positive note, at least that limited the amount I spent on food that day! Many people love this ride and have no motion sickness issues. If you're prone to motion sickness you may wish to pass on this one.

The roughest ride in the "ship" is said to be in the back row. It may be smoother in the front or even middle seats. Ask a cast member to seat you if you have a preference.

Multiple light effects are used in this attraction, including flashing lights, twinkling stars, laser lights, blinking buttons on control panels, bright explosions and moving at "light-speed" through the stars. The theater is very dark, and some very bright images appear on the screen, often suddenly.

When entering the building to go through the queue, there is a series of ramps, which can be steep for manual wheelchairs. The indoor queue has some interesting things to keep you occupied as you wait.

There is a smoke effect as R2-D2 works on his ship. There are various light effects in the queue, such as blinking console and machine lights, swirling lights and a film that includes stars and planets.

The simulator seats have retractable seatbelts, and a 5-point harness is available if more support is needed. The seats are separated and are similar to bucket seats. They have armrests and padding but do not have head or neck support.

> *Tip - Motionless option:* You can request to have a non-moving ride. Just ask a Disney cast member for a test ride or a motionless ride. They will run the video, sound and any other effects, without the motion.

They will only do this in the less busy times. If the ride is too busy, there are not enough cars running or there are not enough cast members around, they may decline or ask you to come back at a later time. They have to put you in your own "space ship" so it slows down the cue.

To be honest, I felt that the motionless experience was not very realistic and not nearly as exciting as with the motion. Still, Sarah was glad she could experience the ride, even with the limitations. I had no motion sickness with the motionless ride because there was no real sensation of being in a moving vessel. It was more like sitting in a small theater and watching a movie clip.

Extra info:

- Time: Approximately 5 minutes

- If you're in an ECV you will be transferred to a wheelchair to get through the queue, and then transferred from the wheelchair to your seat. It is a diagonal transfer. The Disney cast member will remove the wheelchair and bring it back in for you to transfer when the ride is over.
- Service animals are not allowed on this ride.
- The height requirement is 48" (122 cm) or taller.

The Twilight Zone Tower of Terror
Cautions: Heart problems, blood pressure issues, back or neck problems, motion sickness, vertigo and balance issues, claustrophobia, fear of the dark, fear of elevators, fear of lightning and thunder, fear of falling, pain issues, issues around ghosts and hauntings
Quick Notes: While touring a scary haunted hotel your elevator plunges and free-falls, rises and plunges repetitively. Darkness, occasional jolts.

The concept is that you are touring a hotel that is now haunted, old and in ruins. You will pass through the queue being exposed to several main rooms of the hotel with lots of atmospheric touches. You are told to go into the library to wait for your rooms to be ready. Then the lights dim, and from an old black and white TV you will hear Rod Serling tell the story of the hotel. The screen flickers like an old-time movie.

Finally you board a "phantom elevator" to be taken to your room. You are placed in a seat in an elevator and strapped in with retractable belts. The seats are one-piece hard benches with backs and belts. There are four rows of seats with an aisle down the middle. The seats in the aisle give you more room, while the ones near the wall are tighter. The elevator first ascends but then actually moves horizontally, taking you on a small tour of the haunted hotel.

You will see many creepy and ghostly effects before the thrill portion of the ride begins. At one point people who you were told disappeared in the hotel suddenly reappear. There is an electrical current or lightning type of effect all around them, with thunder sounds. The images of the people flicker. There are also other times when the electrical current or lightning type effect happens. Twinkling star lights appear as well.

The elevator is 13 stories high, and once it reaches the top, the story is that the cable snaps and you begin to plummet. It happens repeatedly: After the drop the elevator rises and then suddenly drops again. To add to the excitement factor, Disney has a system that makes the number of drops you'll experience for each ride unpredictable. It's meant to be creepy and scary, and it is. Once the drop is over, the elevator may rise again only to plunge once more.

The drop is so fast that you need to be strapped into your seat to keep you in it. At times I felt that when the elevator came to a stop, it did not create a jolt, but was more of a gradual but quick and smooth stop. On other drops there was a small jolt upon stopping. There is also an experience of a light jolt just before the first drop when the elevator cable is supposed to be breaking. If someone tests the ride for a disabled person, keep in mind that you can't really go by one experience of the attraction. The random sequencing of the ride can give a different experience every time.

While there were some jolts, I didn't feel that they were particularly strong or harsh. For many people the jolts are minor. We have found Sarah to be extremely sensitive because of her back and neck, so we felt it was best that she not try this ride. Others we have talked to with less severe back problems did not find this attraction uncomfortable. However, if there's any question at all, we suggest that you skip this ride.

If you have a problem with claustrophobia, heights, fear of the dark, fear of elevators, fear of falling, or fear of ghosts, you may want to avoid this ride. It is an attraction that's meant to be creepy and scary. This is also not a good idea with a weak stomach, or if you are prone to nausea.

The elevator goes dark, which can increase anxiety for some folks. The sun comes in the elevator when the doors open just before the drop, and you can look outside onto the park. On a sunny day there is a big contrast between the light from outside and the dark elevator chamber. You're pretty high up at that point—many stories above the ground. Then you plummet. At one point during the attraction your photo is taken, and there will be a bright flash of light.

If you stand outside the ride on the street and watch the tower, you see the doors open and you will hear people screaming every time this happens.

If you decide you don't want to board the ride at the last minute, you can use the exit just before boarding the elevator. Let a cast member know you want to leave. Many people with disabilities will be able to enjoy this ride and enjoy the free-fall effect.

The walkway and the queue outside the hotel is cobblestone, which can be pretty bumpy for wheelchairs.

Extra info:

- Time: There is an approximately 10 minute pre-show. You get the back story here. The ride is approximately 3-5 minutes depending on the number of drops. (This varies.)
- If you're in an ECV you will be transferred to a wheelchair, and then transferred from the wheelchair to your seat. The Disney cast member will remove the wheelchair and bring it back in for you to transfer back into when the ride is over. If you need extra room, you may find the aisle seat more comfortable.
- Service animals are not allowed on this ride.

Live Entertainment

We find that Disney shows are high quality!

Indiana Jones Epic Stunt Spectacular!
Cautions: Allergies, fear of loud noises, actors simulating violence, fire and loud explosions. Some smoke from the fire and explosions.
Quick Notes: Live action show with explosions, fire, gunfire, harrowing stunts

This is a fun, high-action live show that we really enjoy. Several scenes from the movie are re-enacted. You will see live explosions, crashes, fights and battles, chase scenes, a helicopter on the set, people falling from buildings and other harrowing stunts. A car flips and explodes, and the cast extinguishes the fire with a foam spray. They also reveal some of the behind-the-scenes secrets that make the stunts look so real.

There are sudden explosions and fire, and you will even feel the heat in the back rows. There are also extremely loud, sudden noises and gunshots. There are smoke effects; however, any time we've seen the show the smoke has blown away from the audience. This could be coincidence, so keep in mind that it could possibly blow your way.

The seats are hard benches with backs. If you have issues with any aspect of the show including the loud noises, explosions and fire, you can minimize the impact by sitting in the back of the theater.

> *Tip:* We found the bench back to be hard, awkwardly positioned and tough on our backs. Both Sarah and I found that using a rolled-up sweater for cushioning and support behind our backs was much more comfortable.

Wheelchair users should speak to a cast member at the entrance to be taken to the special seating area. Sarah prefers to stay in her motorized scooter rather then transfer to the bench seats, as it's more comfortable for her. The back rows of all the sections have cut outs for wheelchairs and there are a small number of wheelchair spots in the front, but they are all towards the sides. We prefer to be centrally located, but if you wish to go up front let a cast member know.

Crowds start coming pretty early for each show, so you may want to arrive at least 20 minutes before show time. The amount of time you need varies based on the park attendance, so if the park is very crowded you may want to arrive even sooner. When the show ends the crowd is thick and hard to navigate through. Unless you're sitting in the back row and can make a break for the exit, you may wish to allow the crowd to thin out before you try to leave.

The seating is covered and shaded. Towards the back of the theater and in some of the queue areas, there are machines spraying a mist on the crowd. During hot weather this can be a welcome relief. It can get pretty moist in those locations.

The queue is outdoors with netting covering most of the area. It does provide a bit of protection from the sun, but it's not full protection.

Extra info:

- Time: Approximately 30 minutes
- Assistive listening devices that will amplify the audio can be used here. They are available at Guest Relations.
- You can request sign language interpretation with a minimum of seven days' notice. Interpreted performances are available on a rotating schedule at each theme park. Check with Guest Relations for the current performance schedules, or call Walt Disney World Information at (407) 824-4321 [voice] or (407) 827-5141 [TTY].
- You can remain in your wheelchair or ECV for this show.

Voyage of The Little Mermaid
Cautions: Fear of dark, loud noises, lightning simulations, flashing and twinkling lights, steam effect
Quick Notes: Live musical show with actors, puppets, film, special effects. Rain drizzles on audience, and bubbles drift down. Evil octopus character, lightning and thunder sounds.

Sarah especially enjoys this multi-media show, which gives you a 15-minute experience of the story of Ariel, the little mermaid. It should be suitable for young and old and every age in between. It includes live actors, film, large and small puppets, special effects and the music from the movie. We would consider this a major attraction and well worth seeing. Just don't tell my buddies I said that!

The room is dark—at times very dark—though it doesn't seem designed to cause fear as in other attractions. There is black lighting on the colorful neon-like puppets. On a couple of occasions a rain drizzles down on the audience. It feels like a lot of water while it's happening but it's really a slight sprinkle that dries quickly. It's brief and doesn't really soak through clothing. On a hot day it's a wonderful relief to be in this cool, damp environment. On a cold day it could be chilly and uncomfortable. The water itself is pretty cold.

There are some bubbles coming down from above to simulate water bubbles. There is a pretty cool effect on the top of the room with lights and lasers that gives the appearance of waves, so that you feel like you're under the sea. There is a huge, evil, octopus-type character on the stage that may scare some sensitive folks. There are special effects like lightning, a steam effect and loud noises such as thunder sounds. There are some brief flashing lights and twinkling lights.

You are seated in theater-style seats, which are pretty comfortable. You can remain in your wheelchair, scooter or ECV for this show. The back row has cut-outs for wheelchairs.

Before the show you will wait in a nautical-themed room. There are no seats.

Extra info:

- Time: Approximately 17 minutes
- Reflective Captioning is available. Guests should contact a cast member at this attraction.
- Assistive listening devices that amplify the audio can be used at this location.
- You can remain in your wheelchair or ECV during this show.

Beauty and the Beast - Live on Stage
Cautions: Mist effect on the stage, thunder and lightning, mildly scary beast.
Quick Notes: Live show with actors, spectacular costumes, music

This is a shortened stage performance of the *Beauty and the Beast* musical. It's done with the usual Disney style, and we find it very enjoyable! The sets, costumes, effects and music were really nicely done. Though the beast yells and roars a bit, only the extremely sensitive should find him scary. There is a small amount of thunder and lightning on the stage. Other than this, there was nothing we found particularly noteworthy as far as physical or psychological issues concerning the show itself. However, everyone is different, so it's important to judge for yourself.

This is an outdoor stadium with hard bench seating that holds 1500 people. The seating is outdoors under canopy cover. There are seats for people in wheelchairs, which the cast members will direct you to.

There is a minor mist effect on the stage. We did not notice it spreading over the audience. If this is a concern for you, consider sitting towards the back of the theater.

Extra info:

- Time: Approximately 25 minutes
- Assistive listening devices that amplify the audio can be used at this location.
- You can remain in your wheelchair, scooter or ECV.

Playhouse Disney – Live On Stage!

Cautions: Swirling, flashing lights and other light effects. Most people will have to sit on the floor, as there are very few seats.

Quick Notes: Live show with Disney characters singing and dancing, and encouraging children to get up and join in. Bubbles released from above.

This is geared towards the littlest kids with characters from shows including Bear in the Big Blue House and Winnie the Pooh. Although it's really cute, adults without small children may wish to bypass this attraction.

The queue is outdoors and in the sun. There are a small number of benches in the back of the theater, but most people sit on the carpeted floor. Wheelchairs go in back behind the carpeted area. There are some bubbles that are released from above the audience, as well as streamers. Kids are encouraged to get up and dance, and they chase the bubbles. This might feel chaotic for some people.

There are a variety of light effects including light images of different shapes projected on the walls and swirling lights.

Extra info:

- Time: Approximately 20 minutes
- Assistive listening devices that amplify the audio can be used at this location.
- Handheld captioning is available here.
- Closed captioning is used when film is shown.
- You can remain in your wheelchair or ECV.

Lights, Motors, Action! Extreme Stunt Show

Cautions: Fear of loud noises, fear of fire and explosions, occasional smoke, actors simulating violence

Quick Notes: Live stunt show with car, jet ski and motorcycle chases. Stunt person falls from building. Shoot-outs, explosions, fire blasts.

This fairly new and amazing show is adrenalin pumping! It is a live car stunt show that comes to Disney from their Paris location. Specially designed cars, motorcycles and sometimes jet skis perform well-orchestrated stunts. There are car chases, explosions, fire blasts, stunt person falls and gun shoot-outs. There is even a stunt person set on fire. They show you how some of the stunts are accomplished, and they show you how the entire thing is cut together into a movie on the massive screen above the action. It's truly exciting, though there are some waiting periods during the show as they change the sets.

The amphitheater, which seats 5000, is huge. The wait for entrance is outdoors in the full sun. It can be a challenge to ride a wheelchair through the crowds to get into the amphitheater. At this attraction we have found folks so anxious to get inside that they are often not watching out for a wheelchair, or allowing passage. It may be very challenging to navigate without running people over. We suggest you take it slowly and give yourself plenty of time. If crowds are a problem for you, it would be a good idea to get there early and wait at the front of the crowds.

The seats are pretty uncomfortable metal bleachers with no backs. You can watch the show in your wheelchair, which Sarah prefers here. If you are in a wheelchair or have a GAC, approach a cast member at the entrance for special seating. Although it's my understanding that there are wheelchair seats in the middle as well as the front and the back, we have always been taken to an elevator and seated about halfway up the theater. We found this elevation to be fine for viewing. Sarah prefers to keep her distance from the smoke from the special effects.

Once seated, you may have to wait some time before the show starts. The amphitheater has a cover over much of the seating areas to help with sun exposure, but if it rains you may get wet from sideways-falling rain. The higher up you're seated, the better the coverage.

There are explosions and a use of fire at times. We could feel the heat even at our elevated point, though it was not uncomfortable. There is the occasional smell of smoke, which usually blows away. Sensitive folks may wish to have a cloth handy to cover their noses. The car engines roar quite loudly, and of course the explosions and gunfire are loud.

Extra info:

- Time: Approximately 30 minutes
- There is a restroom on the first level by the entrance.
- Assistive listening devices that amplify the audio can be used at this location.
- You can remain in your wheelchair or ECV.

Disney-MGM Studios Backlot Tour

Cautions: Back or neck problems, difficulty keeping yourself upright as a car tilts, difficulty standing if you don't have a wheelchair, problems with loud noises, fear of fire, floods, explosions, getting wet

Quick Notes: Four-part attraction includes the following:
1. Harbor Attack: Gunshots, fire and explosion effects. Some people will get wet.
2. Warehouse Walkthrough: Behind-the-scenes walking tour. Some very narrow aisles may be challenging for wheelchairs and ECVs.
3. Catastrophe Canyon: Tram ride trembles, shakes and tilts at one point. Floodwater seems to rush at you. Explosions, fire.
4. American Film Institute Showcase: Displays of costumes and some scary figures such as the monster from the movie *Alien*.

This is a multi-part tour, and each part is very different from the others. During the first portion, you will see how a harbor attack movie is filmed. The second part is a walk-through of a warehouse where you will see many objects and set components from various movies. The third part is a tram ride through various backstage production areas including costuming, props, sets, and finally through "Catastrophe Canyon." Finally, you are released from the tram to exit through a small museum called the American Film Institute Showcase filled with costumes and props representing "villains" from various movies.

Harbor Attack: Prior to the show the wait in the queue is shaded. There is no seating. There are overhead monitors that show a video as you wait. The harbor attack show is also a standing portion of the tour with no place to sit, though you can stay in your wheelchair. There is a lot of water splashing in this show. If you wish to stay dry, look for the water marks on the ground and stay outside of them.

Volunteers from the audience participate in this show, which is themed around making a sea battle movie. The participants act out the scenes and then the movie is shown on overhead monitors. Though participants wear full rain gear, they get pretty soaked and one volunteer has to handle some high-pressure water splashing right at them. If this is a problem for you, avoid volunteering.

There are some loud noises from the charges that simulate gunshots and explosions. There is also some fire coming up from the water. You can feel some heat.

You can use the bathrooms after this part of the attraction.

Warehouse Walkthrough: This is a walking tour through an area containing sets and costumes. It is a fairly short walkthrough and is pretty interesting if you are a movie buff. The one potential issue is that the aisles are quite narrow and it's very difficult to maneuver an ECV or wheelchair around the sharp turns. It may require multiple attempts to get around the corners, but just take your time and don't worry! You're there to relax and have fun.

Backstage & Catastrophe Canyon Tram Ride: The first part of this tram tour is pretty easy and relatively smooth. The trams have a canopy covering and bench seats with backs. You are driven through soundstages; the camera, props and lighting departments; the wardrobe department; and various outdoor cityscapes and large movie props such as planes, cars and space ships.

Then you reach Catastrophe Canyon. This is the portion of the ride that can be scary for some people. Suddenly there appears to be a problem according to your tram driver. The ground starts shaking and you face rushing waters, flames and explosions. It looks like the water will reach you, but of course it doesn't, except for a bit of spray. The tram trembles, shakes and tilts. It's pretty brief—maybe a minute or less, though we haven't timed it. The motion is not terribly violent with the strongest sensation we felt being a sudden tilting of the tram.

If you have pain, neck and back issues, it could be uncomfortable. Several people we've spoken to with these issues have been able to tolerate this motion with no problem at all. Sarah skips this portion of the tour because of back and neck pain, as well as issues with her joints. Holding on when the tram tilts is a concern. If you are very sensitive, or there's any question at all, it's best to skip this section of the attraction.

When the flames begin, you can feel the heat. If you sit on the left you will be closer to the action, flames and water. For those who might be scared by this action, it's best to sit on the right side of the tram.

The entire tram experiences the motion, and it is not possible to ride this part of the attraction without the motion. You can remain in your wheelchair or ECV; however, even the section of the tram that holds wheelchairs and ECVs feels the motion.

American Film Institute Showcase: This is the final drop-off point. It's quite a small display, but we find it very interesting. When the crowds get off the tram and move through this place, it can be a challenge to navigate a wheelchair. We've found it was best to take our time and allow the crowd to get ahead of us. There are costumes and props from *Star Wars*, *Planet of The Apes*, and many other classics. A couple of the figures may seem scary to some people, such as the monster from the movie *Alien*.

> *Tip:* You can take most of the tour and bypass the tram and Catastrophe Canyon portion of the attraction. Just let a cast member know you would like to do this. There is no way to participate in the tram ride without going through Catastrophe Canyon, so it's necessary to skip that entire portion of the tour. When I boarded the tram, Sarah was led to the American Film Institute and lingered there until I arrived. One perk was that she was able to view the Institute's displays with pretty much no one else in there.

Extra info:

- Time: The tour is approximately 40 minutes long. The entire attraction can take up to an hour.
- Assistive listening devices that amplify the audio can be used at this location.
- Handheld Captioning is available at this attraction.
- Filmed portions of the attraction are closed captioned.
- Guests can use attraction translation device units.
- You can request sign language interpretation 2 weeks prior to your visit.
- You can remain in your wheelchair or ECV. Alternately, you can use the regular seats on the tram and the cast members will have your wheelchair or ECV waiting for you at the drop-off point.

Disney Stars and Motor Cars Parade
Cautions: Except for the fact that this is outdoors, allowing exposure to the elements, we did not observe any noteworthy obstacles, impediments or challenges, but please judge for yourself as everyone is different and attractions may change.
Quick Notes: Outdoor parade with Disney characters and cars

The Disney parades are just simply fun for any age. This parade consists of cars decorated for and filled with Disney characters. Other characters walk in front of the cars, at times dancing, with some interaction with the crowds. People start lining the streets fairly early.

You can find a curb to sit on, stand or sit in your wheelchair. There are two wheelchair sections roped off. One is at the end of Hollywood Boulevard in front of the Giant Mickey's Sorcerer hat, and the other is in front of the Keystone Clothiers shop. Although we got there just a minute or two before the parade on our last visit, we were still able to squeeze into the wheelchair viewing area. However, during peak crowd times you may need to get there early.

Fantasmic!

Cautions: Fear of fire, dragons, Disney Villains, loud noises, light effects and strobe lights, laser lights, fireworks, possible smoke

Quick Notes: Outdoor nighttime show with fireworks, live actors, puppets, water effects, boats, lasers, animation, music. Fire breathing dragon may be scary to some. Those sitting up front may get wet.

This nighttime outdoor show is absolutely wonderful and not to be missed. It includes your favorite Disney characters "live" and also in movie form. (I won't give away *how* they show the movie, as this is part of what makes this amazing!) It also includes a fire breathing dragon, water effects, light effects, laser, animation, fireworks, fire, boats, live action and of course music. The story is that Mickey has a nightmare and faces off against Disney villains. Although there is a happy ending, it is possible that it can be scary to children or those with corresponding fears.

The stadium is near the Tower of Terror. Though the stadium is huge, allowing almost 10,000 people including wheelchairs and standing room, it actually starts filling up pretty early. The theater usually opens 90 minutes before the show begins, and at peak crowd times it can fill right up. Each night, weather permitting, there are one or two shows. At very busy times people may start lining up outside the stadium as early as two hours in advance. This is especially so when there is only one show that night. During smaller crowd times we have rushed in ½ an hour before the show started and gotten seats. When there are two shows, it is usually easier to get seating for the later one.

The seats are built around a moat that fairly large boats actually ride through, and on the other side of the moat is the stage. Also on the moat there are water effects and lots of flames at times. The flames are pretty close to those sitting in the lower levels, and you can feel the heat.

There are many light effects including lasers, spotlights, strobe lights and sudden bright flashes. There are perhaps thousands of tiny twinkling lights decorating the ships that pass in front of the audience. There are sudden bursts of flames and fireworks. There are loud explosions. Keep in mind that the fireworks are extremely loud, and there is always the possibility of some smoke settling.

There is a lot of water used in the show, and sitting in the seats up front can get you damp. Really you can see from pretty much anywhere in the stadium. You can bring food inside with you, and you can buy some basic snacks and drinks inside the stadium.

You can also get reserved seating by buying into a Fantasmic! Dinner Package. This allows you to have dinner at one of three restaurants, and then to enter the stadium 30-45 minutes before showtime without waiting in line. We did this once, and the seats were fairly far over on the right side of the stadium. We do usually prefer to be seated more centrally; however, we could see everything from there just fine.

The three restaurants you can choose from for the Fantasmic! Dinner package are:

Mama Melrose – The dinner includes your choice of appetizer, soup or salad, entrée and a dessert.

Hollywood Brown Derby – Choose one wood-fired flatbread to share, family style salad, choice of entrée, and a dessert.

Hollywood & Vine – An all-you-can-eat buffet.

Please see our reviews of the restaurants in the restaurant review section of Hollywood Studios.

Be sure when you make your reservation to leave enough time to eat and then to get to the stadium. Last time we did Fantasmic! as a dinner package, we barely had enough time to eat. They actually started removing the foods from the buffet and telling us we would have to leave shortly. We felt we had cut it way too close to really enjoy our meal. Depending upon your restaurant location, you may wish to plan on leaving the restaurant around 1 hour to 1 hour and 20 minutes before the show to get to the stadium and take your seats. Also, when you make your reservation, ask what time the restaurant stops serving food.

Wheelchairs enter Fantasmic! through the regular queue, staying to the far right side. You will be directed to the wheelchair seating area by a cast member. The seats in the stadium are uncomfortable hard stadium benches with no backs. The back row of the bleachers is exclusively for wheelchair users. The bleachers directly in front of the back row are for members of their party. There are a couple of wheelchair seats in front, also. You may get wet, though. See a cast member if you prefer this location.

Extra info:

- Time: Approximately 25 minutes
- There is a bathroom near the entrance to the stadium, and refreshment stands.
- Reflective Captioning is available.
- Assistive listening devices that amplify the audio can be used at this location.
- You can stay in your wheelchair or ECV.
- There may be some smoke from the fireworks.

Other Attractions

Muppet Vision 3-D

Cautions: Loud noises, minor explosions and gun shots, light effects. Some people with epilepsy have difficulty with 3-D effects.

Quick Notes: 3-D movie and live special effects. These can be startling but not usually scary except to the occasional very sensitive child. Effects include pyrotechnics, cannon shot, bubbles, water spraying, air blowing, light effects.

This is fun for adults as well as kids. It's a very cute 3-D tour of Muppet Labs where things go awry. The 3-D effects are really amazing and a lot of fun. Sometimes it does feel like things are flying right at you, which could be "jump out of your seat" startling. There are also live puppets, animatronics, pyrotechnics and effects around the theater, including sensory effects.

There is a pre-show, which has no seating and can get quite crowded. Before using an ECV, Sarah would sit on the floor during the wait. I stood by her to keep people from stepping on her. The floor in the pre-show area slopes down pretty sharply. Lighting is fairly dim in this area, though not dark. It allows for better viewing of the monitors. Wheelchair users should make their way to the right side of the room to enter the theater.

There are overhead monitors with an entertaining 10 minutes of Muppets on multiple monitors. The

Muppets actually seem to be moving from one monitor to the other, which is a really impressive effect.

The main show has theater-style seating. The seats are reasonably comfortable, but you can also stay in your wheelchair. Contact the cast member to direct you to the entrance for the back row, which has cut-outs for wheelchairs.

You must wear the 3-D glasses provided by Disney in order to get the 3-D effect. These will fit over your own glasses. There are a variety of effects in the theater including water spraying at the audience, bubbles floating down from above onto the audience and air blowing at face level. There are some loud noises and explosions in this show. At one point there is a live audio-animatronics Muppet shooting a cannon, which blows holes through some walls. At the same time the 3-D movie shows debris flying at the audience. It's a quick but surprising moment that occasionally can scare sensitive people. Though this 3-D does not seem to be attempting to scare guests, we have occasionally seen it bring young children to tears.

Extra info:

- Time: There is a 10-minute introduction and an 18-minute film.
- Reflective Captioning is available here.
- Video Caption-ready monitors are available.
- Assistive listening devices that amplify the audio can be used at this location.
- Guests can use attraction translation device units.
- You can remain in your wheelchair or ECV.

Journey Into Narnia: Creating The Lion, The Witch and The Wardrobe

Cautions: Fear of dark

Quick Notes: Guests stand in a Narnia set and view a brief movie and a monologue by a live actress playing the White Witch.

This is based on the wonderful movie of the same name. The first waiting area is outdoors. Then there is an indoor waiting area with no seating, which is fairly dark and can be crowded. In the waiting room, there is a large replica of the wardrobe door from the movie. At some point they had the wheelchairs come through the crowd and up in front of the doors, but once the doors were opened to admit the crowd it was difficult to enter as the crowd behind just pushed in front of us.

You are led into a dimly lit room, which is designed to look like the winter scene by the light pole from the movie. It's somewhat chaotic as the crowd moves in, and there is no real direction as to where people in wheelchairs—or anyone else—should go. Really, we feel that anywhere in the room will usually provide a reasonable view, so we don't recommend struggling to try and get into any special position.

After a wait, there was a brief movie clip that seemed like a promotional trailer for the movie. Then an actress appeared on a balcony above the crowd to the right of the room. She was dressed as the White Witch and did a brief monologue. More of the movie is shown, and afterward, the crowd was released to another area to view a small sampling of props, art and costumes from the movie. The crowd pressed by this quickly and, before we knew it, we were outside again. If you wish to see this small display, you might try allowing the crowd to pass you by so that you can stay and view the area at your leisure.

Extra info:

- Time: Approximately 7 minutes, though this can vary
- You can remain in your wheelchair or ECV.

Sounds Dangerous - Starring Drew Carey

Cautions: Fear of the dark, problems with loud noises, fear of bees, fear of clowns or circus acts

Quick Notes: Movie with headphones that utilizes sound technology to create special effects. Part of the show is in complete darkness. Sound of swarming bees, loud noises.

This is another of our favorites. Drew Carey creates a lot of fun in this movie as a bumbling detective going undercover. You will experience a wide variety of entertaining and even amazing sound effects.

The queue is shaded fairly well with monitors showing a pre-show film. The movie is shown in a theater with fairly comfortable theater-style seats. You can stay in your wheelchair. Just ask the cast member to direct you to the special seating area. The back row has cut outs for wheelchairs with headsets that can reach you in your wheelchair. The theater seats may be small for some people, but there are a few seats with arms that can go up to give you more room.

You must wear a headset over your ears to hear the movie. Sarah sometimes has a problem with earphones because of jaw pain with TMJ. This headset was not particularly tight or uncomfortable, and she was able to tolerate it. It allows for different sounds to come in through the left and right ear to create the fascinating effects you'll experience.

More than half of this movie experience takes place in complete darkness. The idea is that Drew Carey loses his camera feed, and now you can only tell what's going on by hearing the audio. This enables you to focus completely on the sound effects, but if you fear the dark you may find it stressful. If you can relax and pay attention to the sounds, it's really a cool experience. The exit signs stay lit, and you can keep your eyes on these as a way to deal with the dark. Sit near an exit if you feel you may want to leave.

There are some loud noises, and one of the effects sounds like bees swarming. It's fairly brief, though, and done in a comedic context. You can remove the headset if a particular sound is a problem.

Those with hearing impairments may not get the full experience. It may be quite dull if you can't hear well in both ears.

Extra info:

- Time: 12 minutes
- Handheld Captioning is available.
- Assistive listening devices that amplify the audio can be used at this location.
- Guests can use attraction translation device units.
- You can remain in your wheelchair or ECV.

The Great Movie Ride

Cautions: Fear of dark, some scary movie scenes, loud noises, violence, fear of snakes (robotic), mock gun fights with live actors and audio-animatronics, fear of skeletons, fear of witches, allergies, flashing lights. See descriptions below for more.

Quick Notes: Ride through various movie sets with audio-animatronics characters as well as live actors. Some mildly scary scenes, gun shoot-out, lightning.

This is a ride that combines film clips, audio-animatronics (speaking robots) and live performers. You board a vehicle and pass through a re-creation of the door of the Chinese Theater in Hollywood. You are then brought on a tour that takes you through sets from films including *The Wizard of Oz*, *Casablanca*, *Raiders of The Lost Ark* and *Alien*.

The outdoor queue is in full sun. The indoor queue is cool and pleasant with a few really interesting objects of movie memorabilia. These include the carousel horse that Mary Poppins rode and the fur coats the children wore in Narnia. There is no seating in the queue, but you can lean on the railings. Within the next part of the queue you can see interesting clips of movies repeating while you wait to be let into the boarding area. The film can be quite loud, and the room is fairly dark.

Wheelchair users can ride the attraction in a wheelchair or transfer to the ride car seat. Let a cast member know what you wish to do and they will direct you. The ride cars are slow moving and pretty smooth. You can feel very faint bumps on the track, but they should be minor for most people. The track is level. The seats are bench seats with backs and are quite wide.

A cast member goes with you on the tour at the front of the ride car and becomes part of the live action in a "shoot-out" scene. Another actor "hijacks" the ride car, but the original cast member does reappear later. Sound effects can be quite loud.

Though the scenes are not completely realistic, some very sensitive folks may be scared. For example, there is a scene from the movie *Alien*. You pass through the ship and the alien animatronics pops out slightly from the wall. We don't find it to be an intensely startling thing. You could miss it if you weren't looking around for it. Some people may find the shoot-outs to be scary, but most won't. Just know it's coming and that it's really just pretend.

There are a variety of light effects including lightning, flashing lights like those you see in a movie theater marquee, light flashes to simulate gun shots, twinkling stars, swirling and flashing lights in the Alien spaceship set, and other light effects. Other types of effects include a small flame at one point that you can smell. There is some steam used for effect. You pass through the Indiana Jones scene where there are many, many snakes (not real, of course). There are some characters that may scare the very sensitive, including skeletons and a witch. Some of them are animatronic and move. There are old time movies that flicker. Some scenes are quite dark.

After riding through the movie sets you will ride into a theater room where your vehicle parks. You face a large screen where you view many of the most memorable scenes from a wide variety of movies. This theater is quite dark and the movie clips do go on for some time. Once they're over, your vehicle moves again and takes you to the disembarking area.

Extra info:

- Time: There is a 3-minute pre-show with an approximately 18-minute ride.
- Handheld Captioning is available.
- Assistive listening devices that amplify the audio can be used at this location.
- Guests can use attraction translation device units.
- Guests with service animals should check with a cast member to be sure their animal will be comfortable with this ride.
- Guests must transfer from the ECV to a wheelchair. You can remain in a wheelchair during the ride or transfer to a ride seat. See a cast member to direct you.

The Magic of Disney Animation
Cautions: We did not observe any noteworthy obstacles, impediments or challenges, but please judge for yourself, as everyone is different and attractions may change.
Quick Notes: Movie, tour and interactive area teaching the process of animation

This attraction is a behind-the-scenes look at the process of animation.

The first part of the attraction is a fairly pleasant short film that is narrated by an animator and Mushu, a character from Mulan. Together they describe the process of creating an animated film. The seats are theater style and you can stay in your wheelchair or transfer.

You are then led through an area with some displays, and you can view an artist's area where there is usually an artist or two working. Finally your tour will end up in an interactive area where you can "paint" animated pictures by computer, do voiceover on an animated sequence or participate in other activities. It's moderately interesting if you haven't seen it before.

The queue is mostly shaded outside. Sarah actually was able to go behind a large post near the entrance and lay on the ground to rest her back in relative privacy during our wait. Inside, there were some ramps to go down. There was nothing scary, and the only challenge was that at times it was tough for Sarah to stay in front of the crowd on the ECV so she could see the exhibits.

Extra info:

- Time: The movie lasts approximately 20 minutes. The amount of time you spend with the rest of the attraction is up to you and depends on your level of interest.
- Reflective Captioning is available.
- Video Caption-ready monitors are available.
- Assistive listening devices that amplify the audio can be used at this location.
- You can use attraction translation device units.
- You can stay in your wheelchair or ECV.

Walt Disney: One Man's Dream
Cautions: We did not observe any noteworthy obstacles, impediments or challenges, but please judge for yourself, as everyone is different and attractions may change.
Quick Notes: Movie about Walt Disney's life and career

This was created to commemorate the 100th anniversary of Walt Disney's birth. It includes a gallery exhibit with Disney memorabilia and old recordings. You also see a film about Walt Disney's life and career. We found it very interesting to see how everything unfolded.

The seats for the movie are theater style. People in wheelchairs enter through the same entrance as the regular queue.

Extra info:

- Time: Approximately 20 minutes
- You can stay in your wheelchair or ECV.
- Handheld Captioning is available at this attraction
- Reflective Captioning is available here.
- You can use attraction translation device units.
- Assistive listening devices that amplify the audio can be used at this location.

Disney's Hollywood Studios Dining

Some of Disney's most original dining experiences are in Hollywood Studios. The themes are original and so well played out. We make it a point to dine in Hollywood Studios whenever we can.

Better Quality Dining

The Hollywood Brown Derby

This is themed after the sophisticated Hollywood Brown Derby where the stars hung out in times past. The décor is mahogany wood and brass, with many caricatures of celebrities. The main dining room is sunken, with some seating around it on the entrance level. Seats are wood with padded seat bottoms. There are also some booths. Outdoor dining is available, but only attempt this on a cooler day!

It's Hollywood Studios's most upscale restaurant, and the prices are higher than most of the others. It has American-style food including fish, chicken, pork tenderloin, steak and one or more vegetarian dishes. We've found the food to be tasty. The service is excellent with white-jacketed waiters, and the ambiance is pleasant.

Last time we were there, there was a roaming actor mingling with the guests. He sat down at our table and chatted with us in character.

If Sarah's TMJ is acting up, they have a finely chopped Cobb salad which is very easy for her to eat.

It's best to make a reservation in advance here, especially during busy seasons.

The Fantasmic! Dining package is available here.

Sci-Fi Dine-In Theater

This is an incredibly unique environment. This restaurant is indoors and made to look like an outdoor drive-in movie theater. The tables are small vintage-style cars with padded bench-type seating. We did not find it very comfortable on our backs, but it was tolerable. Most of the cars hold six people in three rows. There is a tray table that fits over your legs. There are a small number of regular tables with armless chairs, and even a regular wood picnic table if you prefer.

There is limited bench seating in the restaurant waiting area. There is a sample car outside that you can try out first.

The room lighting is dim. There is enough light to see your food and each other, but it's dark enough to see the movie screens and to create the atmosphere of a nighttime drive-in.

The movies are short clips and trailers for very old, horror and sci-fi movies and cartoons. There really isn't enough of any one clip to get involved in a story line.

The food includes various sandwiches, burgers, salads and shakes, as well as more elaborate dishes such as vegetarian selections, seafood, pasta, fish and ribs. If money is an issue, you may consider going here for lunch and sticking to the less expensive items, or even just going for dessert to experience the place. The ambiance is worth experiencing!

It's necessary to make a reservation here, especially during busy seasons.

Assistive listening devices that amplify the audio can be used at this location.

50's Prime Time Café

This is our absolute favorite Hollywood Studios restaurant, and maybe one of our favorite restaurants anywhere. It's not so much the food, which is good and plentiful, with some incredible desserts. It's more about the experience. When you walk into 50's Prime Time Café, it's like walking into your parents' house in the 1950's. All of the furniture and tables are realistic, and the place is filled with authentic decorative pieces found from that time period. Black and white old-time televisions are everywhere showing continuous clips from the 50's.

Here's what makes the experience even better: Your waiter or waitress is your "cousin" and the idea is that you are home having a meal back in the day. Depending on who you get, the experience can be hilarious. The waiters and waitresses are really interactive role players, and most seem to really enjoy it. Some are better than others, but we've almost always had great fun. In our many visits we've only gotten one waitress who did not get into the part.

If you don't want to participate, let your waitperson know. It's still fun to just watch what goes on at the other tables.

Meals include fried chicken, pot roast, meatloaf, healthier choices such as grilled chicken and fish, and a vegetarian meal. They have sugar-free ice cream here and very enticing, homey desserts such as a combo of marshmallows, chocolate and graham crackers! They have consistently honored our special dietary requests, even when we did not have advance reservations.

You can get a table with booth seating and/or pull-out chair seating.

> *Tip:* Eat everything on your plate or your wait staff might play the airplane game with you. I've been made to eat my string beans like this on multiple occasions! You'd think I would learn. Keep your elbows off the table (or keep them on if you want to engage your server), and most of all have fun!

It's best to make a reservation here, especially during busy seasons. We have gotten in without them at off times without too much of a wait.

Hollywood & Vine

The theme here is the Golden Age of Hollywood. It has a very simple art deco look. The food is an all you can eat buffet which we found decent but not memorable. It's fine if you are looking for variety and plenty of food. The noise level is high in here because of the acoustics in the room. The seats are metal without arms.

The food items on the buffet vary depending on whether it's lunch or dinner. They may include field green salad, shrimp salad, pasta with seafood, beef dishes, rotisserie turkey, fish choices, vegetarian selections, mashed potatoes and desserts.

It's best to make a reservation here, especially during busy seasons. We have found it nearly impossible to get in without a reservation.

The Fantasmic! Dining package is available here.

Mama Melrose's Ristorante Italiano

This is pretty much themed like a moderate neighborhood Italian restaurant. The cast members do not interact according to the theme, and the décor is fairly simple and like many restaurants we have visited locally.

The tables are close together, and we find the booth seats to be awkward and a bit uncomfortable. The booth backs are padded but extremely straight. There are also some wood chairs. It may be challenging to navigate in a wheelchair here, but it can be done.

The food includes wood-fired flatbreads, pasta dishes, bruschetta, calamari and a vegetarian selection. Gluten-free pasta is available upon request.

This restaurant is not centrally located, and there may be a better chance of getting in without a reservation here, though reservations are always a good idea.

The Fantasmic! Dining package is available here.

Quick Service Restaurants

In the quick service restaurants, there may be some minor special requests that can be filled, but for the most part, what you see is what you get.

ABC Commissary

This is in the style of an ABC Commissary where the stars would eat in between shooting. Really it's a very simple environment without strongly themed decor. The food is adequate, and when we can't get into one of our favorite restaurants we go here if we're in the area.

There are vegetarian and low-fat selections and dishes such as a vegetable noodle stir-fry, fish 'n chips, and tabouleh wraps, as well as Cuban sandwiches and cheeseburgers.

The first register on the left is wheelchair accessible. There is indoor and limited outdoor seating. Indoors there are television monitors featuring promos for current ABC shows with closed captioning. The seats are either small padded seats with arms and low backs, or bench seats with backs and padding.

Outdoors there are tables with umbrellas and small metal seats with backs.

Backlot Express

This is themed as a movie studio prop shop and art department. It has a warehouse look to it—it's very casual displaying various objects that could be used as movie props.

They serve burgers, fries, hot dogs, salads, chicken strips, grilled vegetable sandwiches, grilled turkey and cheese, frozen soft drinks and beer.

To ride your wheelchair in, pay attention to the markings for the wheelchair routes, as the main routes involve stairs. Once you're in, the aisle width makes for easy wheelchair parking next to a table.

Starring Rolls Café

You'll find a Brown Derby Cobb salad, turkey on focaccia, smoked salmon on a bagel, vegetarian pita, fresh-baked goods, pastries, deli sandwiches, mini desserts and gourmet chocolates, along with freshly roasted coffee, cappuccino and espresso. You can get breakfast here some mornings.

There is outdoor seating. Service can be slow. The first register on the left is wheelchair accessible.

Studios Catering Co. Flatbread Grill

You'll find some exotic Mediterranean dishes at this open-air grill. They include tandoori chicken and flatbread sandwiches including baba ghanoush and steak gyros. The register on the far right is wheelchair accessible. You can get gluten-free food here upon request. Seating is outdoors.

Sunset Ranch Market

This is an outdoor market setting with various "vendors." Food includes hamburgers, hot dogs, smoked turkey legs, veggie burgers, pizza, french fries, hand-dipped ice cream and fresh fruit. Seating is outside on picnic benches, which are covered.

It can get kind of crowded and challenging to move about in a wheelchair.

Toy Story Pizza Planet

This is more arcade than restaurant, inspired by the movie *Toy Story*. You can get pizza, salad and drinks here, and play arcade games to your heart's content. It's a very colorful environment. The seating is on the second floor. You can take the stairs or the elevator, which is inside the arcade and to the right. The seats are metal with backs. There is some outdoor seating, which is mostly shaded. There are also metal seats with backs. The first register on the right is wheelchair accessible.

Writer's Stop

This little hidden and out-of-the-way place is a favorite of ours. It's cool, usually not very crowded and a pleasant place to relax and get a snack. There is a comfy couch and chairs to relax on. There are books and some souvenirs to browse.

There is a little coffee bar with other appealing choices like baked goods and bagels. The coffee is fresh brewed, and they also serve frozen drinks. You can request iced coffee.

Animal Kingdom

This park is the newest of Disney's playgrounds and also the largest, at 500 acres. It's part zoo, part African culture, and part thrill rides and attractions. Concerning the animals, much of what you will see is created to resemble natural habitats. Keep in mind that Disney does give most of the animals living space where they can be out of the view of their human audience. Many say that the earlier you arrive, the better chance you have of seeing the animals. Often in the heat of the day, they move out of sight and into the shade for their siestas. You may wish to schedule Animal Kingdom on a day where Disney gives Extra Magic Hours in the morning to those staying at a Disney resort.

The rides and attractions at this park are very spread out, so if walking is an issue and you've considered a wheelchair (preferably electric), this is the place for it. Most of the attractions are outdoors, so consider this when planning your day. Although there are many wooded areas in the park, you will often be exposed to direct or indirect sunlight. Many of the walkways are in direct sunlight. As in all of the parks, it's a good idea to bring sunscreen, sunglasses and a good shade hat. If you have problems with heat, plan on stopping regularly in the indoor restaurants for a drink and some air conditioning.

Another option if heat is a problem for you is to spend only the morning at Animal Kingdom. If you buy a park hopper Disney ticket which gives you entrance to all the parks, you can move on to another park such as Hollywood Studios or Epcot, in the afternoon. These parks have many indoor, air-conditioned attractions, which can make the afternoon heat more bearable.

At times Animal Kingdom closes much earlier than the other parks, so a late afternoon visit to this park is not practical. Check with Disney for closing times before you go.

Much of the park has lush landscaping and atmospheric themed towns and attractions. These are as interesting to look at as to participate in. At times you will see live performances given by people from the country the attractions are representing. Disney went all out to keep the various architectural styles authentic. They even brought in experts from Africa to create and maintain the straw roofs on some of the buildings.

With the way the park is laid out it can be overwhelming to walk it all. There is a center island (Safari Village), which all of the other "lands" are built around. Bridges connect each themed "land" with the center island. There will be some backtracking necessary to get from one place to another at times. With the massive distance between opposite lands, it's a good idea to plan your routes before coming.

You may need to build in some flexibility in order to see the shows, as the show times can change from day to day. When you enter the park, get a show time schedule and make any changes necessary to your plan.

Keep in mind that some of the walking paths have hills, some fairly large, and almost all of the paths are textured. They are made to look like a natural path in the jungle with animal footprints, cracks, pebbles and roots running through. Although it adds to the atmosphere, Sarah finds it very uncomfortable to drive over in her ECV. She feels the bumps and cracks jostle her chair continually, and it irritates the condition in her neck and jaw.

That said, most people will have no problem with this at all. It just depends on your level of sensitivity. Sarah is probably on the very extreme end of sensitive. Keep the terrain in mind as you prepare your schedule, especially if you are pushing a wheelchair or using a manual wheelchair by yourself.

Most attractions will have people with disabilities enter through the regular queue. This can be a bit challenging in some places as some of the corners are tight. It may take several tries to get through a corner turn. Just take your time and don't get stressed about the people behind you. Do your best and expect folks to show some decency. Most will!

We find that the walking paths at Animal Kingdom are not as wide as some of the paths at Hollywood Studios and Epcot. During busy times it can feel very crowded, and maneuvering a wheelchair or ECV can be challenging.

On a recent visit during a peak crowd time there was a lightning storm rolling in. As we looked for somewhere to go for cover, we realized that Animal Kingdom does not currently have many places where people can find shelter during a storm. Additionally, we found that the walking paths were narrower than those at Hollywood Studios and Epcot, making the situation seem more stressful as people rushed to take cover. We decided to leave the park and head over to Hollywood Studios. It was crowded there also, but we felt more comfortable as we navigated the wider paths. We also felt there were plenty of places to go for shelter when it rained.

Although we are huge animal lovers, we prefer Hollywood Studios and Epcot to Animal Kingdom. We find those parks to be less physically demanding. Regardless, the main attractions we really love here are the Maharajah Jungle Trek, the Pangani Forest Exploration Trail and the Festival of the Lion King show. If you are able to participate in thrill rides and you really enjoy them, this park may have great appeal for you. Also, the animal attractions are beautifully done and the animals never cease to be fascinating.

> *Tip:* Straws and drink caps are not given out in the park. If you need a straw or cup with a lid for drinking, be sure to bring your own. Disney also has souvenir cups with built-in straws available for purchase.

Park Facts for Disability Issues

You can stay in your wheelchair or ECV during these attractions:

- Conservation Station
- Cretaceous Trail
- Discovery Island Trails
- Festival of the Lion King
- Flights of Wonder
- Fossil Fun Games
- It's Tough To Be A Bug
- Maharajah Jungle Trek
- Pangani Forest Exploration Trail
- Pocahontas and Her Forest Friends
- Tarzan Rocks!
- The Boneyard
- Wildlife Express

These attractions require you to transfer into a wheelchair if you are in a motorized vehicle or ECV, and then into the attraction:

- Affection section in Rafiki's Planet Watch
- Kilimanjaro Safaris
- TriceraTop Spin

These attractions require you to transfer from your wheelchair to the attraction seat:

- DINOSAUR
- Primeval Whirl
- Kali River Rapids

Wheelchair rentals:

- ➢ The main rental location for wheelchairs, strollers and ECVs is at Garden Gate Gifts inside the Main Entrance.
- ➢ Outpost has limited quantities of wheelchairs.

Wheelchair service locations (You can have your wheelchair replaced here also, if they have any left):

- ➢ Creature Comforts
- ➢ Mombasa Marketplace

Companion restrooms: Most restrooms throughout Disney have bathrooms allowing access by guests in wheelchairs. There are companion-assisted bathrooms at the First Aid Station and:

- In Asia right near the Maharajah Jungle Trek
- In Dinoland at Chester and Hester's Dinosaur Treasures

- At Conservation Station at Rafiki's Planet Watch
- Discovery Island just opposite the FlameTree Barbecue restaurant
- At Expedition Everest near the area bathrooms
- In Harambe Village at the Mombasa Marketplace

Attractions with FASTPASS:

- DINOSAUR
- It's Tough To Be A Bug
- Kali River Rapids
- Kilimanjaro Safaris
- Primeval Whirl

Service animal rest stops:

- Primeval Whirl
- DINOSAUR
- Affection Section – Rafiki's Planet Watch
- The aviary area at Maharajah Jungle Trek
- The aviary area at Pangani Forest Exploration Trail
- TriceraTop spin
- Kali River Rapids

Braille map: After you enter the park, walk the path over the bridge. The map is mounted in the shopping area near the Disney Outfitters store and near the Tip Board.

Manipulatives: These are hands-on features around the animal enclosures. They are designed for the sight impaired so that you can touch and feel items that teach you about the animals in that location.

First Aid Station: You will find this is located in Discovery Island just behind the Creature Comforts.

Animal Kingdom Attractions

Animal Experiences

Most of these are designed around walking trails and are experienced at your own pace. If you have allergies, note that these areas are thick with foliage and flowers. Since a large part of this park is experienced outdoors, rainy days may not be best.

It's a good idea to take bottled water on the trails with you, as it can get very hot. There are drinking fountains here and there, but when you are lingering around a particularly interesting view, you don't want to have to leave to search for a fountain.

Wildlife Express

Cautions: We did not observe any noteworthy obstacles, impediments or challenges, but please judge for yourself as everyone is different and attractions may change.

Quick Notes: Train ride to Rafiki's Planet

Although this is not an animal experience itself, this train ride will take you to Rafiki's Planet Watch, which is an animal experience. It is the only way to get there. This area includes the Affection Section and Conservation Station. The wait for the train can take some time. The ride itself is only about 6 minutes each way. The seats face outward with two rows of seats. There is room for one wheelchair per car. This may mean that you'll have to wait for a train during busy times.

The path leading to the Wildlife Express is quite long, but you can see animals and backyard wildlife information posted as you go. After the train ride there, the path to the attractions is also quite long.

Affection Section

Cautions: Allergies, immune issues, fear of being in contact with live animals

Quick Notes: Live-animal petting zoo

Location: Rafiki's Planet Watch

This is an outdoor petting zoo. Interact with smaller domestic animals, many of which are somewhat exotic. The animals include Sicilian miniature donkeys, African Pygmy and a variety of goats, sheep, pigs, chickens and llamas. Children and those who have never had exposure to farm animals may enjoy it.

People with immune issues might consider that these animals can bring exposure to various parasites and bacteria. Although Disney takes exceptional care of their animals, they are still outdoor animals. Those with allergies should use caution. The yard is kept very clean by Disney cast members, but of course animals will be animals. Watch your step!

There is a station for washing your hands. It's a good idea to take advantage of this when you're done! Also watch your belongings. Some of the animals will eat anything, so be careful with anything you don't want eaten.

The area is shaded and the ground is hard-packed sand, suitable for a wheelchair to ride on.

> *Tip:* Llamas spit. I once went eye-to-eye with a llama while petting it in a petting zoo. It seemed so cute and harmless until it spit its lunch at my face. Sarah had a great laugh over this, but I would rather not have experienced it! The lesson learned is that face-to-face meetings with llamas are not always wise!

Guests can participate in wheelchairs here, but the ground is dirt, which can be challenging to maneuver over.

Extra info:

- In light of the interaction with animals, service animals are not allowed here.
- Flash photography is not allowed.
- Guests must transfer from ECV to a wheelchair.

Conservation Station

Cautions: Fear of animals, fear of sounds including thunderstorms and mosquitoes, fear of viewing live surgery on animals

Quick Notes: Educational area promoting conservation. Sometimes a live animal is brought out, and an occasional animal surgery may be viewed.

Location: Rafiki's Planet Watch

This is in the same area as Affection Section. Disney works to promote wildlife conservation awareness here. You can see into examining rooms and feeding areas as the animals are being take care of. There are informational videos, hands-on experiences, Song of Rainforest sound booths and wildlife exhibits. Occasionally a cast member will come out with an animal and answer questions about it. It is possible that you could view a surgery in progress.

Sounds of the Rainforest booths have dim lighting and require the wearing of a headset to hear the sounds. The sounds that you hear will include thunderstorms and mosquitoes, along with the more pleasant bird and animal sounds. Wheelchairs can fit in the booths but must back out.

This attraction is most interesting for children. The message of conservation is a good one; however, adults without children may want to consider the time it takes to get there and get back if your time is limited!

This area is air conditioned, which can be a very big relief on a hot day.

Extra info:

- Assistive listening devices that amplify the audio can be used at this location.
- Video Caption-ready monitors can be used here.
- You can stay in your wheelchair or ECV.
- Sign language interpretation is scheduled on some days. Check with Guest Relations to see if it is available during your visit.

> **Discovery Island Trails**
>
> **Cautions:** Fear of caged wildlife—see below for details.
>
> **Quick Notes:** Walking trails with some caged animals including tortoises, lemurs and cotton-top tamarins

Location: Discovery Island

These are paved trails through lush tropical foliage that also take you around the Tree of Life (described later). Along the way you will see wildlife such as large Galapagos tortoises, lemurs and cotton-top tamarins.

Extra info:

- You can stay in your wheelchair or ECV.

> **Habitat Habit!**
>
> **Cautions:** Fear of caged wildlife—see below for details.
>
> **Quick Notes:** Walking trails with a small number of caged animals, including cotton-top tamarin primates

Location: Rafiki's Planet Watch

This is a minor exhibit along a trail in area where you can see endangered cotton-top tamarin primates.

Extra info:

- You can stay in your wheelchair or ECV.

> **Maharajah Jungle Trek**
>
> **Cautions:** Fear of bats (un-caged), fear of birds (uncaged) fear of wildlife – see below for details.
>
> **Quick Notes:** Walking trails with a variety of wildlife including Komodo dragons, tapirs, tigers, bird aviary and bats. Bats are not fully caged, but separated from guests by structures their wings are too big to pass through. Bird aviary has free roaming birds.

Location: Asia

This is a major attraction with some of the most fascinating animals you will see at Animal Kingdom. It runs through lush forested areas with the theme of the Anandapur Royal Forest of Southeast Asia. There is interesting architecture along the way, even in the make-up of the animal habitats, which adds to the atmosphere. There is some shade, but depending on the time of year it can still get very hot.

Some of the animals you will see include Komodo dragons, tapirs, tigers and the surprisingly fascinating and very large fruit and flying fox bats.

When you enter the bat viewing area, you will see that there is no glass separating them from you. Instead there is an attractive structure that has frames at intervals that prevent the bats from flying through. We have been told by a cast member that there has never been an incident when a bat got through the structures and poles into the viewing area. With their large wingspans of over 5 feet, they are unable to pass through the slender spaces between the frame structures.

Once we got over the initial "freak out" of having nothing visible that seemed to separate us from some very big bats, we spent quite a bit of time there. These are strange and fascinating creatures. By the way, the bats are fruit eaters—not people eaters. You will see lots of fresh fruits hanging for the bats to eat. You can bypass the bats if you are uncomfortable, but they are really worth seeing.

For the tigers, there are several different viewing points. Depending on where the tigers are hanging out in their habitat, you may get to be inches from them separated only by glass. They have their own ruins and a water pool where you may catch them playing. We couldn't get enough of them! They may be quite active in the late afternoon, as it's closer to feeding time.

On most of our visits there was plenty of room to look through the large glass windows. The tigers are pretty popular and the area can get congested. You may have to wait for a spot to open up with a good wheelchair view. There are multiple viewing areas, so if you can't get in at the first one, move further down the trail and you'll see other spots. The first tiger viewing area does have steps, but the other viewing areas don't.

The trail also passes through a bird aviary with over 50 species of birds from Asia. There are benches to hang out on for a while to enjoy the birds and the atmosphere.

Don't be shy about asking questions of the cast members who are stationed with the animals. They always seem quite knowledgeable, and we've always gotten the feeling the cast members have enjoyed chatting with the guests.

The trail is approximately 1/2 mile, paved and quite bumpy, as are many of the paths at Animal Kingdom. You can see the animals from a wheelchair, but if you can stand, the views are better at times.

Keep in mind that there are no bathrooms along this trail, so use a restroom before you begin. There is no set length of time that you might be on this trail, but you can count on at least 20-30 minutes if you're like us. On a nice day we can hang out by the bats and tigers for ages! It's also a good idea to have some bottled water with you. You'll be outdoors and it can get hot. It's important to stay hydrated!

Extra info:

- You can stay in your wheelchair or ECV.
- Service animals can't go in the aviary section. You can use the bypass trail to avoid this area.

Pangani Forest Exploration Trail
Cautions: Fear of spiders, lizards, snakes, wildlife, close contact with free-roaming birds—see below for details.
Quick Notes: Walking trails with a variety of wildlife including those mentioned above, as well as gorillas, hippos, meerkats, antelopes, gazelles. Bird aviary has free-roaming birds.

Location: Africa

This is another major animal attraction that is fascinating and worth the time it takes. This trail is explored at your own pace, so you can linger as long as you like by your favorite sites. Here you will see African wildlife, including an up-close look at a troop of gorillas, Nile hippos (there is an underwater hippo viewing area), meerkats, antelopes, gazelles, birds and others. There are various other displays including African wildlife facts and smaller animals. There is an exotic bird aviary and a savannah overlook. It is also approximately a 1/2-mile trail within a heavily wooded area. Though the trees provide some shade, depending on the time of year it can still get very hot.

Along the way there are some hands-on experiences. As you move in and out of the research center portion of the attraction, you will pass through some heavy doors. Someone in a chair or with a disability may need help with these. The center can be a bit tight for the wheelchair, but it's manageable. You will find spiders, lizards and snakes.

In the aviary there are usually some larger birds roaming free on the walking paths. They are generally pretty passive, but there's the possibility of a bird having a bad day and behaving in a more aggressive or interactive manner.

There are times when the viewing areas can become crowded, and you may have to wait for an opening to get a wheelchair up close.

There are a couple of wooden bridges that you will pass over, which can wobble a bit. You may feel the boards, making for a rougher ride in a wheelchair. Since Sarah finds riding over rough surfaces too painful, I usually ride the chair over the bridges for her.

Keep in mind that there are no bathrooms along this trail, so use a restroom before you begin. There's no set length of time that you might be on this trail, but you can count on at least 20-30 minutes if you're like us. On a nice day we can hang out by the gorillas, hippos and meerkats for ages! It's also a good idea to have some bottled water with you. You'll be outdoors and it can get hot. It's important to stay hydrated!

Extra info:

- You can stay in your wheelchair or ECV on the main paths.
- Video Caption-ready monitors are available in the research center.
- Service animals are not allowed in the aviary. A cast member can direct you on how to proceed.

The Oasis Exhibits

Cautions: We did not observe any noteworthy obstacles, impediments or challenges, but please judge for yourself as everyone is different and attractions may change.

Quick Notes: Walking trails with a small variety of wildlife, some of which may be difficult to spot

Location: Oasis

This is a winding path that has lush tropical trees and gardens with wildlife viewing areas scattered along it. This is pleasant but not as exciting to us as some of the other major attraction areas and trails. There are waterfalls and streams. It's sometimes difficult to spot the animals, some of which have the ability to go out of site. The paths are paved but rough, as are most in this park.

Extra info:

- You can stay in your wheelchair or ECV.

Thrill Rides

Animal Kingdom has some of the newest and most adventuresome rides in Disney World. They can also be quite physically demanding.

DINOSAUR

Cautions: Heart problems, blood pressure issues, back or neck problems, joint or muscle pain, motion sickness, balance or weakness problems, pain issues of any kind, headaches, vertigo, fear of dinosaurs and meteors, fear of dark, allergies, strobe lights, swirling and flashing lights

Quick Notes: Physically intense ride that can be scary, in a simulator/vehicle that takes you back in time to capture an Iguanodon. Severe turbulence, sudden movements and stops, sharp turns, loud noises, smoke smell.

Location: Dinoland U.S.A.

This is a pretty rough ride that lasts approximately 3 ½ minutes. It's extremely turbulent, very dark and loud. You will be jostled, bucked, bounced and swayed pretty intensely. There are sudden movements, sudden stops, sudden sharp turns, loud noises, flashes of light and other very intense special effects. These include ferocious, large audio-animatronics dinosaurs jumping out at you, appearing suddenly or running over the tracks.

The smell of smoke is pumped into the atmosphere. It is apparently a fragrance and not from actual smoke.

DINOSAUR

This is absolutely one to avoid if you have any of the problems mentioned above. We don't consider it wise to see if you can get away with the motion on this attraction if you have health issues. This one can be scary, and not just to children. Many adults find this ride frightening. If you have any problems with blood pressure, anxiety or fear, this may be stressful. Adding to the stress there is a warning counting down the seconds left until the asteroid that killed all the dinosaurs will hit earth. Also consider that this ride is pitch-black at times, with giant, scary monsters jumping out at you from the darkness.

The indoor queue is made to look like a museum where you pass by fossils and life-size replicas of dinosaur skeletons. During the standing pre-show you view a video where you are taught about the destruction of dinosaurs by meteors hitting the earth millions of years ago. You are asked to go back in time and retrieve an Iguanodon just before the big meteors slam to earth destroying the dinosaurs. You are then loaded into your "time vehicle" for a very rough ride.

To get to the ride car and to leave the ride car area, there are a number of steps. You can bypass these steps by using an elevator, which is to the left of the loading area. Let a cast member know you need this. To go on this ride you must transfer from your wheelchair to the ride car.

The ride vehicle seats 12. It is a simulator that supposedly goes through a primeval forest avoiding dangers along the way, including attacking dinosaurs (which just about catch you) and meteorites. The vehicle is open and looks kind of like a safari car. There is a hydraulic pump that makes the vehicle move roughly as if you are traveling over rocks and tree stumps. Although Disney actually toned down the motion some years ago, it is still very rough and jerky. You will have a seat belt. Some may need a shoulder restraint to stay stable on this ride. These seats are pretty narrow and can cause discomfort during the turbulence. There is no head, upper back or neck support. We have heard that the front of the car may have a smoother ride.

There are many effects with lights including a strobe effect, swirling and flashing lights. There is a bright flash when your picture is taken.

Extra info:

- Time: Approximately 3 ½ minutes long on ride portion
- Video Caption-ready monitors are available.
- Assistive listening devices that amplify the audio can be used at this location.
- Guests may use attraction translation device units.
- Service animals are not allowed on this attraction.
- You must transfer from your wheelchair or ECV to the ride car.
- The height requirement is 40" (102 cm) or taller.

Expedition Everest - Legend of the Forbidden Mountain

Cautions: Heart problems, blood pressure issues, back or neck problems, joint or muscle pain, motion sickness, balance or weakness problems, pain issues of any kind, vertigo, fear of monsters, fear of the dark, fear of bats, steam/smoke effect

Quick Notes: High-speed roller-coaster with rough, jerky movements, hard twists and turns, sudden stops, 80-foot plunging drop. It travels backwards at times, with some times of darkness. Scary monster.

Location: Asia

This is a train ride that is also a high-speed roller-coaster ride with some intense twists—literally and figuratively. There are no upside-down loops. The story is that you are taking a train car up Mount Everest, when you are told that the train tracks have been damaged by the Abominable Snowman, otherwise known as the Yeti.

This begins the high-speed thrill portion of the attraction. You'll experience some rough moments, including moving backwards, moments of darkness, plunging down an 80-foot drop, hard twists and turns and sudden stops. This happens with the massive Yeti monster on your trail attacking, roaring and screaming very loudly. This monster can be very scary to some people, and at one point it reaches out to grab you. (Of course it doesn't get you!) It's actually one of Disney's more realistic creations!

The ride goes through some direction changes. It starts forward, stops briefly when you see that the tracks are broken by the Yeti monster, and then it takes off going backwards. Keep in mind that this can all be challenging for someone with health problems such as neck, back, weakness and pain problems. After this it stops again and goes forward for the rest of the ride. This ride does not have an inversion—no upside-down moments. This ride can be very bumpy or jerky. Some of it is very dark.

The ride trains seat two per row with 17 rows per vehicle. Each seat has its own safety bar that you pull down over your lap. It actually should lock in at whatever point you pull it down to. Once it stops moving, it locks in. The seats have a panel that your head can lean back on. There is a test seat that you can try out before riding, which should be by the gift shop that goes with this attraction.

Though the seats are snug, most larger people seem to find the seats a comfortable fit. Some very large people may have a challenge getting the bar down into a position where it locks. You might have to put the bar down until it clicks while still standing, then slide under it to sit. You may want to practice this on the test car to be sure you will fit comfortably.

On sunny days the ride car will move in and out of dark caves and into the bright light, which could be an issue for some people. There are bright flashes of light inside a dark cave when your photo is taken. Bats hang in the caves. There are spots with a steam/smoke effect.

There's an entire back story revealed during your time in the queue, which you will miss if you bypass the lines. The indoor queue area is loaded with details that many find fascinating. It unfolds the story and can keep you occupied during the wait. You can actually go through the queue and decide not to go on the ride. There are exits at various points. Just let a cast member know that you would like to exit.

Extra info:

- Time: Approximately 3 minutes
- Adult supervision is required.
- Service animals are not allowed on this attraction.
- You must transfer from your wheelchair or ECV to the ride car.
- The height requirement is 44" (113 cm) or taller.

Kali River Rapids

Cautions: Heart problems, back or neck problems, high blood pressure, joint or muscle pain, motion sickness, balance or weakness problems, pain issues of any kind, vertigo, fear of fire or water, allergies

Quick Notes: High–speed, white-water raft ride. There are some drops, and the rapids cause some bumpiness and roughness. You will get soaking wet. There is some fire and smoke. Flower fragrance is pumped into the area. The raft can spin and you may travel backwards. You must step down into the raft and up to get out.

Location: Asia

Kali River Rapids®

This is a high-speed white water raft ride. Personally I did not feel this was a violent ride, but it does have its share of motion, which may be challenging for some people. It did not bother my back or neck. Those who like thrill rides often find this too tame, but many will love it. At the very sensitive end of the spectrum, Sarah has chosen not to try this because of the bumpiness of traveling over the white water.

The ride craft is a large, 12-seat round raft with six sets of two-person seats. The raft seats have high backs, which can be supportive. Each person has a seatbelt. There is a round bar in the center of the raft that you can grab onto.

The outdoor queue is covered and is very detailed with displays that fit the theme. The loading area is a large disc that rotates and matches the speed of the raft. You will have to step down into the raft and put on your seatbelt.

For people in wheelchairs or those who move slowly, there is another loading area. The raft is docked and you can get into the raft without the time pressure. They put a flag on the raft so they know you need assistance when you return, and you go through the same procedure getting out. You must step up to get over the raft top, and down three steps.

As all of the Disney rides are, this is not just a water rapids ride but a highly themed experience. Basically, you are taken through a jungle that is being threatened by illegal logging. Part of the ride is through lush vegetation, but then you encounter burned forest. You will smell smoke from the illegal tree burning and feel the heat of the flames. There are also flower scents pumped into the area during this ride.

There are geysers that will spray you and the boat travels over white water rapids. This causes some bumpiness and bouncing. The round raft also does a bit of spinning in the in the water currents. You may travel backwards. There are some times of high speed, and a quick drop of the raft with some impact. The circular boat also rotates or spins around. You could be traveling backwards. There's spraying, dripping and squirting water often aimed at the guests.

Of the 12 people in the boat, at least 10 will get very soaked (and I'm talking drenched). One or two may or may not come out dryer than the rest. There is no way to predict which, if any, of the seats will avoid the water splashes. On my last ride on this attraction, I was the one who came out relatively dry. I got some pretty nasty looks from some of the others on my raft. They were literally dripping and squeezing out the water from their clothes.

On a hot day, this drenching feels wonderful. On a cool day it can be very uncomfortable and even a health concern for some. You may wish to wait for the hottest part of the day to try this ride. Even on hot days, you will probably be going in and out of air-conditioned attractions afterwards, some of which are very cool. Disney sells towels and some dry clothing right after you leave the ride, including socks and underwear. There is also a restroom right outside. You can also store your things in a locker at the entrance of the Animal Kingdom park, though that may not be terribly convenient.

> *Tip:* Be careful with anything you don't want to get wet. Wear a raincoat or Disney rain poncho to keep dryer, though it will not keep you completely dry. You can purchase these at most of the Disney stores and some of the vendors' carts. Bring plastic bags to keep your belongings dry. You can use a garbage bag, or some sealable baggies, depending on what you are protecting.

We have been told that Disney requires you to wear shoes on this ride. If you take them off, a cast member may or may not make you put them back on. That depends on the cast member. You may wish to bring flip flops to change into so you can protect your shoes in a bag. There is a storage area in the center of the raft for your personal items, but in our experience it hasn't been effective at keeping things dry. You may also wish to bring a change of clothing. Even on warm days, wet clothes can chafe as you walk the park.

> *Tip:* For extra fun, people can stand on a bridge overlooking the rafts, and squirt unsuspecting riders with water from an elephant's trunk! Personally, this is my idea of fun!

Please keep in mind that those who are not swimmers or comfortable with water may find this very scary. Especially vulnerable are young kids who are not comfortable with being splashed and are not comfortable with water.

Extra info:

- Time: Approximately 5-6 minutes
- Adult supervision is required.
- Service animals are not allowed on this attraction.
- You must transfer from your wheelchair or ECV to the ride raft.
- The height requirement is 38" (95 cm) or taller.

Other Attractions

It's Tough to be a Bug!

Cautions: Fear of the dark, problems with loud noises, flickering or strobe lights, fear of spiders and bugs, allergies, back pain, strobe lights. Some people with epilepsy have difficulty with 3-D movies.

Quick Notes: 3-D movie experience with sensory special effects. The seat pokes your back. There's smoke created from dry ice, spraying water, wind effects, stinkbug smell, buzzing sounds, giant spiders coming down overhead and from the walls. This could be scary to very sensitive people.

Location: Discovery Island

This attraction's theater is located inside the gigantic 14-story "Tree of Life," which is a manmade tree/building. It has 325 intricate carvings around the trunk depicting wildlife that you can view as you go through the queue, which winds around and then inside the massive tree trunk. The outside path leading to the theater is not shaded and can be quite hot. Disney's most advanced audio-animatronics character made so far is in this show. Hopper is the bad guy of the story, and he has over 70 separate functions that bring him to life.

Once you get in you're given 3-D glasses to take with you to your seat. You are asked not to put them on until the show starts. The pre-show waiting area can be very crowded and can feel a bit claustrophobic to some people.

This is a 3-D movie experience that allows you to see the world through a bug's eyes. Of course, situations ensue in this bug world, and some 3-D as well as 4-D effects happen.

There's actually a sensory effect that pokes you in the back from the back of your theater chair. This is supposed to simulate a stinging bug. The item doing the poking feels small—I'm guessing about the width of a small pencil eraser. It is not at all sharp so it doesn't feel like being stung. Most people will have no problem with this, but it actually poked Sarah right where she was experiencing a lot of pain and made it worse. If you have back pain, you may wish to sit forward in your seat so that your back doesn't touch the seat back while you watch the show. You'll know it's coming when Hopper (a creepy but amazing audio-animatronics character) says, "Arm your stingers and attack."

Some of the other effects include smoke created from dry ice, spraying water, wind effects, stinkbug smell pumped into the room, buzzing sounds and things dropping from the ceiling. At one point the audience thinks it's being sprayed with acid or bug spray. (Of course it's really water.) The effects of this attraction may be of concern for those with allergies.

Another effect that children and adults with fears might be concerned about is that of giant spiders coming down overhead and from the walls. The show might seem quite scary to some children and even some sensitive adults. There's always a lot of screams from the crowd, and this attraction regularly makes children cry. If someone in your party does get scared, taking off the 3-D glasses can minimize some of the on-screen visual effects. Some of the off-screen effects may be less intense in the back of the theater. The scary audio-animatronics character named Hopper is actually in the front to the right of the stage. Sitting in the back left may keep you farther from that character.

There are strobe lights used in this show. It is very dark in the theater.

The theater seats are bench seats with backs. Wheelchair seating is available with slots between regular chairs. If you can transfer to a chair, you do experience more of the sensory effects.

Extra info:

- Time: Approximately 8 minutes
- Attraction translation device units can be used here.
- Service animals are allowed, but you should check with a cast member to be certain that the types of things the animal will encounter won't be a problem.
- The 3-D glasses should fit over your own glasses.
- You can stay in your wheelchair or ECV; however, you will miss some of the sensory effects.
- After leaving the show, turn left to find the exit ramp for wheelchairs.

Kilimanjaro Safaris

Cautions: Back or neck problems, joint or muscle pain, motion sickness, balance or weakness problems, pain issues of any kind, fear of free-roaming animals, allergies, claustrophobia, high blood pressure, heart problems

Quick Notes: Outdoor safari ride in an open-sided vehicle through a 100-acre animal reserve. The ride is rough and jerky over rugged terrain with bumps, ditches and a high-speed chase.

Location: Africa

Kilimanjaro Safaris® with zebras and giraffes

This is an open-sided safari vehicle that takes you on an "expedition" through a 100-acre animal reserve. You will encounter African animals as they roam freely throughout the savannah and hills. You may see giraffes, hippos, zebras, warthogs, crocodiles, elephants, rhinos and lions. The animals can roam in and out of site of the vehicles, so every time you take this tour will be different. They can come right to the truck or they can vanish from view. There are times when I've seen almost nothing close up, and other times when it was great viewing.

The queue is outdoors with a canopy and a few ceiling fans. It can get quite crowded and claustrophobic. You will view a video about the problems of poaching on the televisions overhead. This is to set the tone for the story you will be a part of on your safari.

The terrain is really rugged with bumps and ditches, so the ride is very rough. You will be jerked around quite a bit. The roads are as you would imagine in the wild. You will ride over heavily pitted dirt roads, a bumpy bridge and creeks, and be taken on a high-speed chase. These vehicles are not designed for smooth driving. I didn't find that it irritated my neck or back at all, but those who are sensitive to this type of motion should abstain. Sarah is highly sensitive to this type of motion and has chosen not to participate in this attraction.

The trucks are covered, with open sides and benches with very little padding. The ride may be the least bumpy in the front of the truck. You can place your personal items in a small, netted area.

A few of the safari vehicles can take a single wheelchair. ECV drivers must transfer to a Disney-provided wheelchair or walk to the vehicle bench seat. Service animals are allowed if the can remain lying down during the ride.

Personally, I find that I tend to have more animal sightings walking the main animal trails. We have heard that the earlier you go on this ride, the more chance you have of seeing a lot of animals. Also, late afternoon may be better, since the animals often retreat to shade during the heat of the day.

Don't stand up in the truck. The driver may stop fast to avoid animals. The truck seats 32 guests.

The queue is outdoors and covered.

Extra info:

- Time: Approximately 18-19 minutes
- Attraction translation device units can be used here.
- Assistive listening devices can be used here.
- Service animals are allowed, but you should check with a cast member to be certain that the types of things the animal will encounter won't be a problem.
- Video Caption-ready monitors can be used here.
- Handheld Captioning can be used here.
- You must transfer from your ECV to a wheelchair, or transfer to the vehicle seat.

Primeval Whirl

Cautions: Heart problems, back or neck problems, motion sickness, pain issues, vertigo or dizziness

Quick Notes: This ride looks like a child's roller coaster but is really a thrill ride with sudden drops, sudden stops, hairpin turns, high speeds, tight curves and spinning.

Location: DinoLand U.S.A.

This looks like a child's roller coaster, but is really a thrill ride. It has sudden, unexpected drops, sudden stops, hairpin turns, high speeds and tight curves. Each car spins independently. Based on the programming for your car, it may spin one or two revolutions at a time, or it can come to a sudden, very jarring and abrupt halt in mid-circle. This can be very uncomfortable and painful even to folks without health concerns!

Primeval Whirl® at Disney's Animal Kingdom® Theme Park

Someone may get squashed by the person next to them during a spin, especially if they are smaller. Seats have a low bar. You may go backwards at times, and you will be taking corners and curves with a lot of force.

At one point a dinosaur tries to bite your ride car. It's not a particularly scary ride as far as the effects go, but it is physically demanding and roller-coaster thrilling/scary.

The spinning and other roller coaster moves can induce motion sickness.

The ride vehicles move slowly when guests are loaded. If you can't embark on your own, let a cast member know and they should be able to stop the ride.

Extra info:

- Time: Approximately 2 1/2 minutes
- Service animals are not permitted.
- You must transfer from your wheelchair to the vehicle seats.
- The height requirement is   48" (122 cm) or taller.

Triceratop Spin
Cautions: Motion sickness, dizziness, fear of heights
Quick Notes: Children's spinning ride with elevated cars that allow you to set how high you fly

This minor children's attraction is a spinning ride with elevated cars that allow you to control how high or low to fly. Four people can ride at a time, in two rows. Whoever is in the front row gets to control how high or low you go. Those in the back can tilt your dinosaur car forward and backward, though the tilt is not dramatic.

You can stay in a wheelchair or transfer from your ECV to a standard wheelchair. It's a hard bench seat with a back. Of course, if motion sickness is an issue, stay away from this one.

Extra info:

- Time: Approximately 2 minutes
- You can transfer from your wheelchair or ECV to the car. There are some wheelchair accessible vehicles. You would need to transfer from your ECV to a standard wheelchair. Let the cast member know if you wish to ride in a wheelchair.
- Service animals are not allowed on this ride.

Live Entertainment

Festival of the Lion King
Cautions: Fire twirling act may create some smoke. Flashing lights, mist effect, stimulating.
Quick Notes: Dazzling live show featuring dancers, huge puppets, floats, acrobats, fire twirling, music

Location: Camp Minnie-Mickey

This is one of Sarah's favorite live shows at Disney. It's a truly spectacular and beautifully done production featuring songs and characters from the film. It tells the touching story with a combination of dancers, huge puppets, floats, acrobats, fantastic costumes, makeup and a lot of high energy! The entertainers may interact with some of the folks in the front rows. There is usually so much going on at one time it's hard to pick something to focus on. It's really a dazzling feast for the senses, and in our opinion Disney at its best!

People with conditions that require a calmer, less stimulating environment should keep in mind that this show could be considered very stimulating. For some people this is the perfect show: There's so much going on that it can keep the attention of those who need a great deal of stimulation.

The seating is limited, so you may want to arrive a half hour before the show to get in. Guests are usually seated approximately 15 minutes before the start of the show. The outdoor queue is uncovered and very exposed to the sun. It can get stuffy here, and there are often crowds waiting to get into this popular attraction. Going to the first or last show of the day may be less crowded. Another good time to try to miss the crowds is around parade time.

This is a theater in the round. The seats are rows of hard bleacher seats with no backs. People in wheelchairs and their companions sit in the front row. You must climb stairs to get to the second row or above. The theater is air conditioned.

There is an act with fire twirling. The lights in the room are dimmed, and the fire twirling creates a bright spinning light. We were not really aware of the smell of smoke or fuel, but it's possible that it could be a factor depending upon where you are sitting. Some flames also shoot from the stage, and even cover a portion of the stage. Many people take photos of the show, which creates a lot of flashing lights. There are many spotlights and flashing lights, which usually seem to move with the music.

It's a good idea to get there early if you need special seating. Wheelchairs are seated before the general public is let in. If you have a GAC and need to sit in the front, be sure to let a cast member know. Enter through the regular queue, but look for the signs for a path that wheelchair users should follow.

Extra info:

- Time: Approximately 30 minutes
- Service animals are permitted, but check with a cast member to make sure your animal will be able to handle all of the activity.
- Assistive listening devices can be used here.
- Sign language interpreters can perform here on a designated day. Call (407) 824-5217 to make arrangements.
- You can stay in your wheelchair or ECV.

Flights of Wonder

Cautions: Fear of live free-flying birds

Quick Notes: Outdoor bird show with free-flying birds and unrestrained walking birds, centered on conservation and preservation

---

Locations: Asia

This is a bird show on an outdoor stage with free-flying (and walking) birds. The theme of the show is conservation and preservation. You will see birds such as vultures, owls, hawks, falcons, macaws, crowned cranes and the American Bald Eagle up close.

There is hard bench seating without backs. The theater is mostly shaded. There isn't a formal queue—you just wait outside for the theater to open. Some of the birds are very large, and some fly low over the audience. If you are in the front rows, you will be close to live, unrestrained animals. Some people find this a little bit disconcerting but most people don't have a problem.

Extra info:

- Time: Approximately 20-25 minutes
- Service animals are permitted, but check with a cast member to make sure your animal will be able to handle all of the activity.
- Assistive listening devices can be used here.
- Sign language interpreters can perform here on a designated day. Call (407) 824-5217 to make arrangements.
- You can stay in your wheelchair or ECV.

Pocahontas and Her Forest Friends
Cautions: Fear of animals such as rats, snakes, skunks
Quick Notes: Outdoor animal show with unrestrained animals including a porcupine, skunk, snake and rats

Location: Camp Minnie-Mickey

This is another outdoor stage with a theme of protecting the forests. We find that it is probably most appropriate for young children. It includes animals like a skunk, porcupine, snake and rats. A "mystical" discussion occurs between Pocahontas and Grandmother Willow, a talking willow tree. If your time is limited, and you don't have young children, you may wish to pass on this attraction.

The theater has hard bench seats with no backs and partial shade. If you are in the front rows, you will be close to live, unrestrained animals. The queue is outdoors with very little shade. The first several rows are for children. If adults sit there they will be asked to move.

Extra info:

- Time: Approximately 10-13 minutes
- Service animals are permitted, but check with a cast member to make sure your animal will be able to handle all of the activity.
- Assistive listening devices can be used here.
- Sign language interpreters can perform here on a designated day. Call (407) 824-5217 to make arrangements.
- You can stay in your wheelchair or ECV.

Finding Nemo – The Musical
Cautions: This new attraction has not been fully reviewed. Please see below for preliminary information.
Quick Notes: Live show featuring actors, puppets, aerial acts and original music. This new attraction has not been fully reviewed as of yet.

Location: DinoLand U.S.A.

As of this writing this attraction has only just officially opened. We did go to see it; however, due to technical difficulties we were not able to view the show. Though we have not had the chance to experience it firsthand, we'll share information from our research. Please keep in mind that this information may not be complete and that we have not been able to visually verify it. There may be cautions that I would normally share with you that we have not yet discovered.

This is one of Disney's newest live shows, replacing the Tarzan Rocks show. It is a multi-media musical based on the film, which actually was not originally a musical at all. It includes live actors (mostly puppeteers that you can see), puppets, an aerial act and original music. The puppeteers actually dance and become a part of the show, unlike typical puppet shows. There are villainous fish involved, including a shark. There is a mist effect. The theater is kept quite dark so you can see the puppets on the stage.

It is in the theater that Tarzan Rocks was in, but it's been remodeled to be an indoor theater. We hear that it is air conditioned, but it has the same hard bench seats that are in most of the outdoor theaters. It seats 1500 people, so if the queue is long and you're towards the end, don't worry! There's a good chance you'll get in.

Wheelchair users should see a cast member to be directed to the proper seating.

We did have a chance to experience the queue before being informed that the show was cancelled. Most of it is in full sun. I spoke with cast members and requested that we be allowed to wait out of the sun. They said that was not an option for this show's queue. They would not allow us inside the theater. It was intensely hot, and after we persisted they finally allowed us to go wait at the front of the line, which is on the top of a hill where there was a shade tree.

Extra info:

- Time: Approximately 30-40 minutes (This may change as they work out the bugs)
- Service animals are permitted, but check with a cast member to make sure your animal will be able to handle all of the activity.
- Assistive listening devices can be used here.
- Sign language interpreters can perform here on a designated day. Call (407) 824-5217 to make arrangements.
- You can stay in your wheelchair or ECV.
- Video Caption-ready monitors can be used here.
- Handheld Captioning can be used here.
- Reflective Captioning is available. Guests should contact a cast member at this attraction

Animal Kingdom Dining

There are very few dining options within Animal Kingdom compared to the other parks. Food and the dining experience is not a focus of this park, in our opinion. Even fast-food options are limited here. The one unique experience is the Rainforest Café, which we feel is worth trying. We will cover that restaurant, as well as a couple of the fast-food locations.

Better Quality Dining

Rainforest Café

This is the only table service restaurant in Animal Kingdom. The real appeal of this place is the décor, which is unique, interesting and highly themed. Kids will love it, as will many adults. There are cascading waterfalls, lots of greenery, erupting volcanoes, animatronics jungle creatures that may come alive and periodic thunderstorms. The food is usually decent in our experience. The service can be slow, and the wait to get in can be really long. Reservations are advised.

You can eat here without going into the park, as there are entrances on both sides. There is another Rainforest Café in Downtown Disney. The tables are pretty close together, and getting to your table in a wheelchair may be challenging. The restaurant can get pretty loud, especially when the effects start. They don't usually last very long, though. The restaurant is on the dim side. They seem to be trying to create an atmospheric feel of a cool, dark forest.

Food choices include various salads, Caribbean coconut shrimp, chicken fried chicken, pepperoni pizza, Hong Kong stir-fry, steak and shrimp, ribs, lobster and various fish dishes. Breakfast is served here in addition to lunch and dinner.

Quick Service Restaurants

Flame Tree Barbeque

This has outdoor seating with shade. The menu includes barbecued ribs, smoked ½ chicken, smoked pork sandwiches, smoked beef sandwiches, smoked turkey sandwiches and barbecued chicken salad. There is also a fruit plate with yogurt.

Lots of little animal critters like to hang around the area. The birds and squirrels are pretty fearless and even aggressive at times.

Pizzafari

Pizza is served along with deli sandwiches and salads. You can get meatless pizza here. Indoors the seats are wood with no arms. The tables can be close together.

Outdoors there are a small number of tables under a covering. The chairs are metal with padded seat bottoms and backs, but no arms.

Restaurantosaurus

This is counter service with indoor seating. This place has a morning character breakfast, which is a very basic buffet. Make your reservations in advance. For lunch and dinner it's a burger place with burgers, fries and a mandarin chicken salad.

Tusker House Restaurant & Bakery

Currently this is counter service with indoor seating. Meals include rotisserie chicken, fried chicken sandwich, turkey wrap, vegetable sandwiches, salmon and chicken salad. The seats are wood with no arms.

Starting November 18, 2007, this will be converted from a quick-service restaurant to a buffet restaurant. It will offer a character breakfast buffet and a non-character lunch/dinner buffet. At this writing the restaurant is expected to be closed for refurbishment from mid-August to November 18, 2007.

EPCOT

This massive 300-acre park is tied with Hollywood Studios as our favorite Disney park. Adults will especially find much to really enjoy here. We love the atmosphere of the park, as well as many of the attractions.

Epcot includes two very distinct "worlds." The World Showcase is as the name indicates—a small representation of various countries all around the world. This includes architecture, culture, cuisine, people, shopping, live entertainment and beauty. In fact, each country is actually staffed with people from that particular country, for a more authentic experience. The World Showcase opens around 11 AM.

The front of the park is Future World, which opens earlier in the day than the World Showcase. Future World is filled with fascinating and fun attractions representing a variety of topics. Sections of Future World usually close by 7 PM, while World Showcase is usually open later.

Dining at Epcot can be a big part of the experience. You can actually eat your way around the world as you walk around the World Showcase. Most of the countries offer at least one over-the-counter restaurant, as well as a fine-quality, full-service restaurant. Many of them are really worth the money. Some have great food, some have great atmosphere, and some have both. Even in Future World you will find some interesting dining options worth trying.

When entering Epcot, you can make dining reservations at a number of stations. We suggest that you make your reservations by phone as far in advance as possible. If you need to make reservations there in the park, you can make them at Guest Relations east of Spaceship Earth, or at the kiosk near Germany in the World Showcase. You will find WDW-DINE phones there.

There are times when we have made reservations once we got to the park, or even just walked into a restaurant on the spur of the moment. Sometimes we've gotten in and sometimes we haven't. We have found that even during slower seasons the restaurants at Epcot can be booked up and difficult to get into.

When attractions are inside a pavilion, we will mention their locations. Attractions such as Test Track are obvious on the maps and need no explanation.

The majority of the walkways at Epcot are smooth, wide and fairly level. We'll mention some of the locations that are different. The walkways throughout most of the park are fairly wide, which makes this park feel less crowded and easier to navigate than Magic Kingdom or Animal Kingdom.

Park Facts for Disability Issues

You can stay in your wheelchair or ECV during these attractions:

- Cranium Command
- Goofy about Health
- Honey, I Shrunk the Audience
- Impressions de France
- Innoventions East & West (There are some attractions within these pavilions where guests in wheelchairs may need to transfer to an attraction seat.)
- Journey Into Your Imagination with Figment
- Canada!
- Norway: Stave Church Gallery
- Reflections of China
- Test Track
- The America Gardens Theatre
- The American Adventure
- The Circle of Life
- The Making of Me
- The Seas with Nemo & Friends

These attractions require that you transfer into wheelchair if you are in a motorized vehicle or ECV and then into the attraction:

- Ellen's Energy Adventure
- Gran Fiesta Tour Starring the Three Caballeros in Mexico
- Living with the Land

These attractions require you to transfer from your wheelchair to the attraction seat:

- Body Wars
- Mission: SPACE
- Norway: Maelstrom
- Spaceship Earth
- Test Track
- The Land: Soarin'

Wheelchair rental & service locations:

- ➢ The main rental location is at the Stroller and Wheelchair store inside the Main Entrance to the left, near Spaceship Earth. You can also rent ECVs here.
- ➢ The International Gateway in World Showcase rents wheelchairs and ECVs.
- ➢ The Gift Stop just outside Main Entrance has limited quantities of wheelchairs. They do not have ECVs.
- ➢ The Glas und Porzellan in Germany Pavilion is a replacement location only.

Companion restrooms: Most, if not all, of the restrooms throughout Disney have bathrooms allowing access by guests in wheelchairs. You can find companion-assisted bathrooms at the First Aid Station near the Odyssey Pavilion, as well as at the following locations:

- On the east side of Spaceship Earth
- Future World East just opposite of Test Track
- Future World West just opposite of The Land
- Germany Pavilion on the right side
- Morocco Pavilion on the far right side
- Norway Pavilion on the right near the Viking ship
- Near the Canada Pavilion

Attractions with FASTPASS:

- Mission: Space
- Test Track
- Living with the Land
- Honey, I Shrunk the Audience
- Norway - Maelstrom

Service Animal rest stops:

- To the left of Universe of Energy
- By the gates toward the right side of Imagination!
- At the Kennel main entrance
- At the International Gateway just behind the World Traveler
- Mexico on the right side by the gates
- To the right of The American Adventure

Braille maps: In Future World the maps are located by the Electric Umbrella restaurant and at the Guest Relations office. In World Showcase a map can be found on the International Gateway walking path.

First Aid Station: In the Odyssey Center by Spaceship Earth, at East Block across from Test Track and at West Block across from the Land.

Future World

Location: Mission: SPACE Pavilion

You can now participate in this ride with two different versions. One includes spinning, and the other does not. The spinning version simulates a space ride with an intense lift off, re-entry, real G-forces and actual weightlessness. There are G-forces that can create a feeling of pressure, particularly in the chest and abdomen. It is very cool but very extreme, physically.

Have you ever seen the movie clips where astronauts are training for space by going in a spinning container? This ride actually spins to create the experience of weightlessness. Although you don't feel like you're spinning, you certainly are. While the ride is really cool, it can be much too physically challenging for some people. On the ride without the spinning, the simulation motion is still there, but you will not have the intensity and issues that go with the spinning feature.

Don't attempt the spinning version of the ride if you have any conditions that could even remotely be an issue. Several people have been taken to the hospital after going on this ride, and there have been at least two deaths reported. These people were found to have pre-existing conditions. If you have any question at all, we strongly recommend that you avoid using this ride with the spinning feature.

Even if you feel you have only a mild problem, and may get away with it, we suggest you skip it. We have heard over and over that entire vacation days were ruined by motion sickness from the spinning ride. We hear that even people who really never get motion sickness can get it from Mission: SPACE.

After coming off this ride, I couldn't really shake the nausea, and it really impacted my entire day. They do provide motion sickness bags for guests—that just tells you that it's a frequent problem. That said, some folks love the spinning version and have no problem whatsoever.

> *Tip:* I can't stress how important this is. If you do the spinning version, it's necessary to keep your head straight with your eyes forward and opened at all times. Avoid leaning forward and keep your head back against the headrest. Focus on the screen, and it will help prevent nausea and dizziness. Do not look to the side, and keep your head in one place at all times. You should not try to look at the person beside you. Don't give in to temptation, or you may have a problem with motion sickness. We've heard several accounts of people who gave in, looked to

the side and became severely nauseated. Also, make sure you're not holding your breath. If you find that you are, take some nice deep breaths. These techniques can help even on the non-spinning version.

Even without the spinning, I really enjoyed this ride. The lift-off is exhilarating, and I can imagine that it's close to what a real lift-off feels like. I also did not experience motion sickness from the non-spinning version, though some people may as in all the simulator rides.

When you approach the queue area, you will be asked if you wish to go on the spinning or non-spinning version. A cast member will direct you into one of two queue lines. Your party may be split but you can reunite at the end of the ride. Be certain you go into the correct queue line.

There are several other things to consider with this ride, even without the spinning. You are placed in a small, four-person chamber, which is likely to be a problem for people with claustrophobia. When the ride is about to begin the chamber doors close and the front panel moves in closer to you, increasing the potential for claustrophobia. You face your own control area and viewing "window" (video screen). It's quite close to you, as you will be reaching for the controls in front of you, though you don't actually have any control.

Though the chamber seats 4 people and is small. The seats have adequate room. Many larger people find they are able to fit comfortably in the seat. The seat has a padded, harness-type restraint that goes over the shoulders and is locked. Each seat has its own sound system. It can be very dark at times and loud. At one point there is a sudden alarm sounded, which can be quite startling. There are some small lights on the "control panels" that can blink, and there is a bright flash when your picture is taken during the ride. There is a compartment in front of your seat that can hold your belongings.

In both versions the entire chamber moves. There is some turbulent motion, which can be a problem for some people. Though most of the motion is generally smooth, there is a lot of motion that happens fast and frequently. Picture yourself in an actual space vehicle and imagine how you would be positioned as the ship changes angles. The ship rotates forward as if you were diving downwards, and also backwards as if you were flying into space. It also moves side to side—for example, when you are passing through a meteor shower trying to avoid the meteors. When diving downwards, I felt the restraints putting pressure on my chest area, but not on my shoulders.

I have experienced some jolting motions mainly when we supposedly land on the planet and the ice below the ship cracks. In my opinion it's not severe jolting. There is also some vibration when the ship first takes off into space. I found this to be light vibrating.

Some folks describe the turbulence to be about equivalent to what you experience on Star Tours.

This ride does not seem to be designed to scare. It's more of a thrill experience. There is one point at the very end where you've landed and the ice the ship is on starts to crack. This is very brief and not all that scary, except to the very sensitive. It's similar to the commercials Disney put out when this attraction first opened. There's a lot of excitement and amazement.

The queue is indoors, and it's quite long and winding. There are movies shown, narrated by actor Gary Sinise, with closed captioning. There are many cool things to see, such as areas that look like the inside of a space station.

Tip: There is an interior of a ride simulator that you can see inside the entrance to the ride. Let a cast member know you wish to view it. They are happy to answer any questions you may have.

Tip: If you are unsure about taking this ride, you can go through the queue and look at the actual ride vehicle. Let a cast member know that you want to just look at the ride vehicle and make your decision from there. If you wish to decline once you get there, they will show you how to exit without going on the ride.

Tip: If you are not planning to go on the ride, but wish to experience the queue, you can go through it and leave before getting in the ride car. Just let a cast member know.

Tip: If you are looking for input to help you decide if this ride is okay for you, cast members can help. However make sure the cast member has gone on the ride. The last cast member we questioned made it sound like a walk in the park. When we asked if he had ever gone on the ride, he said, "No way!" He had claustrophobia. When we asked the same questions of another cast member who had been on the ride we got very different answers.

Tip: You will find several games at the exit of the space ride. There is one that is particularly fun if you like video games, called Space Race. It's a live video game competition. You must be able to use very simple hand controls. It may be hard on your hands if you have arthritis or carpal tunnel syndrome.

When I've gone on the Mission: SPACE ride, Sarah goes right to this game area and waits for me there. It's also a good location to meet up if your party splits to go through the separate queues for the non-spinning and spinning version.

Extra info:

- Time: There is approximately a 7-8 minute pre-show. The ride lasts approximately 5-6 minutes.
- If you wish to try the ride without spinning, tell a cast member. Then be sure you are going in line for the non-spinning version.
- You must transfer from your wheelchair or ECV to the seat in the space capsule.
- Service animals are not allowed on this ride.
- The height requirement is 44" (113 cm) or taller.
- Video Caption-ready monitors are available.
- Guests may use attraction translation device units.
- Closed captioning for the pre-show is used.

Test Track
Cautions: Heart problems, blood pressure issues, back or neck problems, motion sickness, difficulty keeping yourself upright at angles, pain issues of any kind, headaches, problem with sudden temperature changes, fear of the dark, and lights with a spinning motion
Quick Notes: Drive in a car through its testing with sharp hairpin turns, sudden braking, skidding, and riding over bumpy surfaces, through hot and cold chambers, and over 50-degree banked curves at high speeds.

This is one of Epcot's newer and more popular attractions. The story is that you are taking a car through testing—taking sharp hairpin turns, sudden braking, skidding, riding over bumps and harsh road surfaces, going through very hot and freezing cold chambers, sudden acceleration, climbing a hill and riding along 50-degree banked curves which have you almost sideways at 60 miles per hour. The top car speed is 65 mph, but it can feel faster as you are in an open car. You also go in hot and cold temperature chambers with a 100-degree difference in temperature between the rooms.

Personally, I find that this ride is not roller-coaster scary or even as physically demanding as most of the thrill rides. I did not experience any irritation or discomfort with my back or neck, nor did several others that we've heard from who have back and neck issues.

Sarah has chosen not to ride this one. The cars travel over different types of surfaces, such as bumpy cobblestone. This bothers her even in a real car on a real street. Though not very severe for most people, the series of bumps could be uncomfortable for people with very sensitive back and neck problems. If this would bother you in a regular car in the real world, then you should definitely avoid this attraction. Sudden stops as well as 50-degree banked curves may put a demand on the body as well.

Test Track with yellow vehicle

There is one moment where it looks like you will crash through a wall, but of course you don't. There is also a point where they are supposed to be spraying corrosion fluid at your car, but it's only water and you don't really get wet. Still, this ride could be challenging for some conditions.

While you're in the queue you will see safety tests happening with dummies inside. They are fun to watch and help make the wait easier. The crashing and test sounds can be quite noisy. There is a pre-show which is standing room only. The queue can be a little tight at some turns for ECVs to navigate. Take your time and don't get stressed! You can do it, even if you have to back up and try again.

The ride car is a 6-passenger (two rows of three people) ride car with no top. The seats are like auto bucket seats with a headrest. The people in the outside seats have shoulder/lap-style belts, and the people in the middle have only lap belts. The back row is tight on legroom. The front row has more legroom.

You must transfer from a wheelchair into a ride car. You will need to make a parallel transfer stepping over the side of the car and then downward to the car seat. If you feel you may have trouble doing this, let a cast member know. You can practice on the stationary vehicle that they have for this purpose. They can give you a supplementary pamphlet with some extra boarding instructions, which may be helpful.

Also let a cast member know if you need a grab bar, which is available to help you pull yourself from the wheelchair into the ride car. You can request a seat cushion. If you feel you will have trouble stepping down into the car, you can request to transfer at the seatbelt stop. There is a shorter step there.

There is light that spins in the queue, and you will also see this many times during the ride. You will pass by many still lights in darkened areas. There is one point where it looks like a truck's headlights are coming at you. If you are riding on a sunny day, there's a section where you go from a dark indoor area to bright sunlight. During the heat test, there are several rows of bright heat lamps on both sides of the vehicle.

There is a post-show ride with a simulation and a film called Dreamchaser, which is more of a cartoon advertisement for GM. It may be more appropriate for children. The seat moves and can be uncomfortable for some people. You can request a non-moving experience.

Since part of the ride is outdoors, they will shut it down if there is thunder and lightning, and even light rain. If rain threatens, you may wish to skip this attraction and come back another time. Some folks find the outside portion more exciting at night, as the darkness can make for more of a thrill. Unfortunately, this ride is known for breaking down more frequently than some of the others. If you happen to be on it at the time, don't panic. They'll get you going again soon. If they need to evacuate the guests, you will either need to walk over stairs and through narrow passages, or wait to be evacuated by cast members.

Extra info:

- Time: There is approximately a 3-minute pre-show. The ride is approximately 5 minutes.
- You must transfer from your wheelchair or ECV to the ride car.
- Service animals are not allowed on this ride.
- The height requirement is 40" (102 cm) or taller.
- Video Caption-ready monitors are available.
- Assistive listening devices can be used at this attraction.
- Attraction translation device units can be used at this attraction.
- Guests may use attraction translation device units.

Wonders of Life Pavilion: Body Wars, Cranium Command, The Making of Me

---

This pavilion is open seasonally (when the crowds are at their highest), so call Disney in advance to see if it will be open during your visit. Call (407) 824-2222.

To enter the pavilion you have to go up a ramp and then down an indoor ramp to get to the attractions.

Body Wars

Cautions: Heart problems, back or neck problems, motion sickness, pain issues, problems with strobe lights, flashing lights and electrical current lights, headaches, loud noises

Quick Notes: Turbulent simulation ride where your ship is "shrunk" and placed in the bloodstream of a human body. It has quick turns, dives, jerkiness.

Location: Wonders of Life Pavilion

This attraction is only open seasonally. Check with Disney to see if it will be open when you go. Call (407) 824-2222.

Ever want to be shrunk and put into a human body as they did in the movie *Fantastic Voyage*? I always thought that would be pretty cool, and this ride simulates that experience very well. The special effects make you feel that you are aboard a vessel, shrunken to microscopic proportions, and placed in the bloodstream of a human body where you encounter all kinds of challenges. This is a very turbulent ride. As with most simulation attractions, those who are prone to motion sickness might really want to skip this one. At the very least, try not to eat a lot close to the time that you go on this ride.

It's a moderate-sized theater/simulator that's spacious enough not to feel closed in or claustrophobic for most people. Forty-four people enter at a time. The front window is actually a movie screen through which you see the action. The entire theater moves to simulate a spaceship-type craft.

Again, this ride is extremely turbulent. You are jostled and bucked around, as your craft simulates the moves of a vessel. You do feel like you are in a moving craft. Your seat simulates motions such as dives, quick turns, turbulence and jerkiness. With the action on the screen corresponding to the motion of your seat, the effect is that you really feel like you're in a moving vessel! It can be very painful for those with back, neck or other pain problems. It can also be very stimulating. The roughest ride in the "ship" is in the back row. There is also a short period of strobe lighting along with flashing lights and lights simulating bolts of electrical current.

With all of the dives, hairpin turns and other effects, this ride can be nauseating for those prone to motion sickness. As with Star Tours at Hollywood Studios and Mission: SPACE, I personally couldn't shake the motion sickness for the entire day.

ECV riders must transfer into a wheelchair to go through the queue. You then must transfer diagonally into the attraction seat. This may be difficult for some people as it can be a bit tight, and it may be a challenge to get parallel to the seat in order to transfer. The seats are theater style but hard, with armrests that can get in the way. The seats have seatbelts. The cast member will take the wheelchair away and bring it back to you so you can transfer to exit.

Extra info:

- Time: There is approximately a 1 to 2-minute pre-show. The ride lasts approximately 5 minutes.
- You must transfer from your ECV into a wheelchair to go through the queue, and then into the ride car.
- Extra 4-point harness restraints are available. Just ask a cast member.
- Service animals are not allowed on this ride.
- The height requirement is 40" (102 cm) or taller.
- Video Caption-ready monitors and assistive listening are available for the pre-show.

Cranium Command
Cautions: We did not observe any noteworthy obstacles, impediments or challenges, but please judge for yourself as everyone is different and attractions may change.
Quick Notes: Amusing multi-media show inside a theater showing what happens inside the body of a 12-year-old boy during through a day of life.

This is an amusing look at what happens inside the body of a 12-year-old boy going through a day of life. It's hosted by an animatronic robot, which is kind of interesting in itself. It's filled with comedians and actors like Jon Lovitz and Dana Carvey. We enjoyed it and find it worth seeing.

There is a pre-show in a room where you must stand on a sloping floor. The main show is in a theater that has hard benches with backs. You can stay in your wheelchair or ECV.

The show is situated in a dark theater with multiple screens in a variety of shapes and sizes. There is also a variety of lights and light effects, including blinking console lights, long, thin lights and swirling lights. There are some flashing lights that seem to blink inconsistently. There is a steam effect.

Extra info:

- Time: The pre-show is about 5 minutes. The main show lasts approximately 12 minutes.
- Guests can stay in their wheelchair or ECV.
- Reflective Captioning is available here.
- Assistive listening devices that amplify the audio can be used at this location.

The Making of Me
Cautions: We did not observe any noteworthy obstacles, impediments or challenges, but please judge for yourself as everyone is different and attractions may change. There are some sensitive subjects touched on, but not graphically.
Quick Notes: Movie starring Martin Short, showing the process of pregnancy and birth

This is a look at human development. The process of pregnancy and birth is shown through the eyes of an adult traveling through time from his own conception to birth. The movie stars Martin Short. It doesn't go into the details of sexuality, but parents may want to think about this one as it brushes past some sensitive subjects. There is a bit of kissing. We find this interesting, and even touching at times.

Extra info:

- Time: Approximately 15 minutes
- Guests can stay in their wheelchair or ECV.
- Reflective Captioning is available here.
- Assistive listening devices that amplify the audio can be used at this location.

Spaceship Earth
Cautions: Back or neck problems, pain issues, muscle weakness, problems with flashing lights, claustrophobia, fear of dark
Quick Notes: Ride through a 180-foot geosphere with audio-animatronics, scenes and displays that depict communication through time. Ride is slow, but travels uphill and backwards downhill with an awkward headrest. The ride car pops and jerks harshly over the track. The smell of smoke is pumped in at one point, and there are some very dark portions.

The massive 180-foot geosphere building that this attraction is housed in is amazing to look at. This attraction depicts the journey of communication through time. Starting with cavemen, the scenes progress to the present and end in the "future." Though it's a slow-moving ride, it can present problems for people with pain and weakness issues.

Wheelchairs can enter through an exit door to the left of the main queue entrance. The regular queue is on a moving walkway that has an incline. You must transfer from your wheelchair or ECV into the ride vehicle. For wheelchairs and mobile folks, you will need to step onto a moving platform to board the vehicle. If you need them to, a cast member can stop everything for you so that you can transfer in more easily. The loading platform is pretty slow, though, and moves at the same speed as the ride car.

The ride cars are hard seats with a neck rest that may be too low for taller people. As the ride takes off you move into almost total darkness and the cars go up an incredibly steep slope in a narrow space for some time. This may trigger claustrophobia in those who have that problem. Once you get to the attraction displays, the sloping becomes much less steep, and there is adequate light for most of the time. There is also plenty of space so you don't have a closed-in feeling. For many people with claustrophobia, it may feel reasonably comfortable from this point on.

Though this is a fairly slow moving attraction, we find that the ride car continuously pops and jerks over the track pretty harshly throughout the entire ride. It jerks more than most other comparable rides and may bother those who are very sensitive with pain issues. Personally I had no trouble, and many people with pain issues don't find it too painful; however, it may irritate very sensitive conditions.

Also, the ride car goes uphill very steeply and then downhill and backwards very steeply. Although there is a hard headrest, Sarah finds the position awkward and not very supportive or comfortable. The ride lasts 15 minutes on slopes, which may be too long for some people to manage comfortably.

> *Tip:* Sarah found that she could use her sweater behind her head and neck to make the headrest more comfortable. Without it, her neck was in a lot of pain with the steep angles and uncomfortable headrest.

There is a wide assortment of light effects. These include an effect like strobe lights. There are twinkling lights that look like stars. There are dark areas of the ride where you pass by multiple bright video screens while moving at a slow speed. There are small, flashing lights on a movie marquee, old-time movies that seem to strobe a bit, flickering lights behind windows, long, thin ropes of moving light along with short flashing lights in various colors towards the end, and many small lights simulating traffic and a cityscape.

There is fragrance pumped in, particularly that of smoke at one point. Oddly, we have never been able to spot where the smoke or fire is that the smoke smell is supposed to come from. The first time we took this ride we thought there might be a fire in the attraction. Of course there wasn't, but we still haven't figured out why they are pumping in that smell.

The ride cars may pause unexpectedly but it's usually a brief stop.

Lines tend to be shorter in the afternoon. As people come into the park it's the first attraction they see, so the lines can be huge. It's best to skip this in the morning and come back a little later on. The queue is outdoors and covered.

Extra info:

- Time: Approximately 15 minutes
- You must transfer from your wheelchair or ECV into the ride seat.
- Service animals are allowed on this ride, but check with a cast member to see if there is anything your animal will have a problem with.
- Handheld Captioning is available here.
- Attraction translation devices can be used here.

Ellen's Energy Adventure

Cautions: Allergies, fear of dark, fear of dinosaurs and snakes, fear of lightning and thunder, difficulty with loud noises, flashing lights

Quick Notes: Movie on the "big bang" creation event and a ride back in time. The ride itself is smooth and slow. The big bang explosion is intensely loud. Times of darkness, and not extremely scary dinosaurs. We find this ride musty-smelling.

Location: Universe of Energy

The star of this attraction is Ellen DeGeneres, who falls asleep and takes you with her as she dreams. You are taken through the event of the "big bang" creation moment and then on to meet some dinosaurs. You learn a lot about energy in this attraction. This is a physically gentle, slow-moving ride that runs quite long at approximately 45 minutes.

If you are in an ECV you will need to transfer into a wheelchair at the attraction entrance. They are parked along the wall across from the entrance. See a cast member if you need help. You can board the ride vehicle in this wheelchair. The queue is indoors, but there is an overflow portion that is outdoors and uncovered.

The pre-show is in a dark room with a few benches along the back wall, but mostly standing room, where you receive the back story. The floor slopes fairly gently. The angle depends on which entrance you used to come into the room. You look up at three large screens to watch the film.

After the pre-show, you move to the ride vehicles, which are long bench seats with backs. Each section of seating is made of hard plastic and they are quite large, seating 97 people. There is total seating for 600 people. If you will be riding in a wheelchair let a cast member know, or move over to the far right side of the ride car area, and wait by the back seats. A cast member will provide a ramp for you to drive your wheelchair into the ride vehicle. You will be placed in the last row where you can stay in your wheelchair or transfer to the seat.

Once the guests are seated, the show begins. The ride vehicles remain stationary at this point while you watch a movie on huge screens in a very dark room. There are some brief moments of complete darkness. When you witness the "big bang" occur on the screen as a bright explosion, there is an extremely loud accompanying sound. It is so loud that you can actually feel vibrations. You also hear the loud thumping of dinosaur feet heading toward you. At the end of the attraction there is a huge roaring sound. There is also a sudden burst of light. Some children and those with fear of the dark, sensitivity to sudden light and noise sensitivity may have a problem with this portion of the attraction.

After the film the vehicles begin to slowly rotate, separate and head toward the dinosaur portion of the ride. You will move through a variety of sites. You will see some animatronics dinosaurs that don't seem particularly threatening. Yes, they are huge, and one even hangs over the ride cars. Yet this ride does not seem to be designed to terrify. They don't move much and don't look like they will attack. Still, they can scare some very sensitive people.

We have found this to be a particularly musty-smelling ride. One dinosaur sprays a mist out of his nose. Though it goes over the ride cars, we've never been hit. It seems pretty inconsequential. Another dinosaur sprays water out of its mouth.

In the dinosaur scenes, there is a misty fog around a volcano. It doesn't really seem to contact the guests. There is some thunder and lightning and an erupting volcano. There are also some flashing lights in a very dark area. There is a giant snake-like creature coming up out of the water.

Tip: A few short clips of the film may cause motion sickness. If you find you're having a problem, simply looking down away from the screen may help prevent this.

Extra info:

- Time: The entire attraction is approximately 45 minutes long with an 8-minute introduction and a 37-minute ride.
- You must transfer from your ECV into a wheelchair. You can ride in the wheelchair or transfer to the vehicle seat.
- Service animals are allowed on this ride, but check with a cast member to see if there is anything your animal will have a problem with.
- Handheld Captioning is available here.
- Assistive listening devices can be used here.
- Attraction translation devices can be used here.
- Flash photography is not allowed in this attraction.

The Seas With Nemo & Friends Pavilion

Since there are several attractions here worth seeing, we'll discuss them together. In addition to the attractions mentioned below, there are some aquarium viewing tanks. You can reach these by entering the Pavilion by the side entrance, or by riding the Seas With Nemo & Friends, which drops you off there.

Coral Reef Restaurant

This is a full-service restaurant. It's a pleasant atmosphere with huge aquariums to watch as you eat. Of course, seafood is the main menu feature, but you can also get chicken, steak or a vegetarian vegetable strudel. The lighting is moderately low and the seats are wooden. The menu is fairly small and does not offer a lot of options.

> *Tip:* The fish aquariums are what make this restaurant beautiful and unique. It may be worth a wait to get seated with a good view. You may wish to arrive 15 minutes early and request an aquarium view table on the lowest level.

The Seas With Nemo & Friends
Cautions: Claustrophobia, fear of sharks or fish, fear of dark, motion sickness
Quick Notes: Ride a "clamobile" in a search for Nemo through underwater scenes. Smooth, slow-moving, level ride. One portion passes through a tunnel that could challenge people with claustrophobia. Projected fish on a wall can challenge those with motion sickness. Some rather dark scenes.

This is the newest addition to this pavilion. Guests ride a "clamobile" through the attraction. During portions of this ride characters from *Finding Nemo* are actually projected onto the real and huge aquarium tanks, so that it looks like they are swimming in the tanks.

The queue is indoors and themed so that you begin at the beach but move down under the sea. It's long, winding, dim and cool. The queue turns seem to have enough room for wheelchairs to navigate pretty comfortably. It may feel claustrophobic to the very sensitive because the queue seems to keep winding for quite a long time, and it's dimly lit. However, we didn't have the sense of being closed in by walls. As the scene moves from the beach to the ocean floor, the ceiling above has screens that look like water to give the sense that you're looking up at the surface.

To load into the ride car, or clamobile, you walk on a conveyer moving at the same speed as the clamobile. Cast members can slow down the conveyer, but they can't stop it. Wheelchair-accessible clamobiles are available, but people in ECVs must transfer to a wheelchair. The cast member will help you into the clamobile.

The clamobile is similar in construction to the ride cars in the Haunted Mansion (see Magic Kingdom Attractions section). Of course, these are far more cheerful looking. They look like a giant clamshell. The seats are benches with backs, which felt reasonably comfortable to us. The little door at the front of the clam shell slides closed your ride car enters leaves the boarding area. Be careful to avoid getting any limbs, toes or fingers in the way.

The ride cars generally move smoothly on level ground. They do rotate to change direction in order to point you toward the action. Sometimes you face forward, and sometimes your clamobile turns and you travel sideways facing the show. We could feel the clamshell pop on the track, but it was not severe or uncomfortable, even for Sarah.

At times there are some small flickering lights designed to create an undersea appearance of lights hitting corals or other objects. They appeared to flicker slowly and at irregular intervals. There are also some lights that look like ocean creatures.

At times this ride was very dark. At one point we entered a tunnel. At first it seemed we stopped completely, but then we could see we were moving very slowly. The ceilings were very low, and there were fish in motion being projected as lights on the wall and ceiling across from us. When we first entered this area, Sarah struggled with motion sickness from the fish images because of the way they were moving on the wall. She had to look down to avoid looking at the images but was fine after that. We have heard from others who have also found that this part of the ride brings on motion sickness.

Sarah also struggled with claustrophobia in this tunnel area because we were barely moving in a very confined space. Once she could discern that we were actually moving and not stuck, she was fine. This segment didn't last more than a minute or two.

There are a couple of fish with big, sharp teeth that may scare the very sensitive.

Extra info:

- Time: Approximately 8 minutes
- You must transfer from your ECV into a wheelchair. You can ride in the wheelchair or transfer to the vehicle seat while walking on a moving conveyer belt.
- Handheld Captioning is available here.

Turtle Talk with Crush
Cautions: We did not observe any noteworthy obstacles, impediments or challenges, but please judge for yourself as everyone is different and attractions may change.
Quick Notes: Interactive animated show where the audience and Crush the turtle can converse

This is a new attraction that is fun and amazing. While it's geared towards children, adults will enjoy it also. The technology is remarkable. This is an actual real-time conversation with Crush, the sea turtle from *Finding Nemo*. The audience is told to ask Crush questions, and he answers them. It's a live interaction between the animated turtle and the audience.

You enter a room with backless benches. The further back the row, the taller the bench. You can stay in your wheelchair or ECV. Wheelchairs sit in the back or side. Some folks stand along the walls.

It's fairly dark, and you watch the turtle on the screen in the front of the room. Children are encouraged to sit up front on the floor. What's amazing is that the turtle really converses with the audience, with the appropriate animated motion. It can be quite humorous, and we find it worth seeing.

Extra info:

This attraction is quite new, and as of this writing we have been unable to obtain some of the specifics. What we do know is the following:

- You can remain in your wheelchair or ECV.

- You can request sign language interpretation with a minimum of seven days notice. Interpreted performances are available on a rotating schedule at each theme park. Check with Guest Relations for the current performance schedules, or call Walt Disney World Information at (407) 824-4321 [voice] or (407) 827-5141 [TTY].

Imagination! Pavilion

The main reason to come here is the Honey, I Shrunk The Audience 3-D movie. It's a blast!

Journey Into Your Imagination with Figment

Cautions: Fear of dark, allergies, some effects that can be startling (see below), flashing lights

Quick Notes: Smooth ride with mild inclines with Figment, a purple dragon, teaching about imagination. There is an air blast, skunk smell, pitch blackness for extended periods, and flashing lights.

We have heard that this attraction may be closed, revised or replaced down the road. If you are pressed for time this may be an attraction to bypass. We find it's often easy to get on this ride with very little or no wait, as it's not one of Disney's most popular. Sensitive people may find parts of this ride anxiety provoking.

It's a ride with Figment, a purple dragon character, along with a professor teaching about imagination. The ride cars are hard plastic with bench seats. The cars stop to allow you to get in. There are wheelchair accessible cars, or you can transfer to the ride seat. The ride is pretty smooth with some mild inclines and declines. The cars do rotate to change direction in order to point you toward the action.

The effects include air blasting at you. At one point it blasts from behind and can be startling. There is a skunk smell released and blown at you. It's not very severe and really doesn't do a skunk justice. You are moved away from it pretty quickly. There are several periods of pitch darkness. During one of those periods you will be in pitch black for maybe 10-20 seconds while hearing the sound of a loud train approaching. You are blown with air as it "passes by you" to simulate the gust a real passing train would create.

There are flashing lights, including a dark area with some flashing footprints moving across the walls. There is also a dark room with many flashing colored computer lights. A large slot machine has many moving lights. Flickering lights in the dark simulate stars.

At one point you pass through Figment's house, which is upside-down. You must look upwards to the ceiling to take it all in.

Extra info:

- Time: Approximately 6 minutes
- Handheld Captioning is available here.
- Attraction translation device units can be used here.
- You can stay in your wheelchair or ECV.

Honey, I Shrunk The Audience
Cautions: Fear of mice, fear of snakes, fear of dark, fear of lions, pain and back problems, allergies, problems with loud noises, strobe lights. Some people with epilepsy have difficulty with 3-D effects.
Quick Notes: Fun 3-D movie with sensory and other special effects, some of which are startling or scary to the very sensitive. Very mild seat jolts, small amount of smoke in front of the room, water sprayed.

This movie never gets old for us. Even with age, it does not feel dated and we find it great fun. This is a 3-D experience that includes real-life effects to make it even more realistic. In this movie, Professor Wayne Szalinski shrinks you and the entire audience. The 3-D effects are really convincing. Things seem to really come off the screen and be right in front of your face.

Some of the effects can be startling and even give you a moment of fright. They can be sudden, and when they appear to be within inches of you it can be scary. You can always remove your glasses to see it's just a 3-D effect and not real. We generally prefer to avoid scary attractions, but we find this more fun than scary. Still, some sensitive folks and some children will find this too intense. You will hear screaming throughout the theater as the surprises unfold, usually followed by a lot of laughter. Only the most sensitive will find it really disturbing. We've heard an occasional crying child.

Warning: Don't read the following paragraph if you don't want any scares spoiled in advance!

Some of the effects do seem designed to scare, such as a cat that suddenly turns into a lion and a huge snake that appears to come right to you and snap at you. There are effects you will only experience in the theater seat. For example, in the film a huge number of mice are replicated and supposedly escape into the audience. There is a little tassel-type thing that rubs your legs to simulate the feeling that a mouse just ran by. The audience always screams at this point, but for most it's more fun than truly scary. If you wish to avoid this effect, keep your legs raised or up on the seat if you're limber or small. You can also try explaining in advance that it's not really a mouse, but a tassel on the seat that's supposed to feel like a mouse.

The seats are theater style with backs and some padding. The seats do have some motion, though it is relatively mild in our experience. For example, when you are "shrunk," the entire theater is supposedly picked up by a child who walks away with it. The seats give faint jolts along with the child's footsteps.

If you would prefer to avoid this effect and you have a wheelchair, you may wish to view the show from your wheelchair. You will miss the other tactile effects, though. Sarah is incredibly sensitive to motion, but she is able to handle the regular seats for this attraction. It may be a bit irritating to her condition, but it is not enough to cause any lasting increase in her pain levels.

The entire audience gets sprayed with water when a dog sneezes. There is also some smoke that comes out of the speaker's podium in front of the auditorium. It didn't seem to flood the entire room. If you sit toward the back you should be able to avoid the smoke. There are some loud noises and some wind blown at you. There are light effects including electrical bolts, flashing and strobe-type lights.

A pre-show in a fairly dark room sets up the story for the 3-D movie. There is no seating there, but you can stay in your wheelchair. The floor is slanted, but the wheelchair area in the back is level. There are rows of multiple screens so everyone can see, and there is closed captioning on some of the screens. If you find it hard to stand, you may get away with sitting on the floor all the way to the right. Try to have someone from your party stand to your left so that you don't get stepped on by the crowd.

If you are uncomfortable with the 3-D effects you can watch the monitor to the left of the 3-D movie screen instead. Take off your glasses and watch the show as a 2-D movie. Of course this carries a lot less impact, but that may be better for people who have fears or visual problems.

You must wear the 3-D glasses provided by Disney in order to get the 3-D effect; these fit over your own glasses.

Extra info:

- Time: There is a 5-minute introduction and a 13-minute film.
- Reflective captioning is available.
- Video Caption-ready monitors are available.
- Assistive listening devices that amplify the audio can be used at this location.
- Guests may use attraction translation device units.
- You can remain in your wheelchair or ECV. Please note that because of limited seating only one person can sit right next to the person in the wheelchair. The rest of your party should be able to get seats in the row in front of the wheelchair row.
- Guests with service animals should check with the cast member to be sure your animal can handle this attraction.

Kodak What If! Labs

Cautions: We did not observe any noteworthy obstacles, impediments or challenges, but please judge for yourself as everyone is different and attractions may change.

Quick Notes: Hands-on play center with interactive sound and image experiences appealing mostly to children

---

In addition to the 3-D movie, the only other thing at this writing that's in the Imagination! Pavilion is this hands-on play center. It's a minor attraction focusing on interactive sound and image experiences. Young children may enjoy a brief visit. You can take a digital picture of yourself and email it home or to others.

It's pretty easy to maneuver here in a wheelchair unless it's very crowded.

The Land Pavilion

A couple of things are worth mentioning about the Pavilion itself. It houses Soarin' as well as Living With The Land. To enter the Pavilion you must go up a fairly steep hill. There is a closed-off path for wheelchairs that helps you to avoid the crowds. When you enter, it's a good idea to head right over to either Soarin' or Living With the Land to either enter the queue or get your FASTPASS. Remember you can only have one FASTPASS at a time. One option might be to get a FASTPASS for one, and get in the queue for the other. Though we really enjoy both Living With The Land and Soarin' we would definitely pick the latter if we were pressed for time. Both rides are very popular and often have long waits.

Food Court

This is a nicer quality food court that you might factor into your plan if there's time. In the food court you'll find everything from sushi and Chinese to salads and nice quality sandwiches. We think this is the best spot to grab lunch in Future World. If you time it right, you can have lunch while you wait for your FASTPASS time to come up.

It may be a challenge to get your wheelchair into the dining area, especially during a crowded time. You may need to wait to find a seat on the outside perimeter of the tables. However, it usually can be done.

Chip & Dale's Harvest Feast Garden Grill

This is a higher priced sit-down restaurant. It rotates very slowly and passes over various scenes from Living With The Land. It is possible for some people to experience motion sickness because of the rotation.

The all-you-can-eat menu is served at your table. The seats are padded booths and/or chairs around a round table.

> *Tip:* Soarin', Living With The Land and the food court are on the bottom level. When you enter the building you are up one level, and must go down. If you need an elevator, stay left when you enter the building and take a left turn at the end right in front of the Chip & Dale's Harvest Feast Garden Grill restaurant. Be careful backing out of the elevator, as it's a tight space and there are often other people in wheelchairs waiting to get into the elevator as you're coming out.

The FASTPASS machines for Soarin' are just to the right of the Soarin' entrance in a separate area. All the way to the right side of the building you will find the Living With The Land queue. The wheelchair entrance is to the right of that, on the right side of a large post. The FASTPASSES are in that same general area.

Soarin'
Cautions: Heart problems, motion sickness, allergies, fear of heights or flying, fear of dark, fireworks, nighttime scene with lights that guests soar over at high speed
Quick Notes: Simulation of hang-gliding raised approximately 40 feet off the ground in front of a curved IMAX screen. Very smooth motion, with mild angling of the chair. It feels like you're flying. Smells are pumped into the room, and wind is blown at you to increase the sensation of flying. Momentary darkness at the start and end.

© Disney

Soarin' Lands at *Epcot*®

Absolutely hands down this is Sarah's favorite attraction in all of Disney World. This attraction gives you the sense that you are flying in a hang-glider. It's a wonderful experience as all of your senses are engaged in this incredible simulation. This hugely popular ride can be crowded, but we feel it's worth the wait.

The very long queue is indoors with large panels on the walls that change, bringing you fun quizzes and fascinating information. The queue ramp inclines and declines. There is plenty of space to maneuver a wheelchair, even when the queue is crowded. However, as you near the actual ride area, the queue space thins, the floor slopes more steeply down and the lights dim.

Once you reach your last queue area you will stand and watch a cute and entertaining video on the overhead monitors.

At the end of the queue, just before going into the ride area, you will be directed into one of three lines. The one that's farthest away puts you on the ride seats on the far left. The center queue puts you in the center seats, and the closest queue puts you on the right side of the theater. The seats on the far left side of the theater will rise the highest. You have the sense of flying higher than in the other seats. The front left is the highest of all the seats. The seats all the way to the right rise up the least. Also, the further back the row, the lower you will be.

> *Tip:* If you have any fear of heights, request to be seated in the furthest right section in the back row. If you're looking for a bigger thrill, request the left section, especially the front row. Most of the time we find cast members will try to accommodate you.

> *Tip:* Although every seat is a great experience, the front row gives you a bit more of a view. Except for the first row, you will have a view of the feet of those in front of you blocking the top of the view screen.

Once the doors open, the cast member will direct you to your seat.

Wheelchair riders who can walk can park their own wheelchairs and walk to a seat. A cast member will direct you to a parking area. For those who need to get right up to the ride seat to transfer from a wheelchair, you can drive right up to your seat and park in front of it. The cast members usually direct wheelchair users to the first row because it gives the most space to maneuver. Once you transfer into the ride seat, the cast member will take your wheelchair off to the side and park it for you. After the ride, the cast member can bring you your chair or, if you can, you can walk to it. It stays in the same room as the ride.

There are 3 rows of 10 seats across, and you can usually sit side-by-side with your party. The front row is the highest, with the back two rows on a declining angle once you are in the air. When I think of what a seat would be like in a hang-glider, I think of being in a position like lying down on my stomach. However, this is not what this ride is like. You sit upright in a seat with a high back that supports your back, head and neck comfortably. Each seat has its own seatbelt. There are grab bars on the side of each seat, though we've never really felt the need to use them. There is adequate room to feel comfortable for most people. There isn't really a foot rest, and your feet are supposed to dangle once the seats rise. Sarah keeps one or both of her feet on the little storage compartment below the seat, which is more comfortable for her back.

When the ride starts, the room goes completely dark for a very brief moment while you are lifted 40 feet up into the huge screen dome area. It is a quick and very smooth transition. We did not experience any jerking or discomfort. Suddenly the screen lights up, and you are flying over the clouds. You then fly through one incredible scene after another.

The seats tilt, but very smoothly and gently. The angles are not extreme and Sarah, who is sensitive to this, did not feel any sense of leaning to an uncomfortable degree. The movements were enough to feel like we were flying in different directions, but not enough to put pressure or a strong demand on Sarah's muscles, joints and spine. She did not feel she had to keep turning her head either in order to enjoy the attraction, which made it easy on her neck. We've heard from others with a variety of physical issues who find this to be a physically easy attraction.

As you "fly" a wind is blown toward you in a way that enhances the sensation of flying. To us it feels natural and not uncomfortable at all. As you fly over certain scenes, mild fragrances are pumped in through the breeze. If you aren't paying attention, you might miss the smells altogether. For sensitive people, a washcloth or something similar over the nose can be helpful. We do not feel we need to hold on to the grab bars on this ride, so it wouldn't be challenging to hold a cloth to your nose with one hand. The fragrances include oranges, pine and sea air.

> *Tip:* We experienced smell effects more strongly when riding in the front row on the left side of the theater.

Once the ride is over the lights go out and you are in darkness for the few seconds it takes for the ride seats to come back to the ground. There are some nighttime scenes, and the experience of soaring near planes and fireworks. Nothing about this ride seems to be designed to make you scared but to give you a thrill and an enjoyable time.

For the most part, we do not experience motion sickness on this ride, though it is possible. There is one scene toward the end that might cause motion sickness, and those who have difficulty with some types of lights should take note. It's a nighttime scene where you are flying at high speed over street lights and moving cars. If you have a problem, just close your eyes for the few seconds it takes to get past this scene. You should be fine. It doesn't help to look downward, as the screen is curved and you will still see a part of the scene. In the final scene you are in the air taking a close-up look at fireworks.

> *Tip:* We felt it was pretty safe to leave our belongings in Sarah's scooter basket as it was in the same room as the ride and we were nearby. However, while it's unlikely, there's always the

chance someone could swipe it on the way out before you get to it. Once the ride stops it can take you seconds to be in view of your chair, depending upon where it is. There is an area below your seat on the ride where you can store a small amount of things. You may even want to put your shoes, sandals or flip flops there if you think they may fall off during the ride. You can hold your belongings on the ride if you need to.

Extra info:

- Time: Approximately 5 minutes
- You must transfer from your wheelchair or ECV into the ride seat.
- Service animals are not allowed on this ride.
- The height requirement is 40" (102 cm) or taller.
- Video Caption-ready monitors and assistive listening are available for the pre-show.

Living With The Land
Cautions: Allergies, fear of lightning and thunder, neck pain—a lot of head turning required to see everything, lightning flashes, old-time movie flickers
Quick Notes: The past, present and future of farming is displayed in this smooth, slow-moving boat ride. There is occasional mild bumping of the tracks. You'll pass through various climates experiencing dry or moist air. There are musty-smelling portions.

This is a fascinating and pleasant learning experience about the past, present and future of farming. A very smooth riding boat takes you through various types of climates such as a rainforest and a desert. The air in each of these places reflects the climate. For example, the rain forest is moist and misty and the desert dry. You will encounter some light wind and hear some thunder. You then see different kinds of farming methods through time. It is displayed through a variety of means including scenes with animatronics and film.

The boat ends up in a futuristic indoor greenhouse farm that is a real working Disney farm. Much of what's grown in this place will end up on a plate in a Disney restaurant. You will see some amazingly huge fruits and vegetables, as well as produce grown using high-tech procedures. You will even see some fruits grown into Mickey Mouse shapes. This part of the attraction is our favorite, and it is always changing as they plant new crops.

Tip: Bring your sunglasses. The ride moves through pretty dark areas, and then suddenly you enter a sunny greenhouse-type environment that can be very bright. The ride car does move slowly during this transition, so there's plenty of time to put your sunglasses on.

There is usually a big line to get into this ride. It's also a dull queue to be in, with pretty much nothing to look at while you're waiting. People with wheelchairs and GACs don't use the main queue. See a cast member. (They usually let wheelchairs in to the right of the main queue.) The number of wheelchairs allowed in the queue is limited. You may have to wait at the entrance for a while before they even allow you to enter into the wheelchair queue. At other times we've been let right by, passing a big line in the regular queue.

People in ECVs must transfer to a wheelchair. The chair can go on the boat, or you can transfer to the boat seat. Depending on the cast members, you may transfer to a wheelchair or stay in your ECV. You can sit while waiting in the wheelchair queue, then leave the wheelchair and board the boat. If you need the wheelchair brought to you to disembark, let a cast member know.

The boat seats are hard with backs. The boat ride is slow and fairly smooth with occasional slight bumps as the boat goes over the tracks, which are in the water. One potential challenge on this ride is that you have to turn your head from side to side to see everything, which can irritate the neck. This is a very mild ride.

Portions of this ride have a musty odor. There are some old-time movies projected on large screens that flicker. In the first scene there are some lightning bolt effects.

Extra info:

- Time: Approximately 15 minutes
- Guests must transfer from their ECV to a wheelchair.
- Handheld Captioning is available here.

Circle of Life

Cautions: We did not observe any noteworthy obstacles, impediments or challenges, but please judge for yourself as everyone is different and attractions may change.

Quick Notes: Movie featuring *The Lion King*'s animated characters

---

When you enter the Land Pavillion, off to the right is a theater where you can see a 20-minute film with an ecological message that features *The Lion King*'s animated characters. We consider this to be a minor attraction, but it's a cool and comfortable theater to take a break in if you need it.

The queue is inside, with a few benches. The attraction has theater seating. There are steep steps in the theater, and wheelchairs are seated in the back. There are no regular seats in the wheelchair row, but your party can sit right in front of you in the back row of theater seats. If you wish, one person can stand by the wheelchair in the back.

Extra info:

- Time: Approximately 20 minutes
- You can stay in your ECV or wheelchair.
- Reflective Captioning is available here.
- Assistive listening devices that amplify the audio can be used at this location.
- Attraction translation devices can be used here.
- Video Caption-ready monitors are available.

Innoventions: The Road to Tomorrow - Innoventions East & West

Cautions: We did not observe any noteworthy obstacles, impediments or challenges, but please judge for yourself as everyone is different and attractions may change.

Quick Notes: High-tech displays and hands-on experiences, much of which consist of vendors showing their wares. Includes video games and cars.

Two separate buildings house high-tech displays and hands-on experiences. Various vendors show their current and upcoming wares including video games, cars, home theater systems, and high-tech home technology. There are also some hands-on play areas for children.

Most exhibits are wheelchair friendly. There are benches here and there. Some exhibits are very adult oriented, but some are interactive displays and shows designed for children. One nice thing you can do is to make a postcard with your photo on it and e-mail it to your friends.

Although this takes up two whole buildings, we consider this a minor attraction. Some of it is pure advertising for vendors, though there are a few moderately interesting things for adults, and some play areas that children like. I would suggest that you visit Innoventions after you've seen everything else you want to experience at Epcot.

Wheelchairs can move pretty easily through most areas but there are a few displays and activities that are not accessible. Just ask a cast member for assistance at each individual exhibit if you're uncertain.

Extra info:

- Assistive listening devices can be used for some exhibits.
- Sign language interpretation is available at the House of Innoventions display on certain schedule days. Check with Guest Relations for the current performance schedules, or call Walt Disney World Information at (407) 824-4321 [voice] or (407) 827-5141 [TTY].
- Video captioning is available in some places at this attraction.
- Service animals are allowed, but check with a cast member to be sure there is nothing that will bother your animal.

World Showcase

Built around a large 40-acre lake, the World Showcase is a magical place to travel without traveling. Each pavilion represents a country where you will find a wide variety of shops, dining, live entertainment, interesting architecture, museums, various demonstrations, films about the individual countries and even some rides. World Showcase is generally most appreciated by adults, and we never grow tired of it!

Generally each country's pavilion contains one or more fine dining restaurants and one or more over-the-counter restaurants representing the foods of the country. The prices are generally higher than in the "real world", but many of the restaurants are worth it because of the authentic food and distinctive atmosphere. Most of the staff members in these places are from the country that the pavilion represents. Many of them enjoy interacting with guests and will answer questions about their country.

It's best to make reservations well in advance for the fine dining restaurants. At peak times, it's next to impossible to get in without a reservation. That said, it may be worth a try even at the last minute, as there may be cancellations or no-shows. We generally pick one nice sit-down restaurant to dine in at the World Showcase each time we go.

All of the countries' attractions, restaurants and stores are wheelchair accessible, although there may be a few tight spots here and there. When the park is very crowded, the stores and pavilions become much more difficult to navigate.

Some of the countries have textured walks, such as the cobblestones in France. They are pretty obvious, and easy enough to avoid if necessary, though you may have to skip some nations altogether. The majority of the sidewalk areas are smooth and level with the occasional thin textured strip. A lot of walking is involved here, with the path around the lake measuring over a mile. Then you have to add some more distance for the extra walking within the countries. There are benches placed around the lake and in some of the countries if you need to rest.

You can take a boat across the lake, though the wait can be long. The boat can be tight for maneuvering a wheelchair. The boat is enclosed, except for a few seats on the end that are outside on the back deck. Last time we were on the boat, it was uncomfortably hot inside, and we couldn't wait to get to the other side and get off. We also find that the back, uncovered area of the boat has more exhaust fumes.

You can get an entertainment schedule when you enter the park, and most of the live entertainment is worth seeing. However, these outdoor shows are fairly short and timed sporadically. Personally, we find that it's just too difficult to try and be in any one place at a certain time around the World Showcase. It's just too big to try and navigate like that. We usually just start at the entrance of the Showcase and work our way around the lake until we are back to where we started. We catch shows if we happen to be there at the right time and place. If there is a show you particularly want to see, you may wish to schedule your day around that.

For most outdoor live shows the audience stands or sits on the ground. It can get crowded, making it hard to see if you get there after the show has started. If you are close to the actors and would like to leave before the show ends, it can be hard to get through, especially if you are in a wheelchair. There are a couple of shows that have a few benches around the area, but most don't.

For each country, we list the main attractions. We only go into detail where there is something unusual that may be worth mentioning, or where we have some strong opinions or tips. Generally speaking, for each country you can assume that you will see some unique architecture, cool shops and restaurants and even a few mini-museums and galleries. Several of the countries have perfume/cologne shops, including Italy and France. Avoid these shops if you have sensitivities.

For postings of sample menus and prices at the Disney restaurants go to this web address: http://allearsnet.com/menu/menus.htm#epc

Canada Pavilion

Canada is particularly pretty, though you might miss much of it if you aren't looking. To the right is an entrance to Victoria Gardens, which is a well-manicured and pleasant environment. You can get a great view from the top of the Canada Pavilion. Wheelchairs can take the winding ramp all the way to the top of Canada. The wheelchair ramp is cobblestone, and a fairly rough ride for wheelchairs.

To the left of the pavilion is a stage where you can catch a Celtic rock band.

"O Canada!" CircleVision 360° Movie

Cautions: Motion sickness

Quick Notes: CircleVision 360° movie about Canada

This is an introduction to Canada. There are no seats in this theater. You can stay in your wheelchair or stand. There are rails to lean on. At times we've found that the CircleVison 360° can be disorienting, particularly if you are standing. It might help to hold on to the rails and look down for a moment if you need to get your balance. Some people may experience motion sickness.

The waiting area is kind of tight. The wheelchair entrance is also very narrow and goes over a wooden walkway.

Extra info:

- Reflective Captioning is available here.
- Assistive listening devices that amplify the audio can be used at this location.
- You can remain in your wheelchair or ECV.

Le Cellier Steakhouse

This full-service restaurant is extremely popular and can be difficult to get reservations for, even well in advance. Of course, steak and beef variations are the stars here, with seafood dishes available as well. There is a vegetarian tofu dish. We hear people rave about the cheddar cheese soup more than anything else except the pretzel bread!

The restaurant is rather dark, as it's modeled after a cellar made of stone. It's not our favorite atmosphere, but it's a good place to go if you are a fan of their food specialties. There are wood chairs with no arms here, and there are some bench seats with padded backs.

You enter the restaurant by going to the far right of the Canada Pavilion through the Victoria Gardens.

China Pavilion

The main store in the China Pavilion is one of Sarah's favorites in all of Disney World. It's filled with authentic and beautiful items, which we find to be priced very reasonably. It's a large store with everything from clothing to furniture and rugs.

"Reflections of China" CircleVision 360° Movie
Cautions: Motion sickness
Quick Notes: CircleVision 360° movie about China

This is an introduction to China. There are no seats in this theater. You can stay in your wheelchair or stand. There are rails to lean on. At times we've found that the CircleVision 360° can be disorienting, particularly if you are standing. It might help to hold on to the rails and look down for a moment if you need to get your balance. Some people may experience motion sickness.

Extra info:

- Reflective Captioning is available here.
- Assistive listening devices that amplify the audio can be used at this location.
- You can remain in your wheelchair or ECV.

Live show: Dragon Legend Acrobats and performances on the Chinese harp

This show is really one of the best at the World Showcase, in our opinion. It gets extremely crowded so get there early if you can. It gets really crowded, and there's limited space allowing for a good view. They come out in front of the Pavilion in an area on the right side. If the weather isn't good they can be seen inside in the temple.

Nine Dragons Restaurant

This full-service upscale Chinese restaurant is a nice place; however we've found the menu to be on the expensive side. If you don't have access to this kind of food or atmosphere at home, then it may be worth trying.

The seats are wood with no arms. As with most Chinese restaurants, MSG may be used in the food, so you may want to request your food without it.

Lotus Blossom Café

This is an over-the-counter restaurant that we like if we're looking for a quick meal. Though we would like to see more on the menu, this is a decent and more affordable alternative to Nine Dragons. It has counter service with seating indoors. Chairs are wood with backs and padded seats. You can request no MSG.

France Pavilion

The ground here is cobblestone/brick and rough to ride a wheelchair over. There are perfume shops here, which may be of concern to those with allergies.

"Impressions de France" Panoramic Movie

Cautions: Motion sickness

Quick Notes: Movie tour of France on five large screens

This is a tour of France. It is not a 360° movie, but it is shown on five big movie screens. This theater has theater-type folding seats. There may be some loud volume. This brings you on a tour of France.

Extra info:

- Reflective Captioning is available here.
- Assistive listening devices that amplify the audio can be used at this location.
- You can remain in your wheelchair or ECV.

Boulangerie Patisserie

This is a French bakery that is full of unbelievably tempting baked goods. You can also get sandwiches, coffee, tea and soft drinks. It is truly a challenge to not buy everything they offer.

There are display cases to the left and right. They both carry the same choices. The place is pretty narrow and may be a challenge for a wheelchair, especially if crowded. There are often lines going out the door.

Wheelchairs can enter by the very thin ramp near the entrance and depart through another very thin ramp on the exit side. There is no seating inside, but there are a few metal garden tables and chairs outside. There is inside seating at a small shop inside at the Galerie les Halles, right next door. During warmer weather it's a good choice because it is air conditioned, and it's easy to maneuver a wheelchair in there.

The Bistro de Paris

This is a full-service restaurant on the second floor above the Chefs de France restaurant. You can take the elevator or a steep, winding staircase. The prices are among the highest in the World Showcase.

We had heard that if you could get a window seat at night, you could see IllumiNations. However, we found that there are very few tables that have a good view, and the chances of getting one of those seats are slim. If you are hoping to see the nighttime show, we would recommend that you plan on seeing IllumiNations elsewhere.

Though most seats are padded straight-back chairs, Sarah finds them very uncomfortable. The seat feels unusually high to her, and the padding presses in an awkward way that increases her back pain. Of course, everyone is different, so it might be fine for others. There are a few seats that are padded benches.

There is a dress code here, but not a stringent one. They ask that men do not wear tank tops. They do realize that you are spending the day at an amusement park, and people are dressed accordingly casual.

Les Chefs de France

This is a full-service restaurant. We enjoy the food and the experience here. The atmosphere is pleasant and elegant. Though it's still expensive, it's a little less costly than the Bistro de Paris. You can get some of the classics here, such as escargot and French onion soup.

It can be very noisy in here during busy times.

Germany Pavilion

The ground is textured like cobblestone, giving a rougher ride for wheelchairs.

Biergarten

This is a full-service restaurant that offers a unique buffet in the spirit of Oktoberfest. There's plenty of food, as well as live entertainment with a band, song and dance. During the show the guests are invited to come up and dance. The interior is atmospheric and pleasant. During busy times it can seem quite chaotic, with the wait staff running around and people getting up to go to the buffet. The noise level can run pretty high, limiting conversation at times. You may be seated with strangers, which could be fun or awkward depending on everyone involved. If you prefer to be seated alone, make a request when checking in. They may or may not be able to accommodate you, depending on crowd levels.

The tables are on several levels. The long wood tables are situated pretty close together. It may be challenging for a wheelchair to maneuver. There are armless wood chairs that we feel are not the most comfortable. The backs have a thin metal bar going across the lower back and a wider one going across the middle back. They squeeze quite a few people around each table when it's busy.

During our last visit during a peak park time the lines at the buffet were extremely long. You may consider filling two plates of food during your visit to the buffet, rather than making two separate trips.

The restroom doors are extremely heavy.

Assistive listening devices will work for the performances here.

When you call and make your reservation, ask when the band is scheduled and time your dining accordingly. There can be long breaks between performances.

The menu includes sauerbraten, salmon, assorted sausages, chicken schnitzel, glazed carrots, bratwurst, beef roulade, chicken soup, cheeses, cold cuts, pretzel bread, spaetzle and various salads including herring, cabbage, macaroni and wurst. Kids can have macaroni and cheese, hot dogs and chicken tenders. Of course there are several beer and wine choices. We have been told by several people from Germany that the food is really authentic.

Sommerfest

This is a fast-food alternative with a very small menu including bratwurst, frankfurter, black forest cake and beer. There are a small number of tables with covered seating. It can be crowded and tight making it difficult for a wheelchair to maneuver.

Italy Pavilion

There are perfume shops here, which may be of concern to those with allergies. You can catch the "World Showcase Players" here. We've found that this is pretty much the same show you'll see over in England. It's cute and worth catching. There is also a juggler. These shows often involve bringing audience members into the plot.

L'originale Alfredo di Roma Ristorante

This is a higher-end, full-service Italian restaurant which is scheduled to be closed August 31, 2007. It will be replaced with a restaurant featuring the cuisine of Master Chef Joachim Splichal.

Currently, the menu includes a number of pasta dishes, as well as chicken, wild boar, lamb, veal and steak.

The tables are extremely close together, and it's quite noisy. It may be very difficult to maneuver a wheelchair. You may find yourself seated very close to strangers. This is not the place to go if you are looking for romance. There are regular chairs and some bench seats with backs. If you are on a low-carb or low-fat diet, it may be difficult to maintain here. At times the waiters may sing, and they may have an accordion player.

Japan Pavilion

We really enjoy the large store filled with all kinds of things that we never see anywhere else. By the way, for those with pain, a variety of devices for massage and self-massage are available. Of course there are beautiful Japanese items like kimonos, glass and ceramic products, jewelry, toys, clothes, Bonsai trees and a lot of Hello Kitty products.

There is a group here that plays Japanese drums outside on the deck of the pagoda. They are really fascinating to watch and listen to. Those who are noise sensitive may wish to watch at a distance or bypass this one. It does get extremely loud.

You can also catch a Japanese story teller here, as well as a candlemaking display.

For all the restaurants in this area, food is cooked with peanut oil, so avoid this place if you have an allergy to peanuts. They also use MSG, but you can request that it be left out of your meal.

Mitsukoshi Teppan Yaki Dining Room

This is a full-service restaurant that, in our experience, is just like a popular Japanese chain restaurant called Benihana that cooks for you at your table. If you've never eaten at this type of restaurant, we feel it's worth experiencing.

This is on the second floor, over the store. You can either use the rather long and steep staircase, or a very small elevator to the left of the main store entrance. There is some cushioned bench seating in the waiting area.

Your dinner table has a built-in grill in the center. Be careful not to touch it as it gets very hot. You may be seated with strangers. There are eight seats per table. The chairs are wood with cushioning on the seat, a wood back and no arms. A Japanese chef prepares your food in front of you. Some perform as they cook, but what they do depends on your chef's skill level and how busy they are. It's very entertaining when they go all-out.

The food is on the expensive side. Many items normally included with the main course for the same price in most Japanese restaurants are not included here. You will pay extra for items such as fried rice, salad and soup. Main Teppan courses include fresh vegetables, chicken, scallops, sirloin, and filet mignon. You can also get lobster. You can request no MSG.

Yakitori House

This counter-service restaurant is located in what looks like a very attractive little Japanese house across from the main building. It's surrounded by a Japanese garden with a fountain adding to the particularly pleasant environment. At night the lanterns are lit, adding drama. The outdoor atmosphere is particularly beautiful.

The restaurant has both indoor and outdoor seating. This is a good alternative for a light meal in a pleasant atmosphere. The prices here are very inexpensive compared to the full-service dining options.

You can take the path behind the Pagoda into the building or use the wheelchair ramp that goes through the garden. The indoor seats are wood with backs. It would be very difficult to get a wheelchair into an inner table. If you can walk, the easiest thing to do is to park your wheelchair right outside and walk in.

Outdoor chairs are stools with padded seats. The tables have umbrellas.

You can get teriyaki chicken, chicken ginger salad, sushi Tokyo roll, Japanese curry, miso soup, kaki age udon noodle soup and ginger cake. You can request no MSG, but some foods may not be available without it, as they are not freshly made-to-order.

Tempura Kiku

This restaurant falls between a full-service and counter-service restaurant. There is only one type of seating, which is at a counter like a sushi bar. This is also upstairs on the second floor of the Japanese main building. You can get tempura, which is chicken, shrimp and/or vegetables dipped in a light batter and fried. You can also get tempura sashimi. The tempura is served with soup and steamed rice.

Mexico Pavilion

This pavilion is striking and atmospheric on the inside. It's quite dark and cool inside, which is a big relief from the warm weather. There is some really nice shopping inside with a central plaza area filled with vendor carts, surrounded by some separate shops. There is also an attraction and a very notable restaurant. At times a live Mexican band plays with their singers. They are amazing and really worth catching. There is a huge volcano and Mayan temple as a backdrop for the restaurant and the shopping area, and the interior of the pavilion is very dimly lit.

Wheelchairs can enter the pavilion by a ramp to the right of the main entrance. We don't normally mention wheelchair entrances for pavilions because they are usually obvious or there's a cast member at the main entrance to direct you to it. However, this one is kind of hard to spot. The path is in a wooded area to the right of the building, and it can be easy to walk right by it.

The shopping plaza can get very crowded, making wheelchair maneuvering a challenge.

Gran Fiesta Tour Starring The Three Caballeros Boat Ride

Cautions: Back and neck problems, fear of dark, simulated fireworks, flickering lights

Quick Notes: Indoor boat ride showing Mexico, which includes animatronics, animation, dolls. Smooth ride except mild bumping of the boat against the tracks. Also incline and decline as well as bumpiness when the boat leaves and arrives back at the docking station, as it passes over rollers. At the end boats in line to disembark hit each other. Musty smell in some areas.

This is an indoor boat ride that has recently been updated and is primarily a very calm and physically easy boat ride that shows you Mexico's past and present. Most of the updated ride is the same as the original, but the main difference is that there's fun new animation added. There's animatronics, dolls, a carousel, and a few special effects like simulated fireworks and a bit of mist. You also ride past the smoking volcano.

It's all pretty mild except when the boat leaves and arrives back at the docking station. When you depart, the boat slides slightly downhill over some pretty bumpy, roller-type tracks. From there the ride is smooth, except that the boat bumps the sides of the tracks quite often as it moves along. Still, it's pretty mild and Sarah was okay with it. When you arrive back at the docking station, the boat hits the boats in front of it and is also hit from behind repetitively, before you are allowed to disembark. It also goes slightly uphill and briefly rides over some bumpy, roller-type tracks. Regardless, Sarah found the jostling tolerable, so we feel that most others will also.

You must transfer from your ECV to a wheelchair. You can ride the wheelchair onto the boat. Not all boats have this option, so you may need to wait for an appropriate boat.

This is a water ride, and it smelled musty to us in some areas. There were brief periods that were fairly dark. We noticed small flickering lights around some of the dolls. The simulated fireworks appeared to be made of lights on the ceiling.

Extra info:

- Time: Approximately 7 minutes
- Handheld Captioning devices can be used here.
- You must transfer from your ECV to a wheelchair. You can ride the boat in a wheelchair or you can transfer to a boat seat.

San Angel Inn

This full-service restaurant would be worth trying just for the atmosphere alone. You have a clear view of the river and the volcano mountain with a Mayan temple on it. Every so often it "erupts" but it's quite subtle. You can see the boats for the The River of Time attraction float by. It's fairly dark and cool, which creates a beautiful nighttime scene.

This exotic restaurant gets very crowded. The tables and seats are extremely close together and sometimes uncomfortably so. It can be challenging to navigate a wheelchair through the maze of tables. It can get very noisy also.

The food can be very spicy. The seats are wood without arms. Oversized wheelchairs may have trouble entering the restaurant over the ramp. The ramp is located to the left of the restaurant check-in area near the boat ride. You may need to get assistance from a cast member as they sometimes store items on the ramp and need to move them. They may have to ask people to move who are dining so you can get through to your table.

You can get drinks including margaritas, nachos, tortilla soup, salad and a variety of beef, shrimp, chicken and fish dishes.

La Cantina De San Angel

This counter-service restaurant is located outdoors, across from the Mexico Pavilion. There are many seats that have a great view of the World Showcase Lagoon. This is a popular spot for people to watch the nighttime IllumiNations show, or just to relax if the weather is nice. The seats get taken fairly early in the evening as people eat and drink, lingering for IllumiNations.

The line to order can get very long. The food is far less expensive out here than inside and most people find it good and plentiful. During busy times it can take a very long time to get food prepared with any special requests. We have heard of people waiting even ½ hour for a special request order during busy times.

The tables have big umbrellas for shade. The seats are wood and metal with small wooden backs and no arms. There are also some backless bench seats. The birds can get really aggressive here. Guard your food and don't leave it unattended as the birds will swoop down for a catch if they think they have a shot. They have even been known to swoop while you are sitting there. It's not wise to feed the wildlife here, as you may get more than you bargained for.

You can get a variety of tacos and tortillas, and of course drinks including frozen margaritas.

Morocco Pavilion

We do particularly like the Morocco Pavilion. Not only is it beautiful, but we really enjoy the shops and restaurants. The shops are full of authentic items including jewelry, clothes, ceramics, rugs and other household items. There are many unique and beautifully crafted items. The restaurants are among our favorites. The Moroccan people are very friendly and happy to answer any of your questions about their country and culture.

The Moroccan band, which is accompanied by a belly dancer, plays outside on the stage and in the restaurant. They are really worth catching.

Of note here is that some of the shop areas are a bit tight and may be a challenge for wheelchairs.

Restaurant Marrakesh

This full-service restaurant features a belly dancer and Moroccan musicians. The entertainment happens approximately every 30 minutes to an hour throughout the day, with the last performance around 8 PM. The Disney dining reservations line does not have advance information about the exact performance times. You can reach the restaurant directly by calling the park and asking to be connected to Restaurant Marrakesh. They may be able to inform you about show times for that day. Call 407-824-2222.

Overall the food seems very pleasing to those who enjoy trying authentic ethnic dishes. It's one of our personal favorites at Epcot. The menu may include items such as couscous with lamb shank, shish kebab, lemon chicken and Harira soup made of tomatoes, lentils and lamb. We have heard that this restaurant is not the best pick if you plan to make any special requests with food preparation. If you are dining here, plan on pretty much choosing what's on the menu as it's written. We have heard that the dining room can be uncomfortably warm at times, but we have always been comfortable on our visits.

The show is usually best seen from the center of the room. The music can be loud if you're close to the musicians, so request a seat away from them if noise is an issue for you. There chairs are wood with no arms. There are some tables that have booth seating on one side. We find this to be a comfortable and pleasant atmosphere with enough space between tables to feel open.

Norway Pavilion

Included here is a ride called Maelstrom, which is pretty rough. There are restaurants, shops, live entertainment and a Viking ship play area for kids. The walkways are cobblestone and textured. Some of the shops can be a bit tight and difficult to maneuver with a wheelchair, particularly if there are a lot of people shopping.

There is an authentic Stave Church that is easy to walk right by, but it's worth noticing and walking into. It's small but interesting with displays showing real artifacts, scenes and representations of people from Norway's history. Wheelchair maneuvering is fine inside. The entrance door can be heavy for some people.

You'll catch a small band here playing authentic Norwegian folk music.

Maelstrom

Cautions: Back or neck problems, motion sickness, pain issues, muscle weakness, fear of trolls, fear of dark, storms or rough boat rides, long step down to get into boat, flashing lights, sparkling lights, fear of lightning and thunder, fear of polar bears

Quick Notes: Turbulent boat ride with rough whitewater, traveling down a waterfall where the boat hits the water with impact, and riding backwards. Some scenes may be scary to sensitive people.

This is the only ride with a bit of a kick to it in the World Showcase. It is actually quite turbulent and rough, and was actually very painful for Sarah. It increased her neck and back pain. We believe that this attraction is rough enough that it may be challenging for many people with back, neck or other pain problems. We recommend passing on this attraction if you have any pain issues.

The theme is a trip through a mythical Norway going back in time on a 16-passenger Viking ship. There are trolls and a scary wizard who casts a spell sending your boat backwards into water rapids. You also pass through a storm with lightning. There are audio-animatronics, including large polar bears and various special effects. Most of this is very dark. There is a light that flickers or flashes and groups of some small lights that sparkle. There are scenes that children and those who are sensitive may find scary. This is a very dark ride, and there are parts that are pitch black.

On the ride, you will go quickly up a steep incline and will ride backwards during part of the trip. The most rough and physically challenging part is when the boat goes over white water and down a waterfall. It has a rough landing with impact. There is some turbulence and jerking.

The ride is followed by short film on current-day Norway. You can skip the movie if you wish by walking through the theater and out the exit doors instead. If you wish to skip the ride but see the movie, just let a cast member know.

You must leave your wheelchair or ECV at the dock. You will have to walk a short distance with handrails and step down into the boat. You must be able to walk up and down two steps to board and disembark the Viking boat. The boat seats are hard benches with backs. There is a good-sized step down to get into the boat.

Extra info:

- Time: Approximately 10 minutes
- Reflective captioning available.
- Assistive listening devices that amplify the audio can be used at this location.
- Guests must transfer from their wheelchair or ECV to the ride boat.
- Handheld Captioning is available here.

Restaurant Akershus

This is a princess character dining experience in a medieval castle-like setting, with breakfast, lunch and dinner. It's an all-you-can-eat buffet. The characters go from table to table greeting the little guest princesses. (If you don't have a little princess to bring to this restaurant, it may feel awkward, but you're still welcome!) It can get very noisy here. Dinner foods include sliced meats and cheeses, seafood, salads, breads, salmon, pasta, venison stew, barbecue short ribs, cod and lamb.

It's a pre-set buffet menu so special needs are more difficult to have met. If you have dietary needs, let them know when you make your reservation. Try to do this as far in advance as possible. Chairs are wood with backs. We found that there is adequate space for wheelchair maneuvering.

Kringla Bakeri Og Kafe

This counter-service restaurant has pastries, desserts, open-faced sandwiches and salads. The pastries are hard to pass up, so save room! There are a small number of covered outdoor tables. The interior of the shop is very tight with one line, and would be a challenge for a wheelchair to pass through, especially when crowded.

U.S.A. Pavilion

This pavilion offers a show, a counter-service restaurant and a store, but no full-service restaurant. There are a few simple vendor carts outside. The ground is brick and cobblestone, making for a rough wheelchair ride. There are several shows a day with a group singing patriotic music, most times inside the American Adventure building, and occasionally outside. There is also a fife and drum band that you can catch playing outside.

The American Adventure Theatrical Show

Cautions: Thunder, lightning and firework effects. We did not observe any other noteworthy obstacles, impediments or challenges, but please judge for yourself as everyone is different and attractions may change.

Quick Notes: Multi-media show with audio-animatronics sharing American history

This is a multi-media show that shares American history through audio-animatronics, film and music. Much of the film portion consists of a series of still drawings. The sound system makes it difficult to hear and understand some of the words from the back of the theater, where the wheelchair users are seated. The theater is large, dark and cool, with comfortable theater seating.

There is a thunder and lightning effect, flickering stars and fireworks displays. At one point an audio-animatronics figure uses a tool that creates sparks and light.

Escalators, stairs and an elevator go to the second floor to get into the theater. Wheelchair users should locate a cast member to escort you to the elevator, which is hidden behind what looks like a door. Wheelchair seating is on the second floor. You will wait to be seated in a hallway with a sloped floor. Wheelchair seating is on the top row of the theater.

Extra info:

- Time: Approximately 30 minutes
- Reflective captioning available.
- Assistive listening devices that amplify the audio can be used at this location.
- You can stay in your wheelchair or ECV to view the show.

Liberty Inn

This counter-service restaurant features American favorites such as hot dogs, hamburgers, bacon cheeseburgers, turkey sandwiches, barbecued pork sandwiches, chicken fingers and french fries. There's also a vegetarian salad and a southwest chicken salad. There's a topping bar, so you can choose just what you like. You can get a kosher meal. A really tempting American dessert you'll find here is the S'mores—marshmallows with graham crackers and chocolate. You can also get no-sugar-added vanilla ice cream.

There's indoor and outdoor seating. The chairs are metal with seat cushions and no arms. The outdoor tables have large umbrellas. The ground is all brick and cobblestone inside and outside, so wheelchairs will have rough ground.

United Kingdom Pavilion

The ground is mostly made of brick, so wheelchairs will find the ride rough. There is a talented Beatles cover band that plays here periodically called British Invasion. There are a few benches in the music performance area. There are sign language interpreted performances of the improvisational troupe on pre-assigned days. Check with guest relations for days and times.

Rose & Crown Pub and Dining Room

This full-service restaurant serves British favorites such as potato and leek soup, fish and chips, bangers and mashed potatoes (bangers are English sausages with cabbages and onions), chicken pasty (chicken and veggies wrapped in pastry, topped with cream sauce), beef stew and grilled steak. Curried vegetables are available for vegetarians. It may be a challenge to eat low-fat or low-carb here.

131

There are tables inside and out. Inside the dining atmosphere is pleasant, with dark wood fixtures and wood chairs with backs. There are some tables with excellent views of the lagoon, which are perfect for viewing IllumiNations at night. If your table doesn't have a good view of the IllumiNations show, there is a viewing area inside the restaurant where you can go during the show.

The pub area is attached to the restaurant with an open space between them, and the tables near the pub can get really loud. In fact, whenever we've been inside the pub seems like a very rowdy party atmosphere. We have even noticed a kind of singles bar thing going on at times. There can be some big-time drinking, with lots of yelling, laughing and general noisiness. The restaurant area itself is generally calmer with family diners.

In the dining area, tables are very close together, making wheelchair maneuvering challenging. People in wheelchairs may find it next to impossible to get in the pub area if it's busy.

America Gardens Theatre

This open-air theater features live music from all around the world. There are often American performers here. The seats are long wood benches with backs. They usually have the wheelchairs form a separate line on the left. It's got some partial shade and partial sun. The queues are in the full sun. We often find that the theater is not filled. Many times we have happened upon a concert in progress and just walked right and found a seat. Of course that will depend on the time of year and who is performing.

We have seen the use of special effects at this theater such as fog on the stage.

IllumiNations: Reflections of Earth

Cautions: Smoke from fireworks and torches around the lake. Loud noise from explosions and fireworks.

Quick Notes: Spectacular show including fireworks, lasers, fire, water bursts. Smoke from torches and fireworks are possible.

At the end of the night, folks start to gather around the World Showcase lagoon to see an amazing nighttime show. The sky erupts with over 1,100 pyrotechnic bursts, water bursts and lasers as music is pumped throughout the World Showcase. There's a massive globe the moves over the lake that's covered with lights creating images such as running horses. We find it to be really spectacular and worth viewing!

Check the park show times sheet to get the exact start time. Find a spot at least 30 minutes in advance (and maybe even 45 minutes to an hour or more in advance during very busy times) along the lagoon. During peak crowd times we've seen people begin to claim their spots 2 hours before show time. Spots where trees don't block your view fill up pretty quickly.

As the time nears, large torches are lit around the lagoon. Check the wind direction when picking your viewing spot. If you have allergies, you may want to position yourself so the fumes don't blow on you.

Keep in mind that the fireworks are extremely loud.

There are many good viewing spots around the lagoon. Some of the restaurants are ideal with indoor and outdoor locations with great views. There are also some benches along the lagoon that are great. The fireworks themselves do put out a lot of smoke, and it's a good idea to see which way the wind is blowing before choosing your site if you are sensitive. Depending on the wind, you may never get a whiff of anything, or you may catch a lot of smoke.

Once the show is over there is a mass exodus to the parking lot, boat dock and bus terminals. We tend to leave a couple of minutes before the end of the show to avoid the rush, but if it's your first time you may not want to miss the dramatic ending. If you stay for the ending, which by the way is spectacular, you may wish to take your time exiting the park so you don't have to be jostled in the throngs of people rushing to leave. Those in wheelchairs and ECVs will find it very challenging to move within these crowds.

Magic Kingdom

This is the oldest Disney World park, and probably what you think of when you imagine coming to Disney World. Main Street USA and Cinderella's Castle have been featured on TV and film many a time. This park was opened in 1971 and many of the older rides, though maintained and even updated, reflect the relative technical simplicity of the time.

This is often the park of choice for young children, and roller coaster buffs will love the choices here. As adults, and particularly in light of Sarah's physical limitations, we find this park has a limited number of attractions that are appropriate for us.

Much of the park has attractions that are similar to what you would find at your local traveling fair. However, the Disney versions are usually much more whimsical and even beautiful. Originally planned and built over 30 years ago, this is perhaps the least wheelchair friendly of the parks. There has been remodeling to allow accessibility but you may still notice the difference between this park and the others. For example, you will find areas with a tighter fit for a wheelchair than you usually find in the other parks.

There are 7 different park sections that circle Cinderella's Castle (the same one you've seen on TV and movies all your life!). Each area has a distinctive theme. We'll group and describe the attractions within each area.

Entering the park, you will find brick walkways that can be bumpy for wheelchairs. Once inside, most of the ground is smooth. There are areas where large cement tiles are separated by deep cracks, which can create minor bumping for a wheelchair. There are some deep grooves and metal tracks across Main Street.

Most of the walkways in Magic Kingdom are in full sun with very little or no shade to be found. We find that on a warm day the walk through Magic Kingdom is intensely hot.

Park Facts for Disability Issues

Guest Relations: Located in City Hall on Main Street.

You can stay in your wheelchair or ECV during these attractions:

- Ariel's Grotto
- Castle Forecourt Stage: "Cinderellabration"
- Country Bear Jamboree
- Donald's Boat
- Fairytale Garden
- Frontierland Shooting Arcade
- Galaxy Palace Theater
- Judge's Tent
- Jungle Cruise
- Liberty Square Riverboat
- Mickey's PhilharMagic
- Mickey's Country House
- Minnie's Country House
- Shrunken Ned's Jungle Boats
- Toontown Hall of Fame
- The Enchanted Tiki Room
- The Hall of Presidents
- The Timekeeper
- Tomorrowland Arcade
- Walt Disney's Carousel of Progress

These attractions require you to transfer into a wheelchair (available at no charge at the attraction) if you are in a motorized vehicle or ECV:

- Buzz Lightyear's Space Ranger Spin
- It's a Small World
- Stitch's Great Escape!
- The Magic Carpets of Aladdin
- The Many Adventures of Winnie the Pooh
- Tom Sawyer Island
- Walt Disney World Railroad

These attractions require you to transfer from your wheelchair to the attraction seat:

- Astro Orbiter
- Big Thunder Mountain Railroad
- Cinderella's Golden Carousel
- Dumbo the Flying Elephant
- Mad Tea Party
- Main Street Vehicles
- Mike Fink Keelboats

- Mad Tea Party
- Peter Pan's Flight
- Pirates of the Caribbean
- Snow White's Scary Adventures
- Space Mountain
- Splash Mountain
- Swiss Family Treehouse (no actual ride car – you must be on foot for this)
- The Barnstormer at Goofy's Wiseacre Farm
- The Haunted Mansion
- Tomorrowland Indy Speedway

Wheelchair Rentals:

➢ The main rental location is the Stroller & Wheelchair shop inside the main entrance. The also have ECVs.
➢ Mickey's Gift Station at the Ticket and Transportation Center has limited quantities of manual wheelchairs. There are no ECVs here.

Wheelchair replacement locations:

➢ Frontier Trading Post in Frontierland
➢ Tinkerbell's Treasures in Fantasyland
➢ Tomorrowland Arcade

Companion restrooms: Most, if not all, restrooms throughout the Disney have bathrooms allowing access by guests in wheelchairs. You can find companion-assisted bathrooms at the First Aid Station, as well as at these locations:

- At Mickey's Toontown Fair
- In the lower level of Cinderella's Royal Table restaurant
- Next to Space Mountain
- By Pirates of the Caribbean
- By Splash Mountain
- At the Transportation and Ticket Center East Gate

Attractions with FASTPASS:

- Big Thunder Mountain
- Buzz Lightyear's Space
- The Haunted Mansion
- Jungle Cruise
- The Many Adventures of Winnie the Pooh
- Mickey's PhilharMagic
- Peter Pan's Flight
- Space Mountain

- Splash Mountain

Service Animal rest stops:

- Next to Tony's Town Square Restaurant behind the gates, backstage.
- Near Splash Mountain behind the parade gates, backstage.
- Next to Pirates of the Caribbean behind the gates, backstage.
- Near Pete's Garage next to the restrooms and through the gate, backstage.
- Between Carousel of Progress and the Tomorrowland Stage, backstage.

Braille map: There are two here. One is in City Hall where Guest Relations is located, on Main Street. The other one is near the Tip Board, also on Main Street.

First Aid Station: This is located next to the Crystal Palace, which is a restaurant just off Main Street, U.S.A.

Magic Kingdom Attractions

For this park we list the attractions by location.

Main Street, U.S.A Attractions

Main Street is the street you see upon entering the park. We find it to be the most attractive and appealing location in all of the Magic Kingdom.

Main Street Vehicles

Cautions: Pain. For the horse car only – Fear of animals, allergies, must walk up and down steps.

Quick Notes: Ride in a turn-of-the-twentieth century vehicle. Some vehicles are pretty bumpy. One-way trip.

Main Street U.S.A. with Cinderella Castle in background & horse-drawn trolley

In Town Square or in front of Cinderella Castle near Central Plaza, you can catch a short ride in a turn-of-the-twentieth century vehicle. The rides are one-way. You can choose a horse-drawn trolley car, omnibus, jitney, horseless carriage or fire engine.

Most of the time there is a pretty long wait to catch a ride. The queue is outside in the sun. Some of these vehicles can be bumpy, but other than that they are pretty calm rides. There are two or more steps up to get into the vehicles. Some of the vehicles require that you sit sideways.

In the photo to the left you can see Main Street, U.S.A. with Cinderella Castle in the background. There you will see vehicles such as this horse-drawn trolley car, which all add to the pleasant and fantasy-like atmosphere of the Magic Kingdom.

Extra info:

- Time: About 2 ½ - 3 ½ minutes
- You must transfer from your wheelchair or ECV to the ride vehicle.
- Folding wheelchairs can be put in the ride vehicle for a one-way trip except on the jitney. This can't take a folding wheelchair. A member of your party would have to go retrieve an ECV after the ride.

Walt Disney World Railroad

Cautions: Difficulty going up and/or down stairs, difficulty with train motion

Quick Notes: Train ride around the Magic Kingdom

Ride a real steam train around the Magic Kingdom. You can go full circle and end where you started, or you can get off at Frontierland or Mickey's Toontown Fair. Because these locations are elevated, there is a wheelchair ramp next to the station by the Main Street Gallery and another at Frontierland. There's no special ramp at Mickey's Toontown Fair. Wheelchair riders should go to the front of the train and will be loaded into the first car. A cast member will direct you. Please note that the trains don't accommodate ECVs.

Unless you're riding on your wheelchair, you must step up pretty high to get onto the train. The seats are wood benches with backs. The train is covered on the top with open sides. The left side of the vehicle has a side wall, and the right side is open with an arm rest. If you wish to lean on a side wall, move all the way to the left inside of the car. Strollers must be folded up and carried on.

Extra info:

- Time: 20 minutes for the complete circle. Trains arrive approximately every 8 minutes.
- Manual wheelchairs can ride, but ECVs cannot go on this attraction. You must transfer into a wheelchair, or transfer onto a train seat.

Tomorrowland Attractions

Space Mountain

Cautions: Heart problems, blood pressure issues, back or neck problems, motion sickness, difficulty keeping yourself upright under force, weakness, pain issues of any kind, vertigo, fear of heights, fear of dark, problems with flashing lights, difficulty with high-pitched noises

Quick Notes: High-speed roller coaster in the dark, with a very rough ride. Hairpin turns, plunges, twists that jerk you around, flashing lights.

This high-speed roller coaster is a very rough ride. We suggest avoiding this if you have any conditions that may be worsened by it. Many years ago Sarah was still able to ride a coaster. She left Space Mountain feeling battered and bruised from being tossed around and banged up in the ride car. With the format of the ride seat, she felt that she could barely hold on and keep from being tossed out. We have heard from others that the tracks have become rougher with time, making for a very rough ride.

Although there are no upside-down loops, there are high-speed plunges, stops, hairpin turns and twists that jerk you around, with speeds up to 28 miles per hour. This may sound pretty slow compared to other attractions, but it doesn't feel slow when you're on it! The ride is often in the pitch dark, which enhances the sensation of speed. It also makes it very difficult to brace yourself, as you don't know where you're headed.

Tip: Some people feel they are able to discern direction more when seated in the front seat.

The ride itself is very dark, and you rush by a lot of flashing lights and still lights. We have heard that this can be an issue for some people with seizure disorders. One particularly intense portion of the ride is when the car first takes off. There are many long lights inside a tunnel that are meant to simulate a ship taking off in space through the stars at high speed. Towards the end there is another tunnel, which is shorter with a lot of flashing lights.

Most of the queue is dimly lit, with some very long hallways. People with claustrophobia should be aware of this, especially during crowded times when it can feel more confined. There are some interesting space-related things to see as you walk through. As you approach the ride car area you'll hear people who are already on the ride screaming.

If you are using an ECV you must transfer to a wheelchair to go through the queue. You will then transfer from the wheelchair to the ride car. You have to step down into the low-lying seat car. The seats are firm with a backrest and armrests. There is a lap bar. A cast member will bring a wheelchair to you for disembarkation.

There is a moving sidewalk that exits the attraction, and it inclines very steeply. Wheelchairs can roll right onto it. Be certain to lock your wheelchair brakes.

Folks prone to motion sickness may want to avoid eating right before this ride. There are flashing lights and high-pitched noises on this attraction.

Extra info:

- Time: Approximately 3 minutes on the roller coaster
- If you're in an ECV you will be transferred to a wheelchair, and then transferred from the wheelchair to the ride.
- Service animals are not allowed on this ride.
- The height requirement is 44" (113 cm) or taller.
- Some parts of the pre-show have closed captioning.

Buzz Lightyear's Space Ranger Spin
Cautions: Carpal tunnel, flashing lights, swirling lights, fear of dark. Dizziness is a consideration but problems can usually be avoided.
Quick Notes: Ride through a life-size game where you shoot targets with a laser gun. Gentle, slow-moving ride. Each car can spin, but riders control this. There can be jerking when you spin your ride car, but this can be minimized by the rider. There's one area where motion sickness may be an issue.

If you like video games, you might love this attraction. Adults and children alike seem to really enjoy it and even find it addicting like a video game. This is one of the few rides at Magic Kingdom that Sarah can participate in. You are actually inside a life-size game where you shoot at targets with a laser gun. Many folks ride this attraction over and over, trying to better their score. You pilot your own "space cruiser" to fight the space bad guys. The environment is brightly colored, and there is a lot of activity and sound from the target areas, like being in a cartoon. This can be very stimulating.

This is a very gentle and slow-moving ride. It is in an open car with a hard bench seat that has a back. Though the cars can fit 2-3 people, only two people have a laser pistol. Your scores are kept on a score panel in front of you, and you can compete with the person you're riding with.

Each ride car has the ability to spin. This is controlled by a joystick between the two pistols, which you can use to spin or change the direction you are facing. You don't have to turn if you don't wish to; however, there are a couple of times when the ride car gradually turns on its own to face a certain direction.

If you do wish to turn your ride car, you can control the speed of spinning. You can move slowly or quickly—it's up to you. There is a minor jerky motion when turning the ride car. If you turn your car smoothly and slowly, this is minimized. We let Sarah control the spinning, and that way she can anticipate any turns. This helps her brace properly and avoid vertigo and any disorientation. She only turns the car according to her comfort level. The joystick used for turning is easy to move.

> *Tip:* If you have difficulties such as dizziness, it may help for you to take charge of the spinning feature. This way you are prepared to turn, and you can move within the bounds of your comfort level.

The ride is basically smooth and level with a very slight incline at one point. There is a brief period of darkness. There is also a part of the ride where you are passing through a tunnel-like room. There is a film with a "moving through space" scene projected on the walls and ceiling. It gives the illusion that you are traveling at great speeds through space. There are spaceships moving around on it. Sarah felt motion sickness during this part and had to close her eyes. Once she realized that you could fire at the spaceship for more points, the motion sickness stopped. She found that by focusing her eyes on just one ship at a time, she could prevent the queasiness. This part lasts maybe 30 seconds to a minute. You also pass through an area with a red light that projects many lines of light spinning against the walls.

The queue is indoors but can extend to the outdoors in a sun-exposed area if it's very busy. If you are in an ECV you must transfer to a wheelchair to go through the queue. You can stay in your wheelchair on this ride—let a cast member know you want to do this, and they will get you a car that accommodates a wheelchair.

People in wheelchairs will be directed to bypass the queue to go down a hallway to board the ride where passengers are getting off. The hallway itself is fairly narrow and long. It may be a challenge for someone with claustrophobia, but once you are through the hallway, you enter a wide-open space for boarding.

To board and leave the ride car, you will go over a moving walkway. It can be slowed or completely stopped if you need this. The sidewalk speed matches the ride car speed. If you need the walkway slowed or stopped, let a cast member know.

Once on the ride, there are Z's on the targets, and you aim for them with your laser pistol. People with vision problems may have difficulty spotting some of the targets. People with hand or wrist problems might find holding the pistol trigger down will create some discomfort. Sarah has pretty severe hand and wrist pain, but was able to go through the ride a couple of times without any major increase in discomfort.

There is one spot with spinning red beam lights. There is also white light that flashes when pictures are being taken of the guests in the ride cars. It seems to flash at pretty close intervals. The attraction can be really loud with a lot of different noises.

Extra info:

- Time: Approximately 5 minutes
- You can ride this attraction in a wheelchair or transfer to a ride seat. If you wish to ride in a wheelchair and you're in an ECV you will be transferred to a wheelchair.
- Handheld captioning devices can be used here.
- Flash photography is not allowed in this attraction.

Stitch's Great Escape
Cautions: Claustrophobia, fear of dark, problem with strong odors, allergies, neck, head and shoulder pain, flashing and strobe lights, smoke effect
Quick Notes: Multi-sensory show meant to be scary. Guests are confined to their theater seats by a harness, which locks in place. This moves harshly on the shoulders and can cause pain for some people. Chili dog smell is pumped in. Long periods of complete darkness are meant to frighten the audience. Strobe lights, loud and startling sound effects, smoke effect.

Stitch's Great Escape!

This attraction replaced a ride called Alien Encounter and is pretty close to the original. Many people find it very scary, though some don't. It can be physically difficult for some. You will be confined to your theater seat by a harness restraint system. The seats are hard chairs with backs and armrests. There is no neck or headrest. The harness comes down over your shoulders and can create a feeling of being trapped. Actually, Disney staff says you can't remove the harness once it's locked into place. We have heard that if you push it off with force it will give way. The harness comes down over your shoulders and stops when it touches your shoulders. It then locks in place.

Tip: To keep the shoulder restraints from putting too much pressure on your shoulders, sit up in your seat straight, tall and as high as you can. Let the harness come down and lock into place. Once it's stopped and locked, you can relax and sit down lower in your seat, as you normally would. This may help, however there's no guarantee that this will keep you from experiencing some pressure and motion.

The restraint moves roughly up and down on your shoulders during the show to give the effect that Stitch is jumping on it. It can impact the neck as well. This can be uncomfortable for sensitive people and those with pain issues, and even for those without pain problems. We have heard accounts of people without any particular pain issue experiencing bruising from the motion on the restraint.

The individual sound speakers are in the harness. The only way to view this attraction without the harness is to stay in a wheelchair. All seats in this theater have a harness.

At one point there is a strong hot chilidog smell pumped in that's supposed to be coming from Stitch. Some people find this really disturbing and even nauseating. It is a synthesized smell, so those with sensitivities to fragrances should take note. There is use of some bright flashing lights that seem to strobe, as well as small blinking lights and other light effects.

> *Tip:* Consider holding your breath when you hear the words "chili dog" and when Stitch burps. You may be able to avoid the worst of the smell.

There are lengthy times of complete darkness. The sound effects can be loud, startling and disturbing to some people. The show is meant to be scary, and though Stitch is a cute character that a lot of kids love, this show is not for the sensitive. Children often cry out of fear in this attraction.

There are pre-shows where you view a video that sets up the story. When you enter the theater for the actual show, you may want to avoid the first row. Those who are close may get wet. There is a smoke effect that happens in the glass chamber area. Those who are sensitive may wish to pick a row further back.

Extra info:

- Time: Approximately 20 minutes
- If you're in an ECV you will be transferred to a wheelchair.
- Guests with service animals should contact a cast member to see if your animal will be okay on this ride.
- Handheld captioning devices can be used here.
- Assistive listening devices can be used here.
- Video caption ready monitors are available here.
- The height requirement is 40" (113 cm) or taller.

Astro Orbiter
Cautions: Fear of heights, fear of elevators, claustrophobia, dizziness, motion sickness, knee and back problems, weakness. People of size may have difficulty. You must step down into a low-sitting ride car.
Quick Notes: Children's spinning ride that is very high up, and allows you to move upwards and downwards. Those with back and knee problems will find the ride car particularly uncomfortable and challenging to get in and out of.

This is an attraction that is most appropriate for children. It's simply a ride that spins around pretty quickly, and that also allows you to move upwards and downwards. Folks with motion sickness tendencies or dizziness issues will want to avoid this.

You go up to the ride cars by a very small elevator, which often has a long queue. The line is mostly in the shade, but there are some sunny parts. The elevator is really small and often "sardine-can" packed with people. Sensitive people may wish to know that as of this writing, we have heard that there is an uncomfortable smell in the elevator. It's actually very high up, and you get the full impact once you get up to the ride car loading area.

It's a slow-loading ride, so the queue can move slowly. You will enter a ride car that looks like a little rocket that seats two. You must step down into a low-sitting seat. Folks with back and knee problems may have a hard time getting in and out. Larger or taller people may be uncomfortable in these little rockets. There is no upper back or head support. Two people fit in a rocket; the person in front sits in between the legs of the person in back. The spinning motion will create centrifugal force, which can be uncomfortable for children and those who are weak.

You control the vehicle's up-and-down movement. There is a restraint across your lap, though some people feel like they could fall out. Wheelchair users can pull right up to the ride vehicle to transfer into it.

Though it's not posted, if you're in an ECV you may be required to transfer to a manual wheelchair to go up to the ride. Some folks with disabilities will need assistance getting into the ride car, and a member of your party must do this.

Extra info:

- Time: Approximately 2 minutes
- Those in a wheelchairs or ECVs must transfer to the ride car.
- Service animals can't go on this ride.

Galaxy Palace Theater (open seasonally)

This is a theater where Disney presents live musical acts from time to time. It's in almost full sun. The seats are bench seats with no backs.

Extra info:

- Guests can stay in their wheelchair or ECV.
- Assistive Listening devices can be used here.

Walt Disney's Carousel of Progress
(open seasonally – usually during peak attendance times)

Cautions: We did not observe any noteworthy obstacles, impediments or challenges, but please judge for yourself as everyone is different and attractions may change.

Quick Notes: Educational audio-animatronics show displaying technological changes throughout the twentieth century

This attraction actually pre-dates Disney World, having been originated for the 1964 World's Fair. It was then moved to Disneyland, and then finally to Disney World in 1973. It's an educational experience with an audio-animatronics American family shown through the generations, as they experience technological changes throughout the twentieth century. It's a very calm experience and many adults seem to like the nostalgia factor.

The queue is outside and has only partial shade. The film is shown in a theater where the seats actually revolve around a series of stationary stages. The motion is easy and pretty smooth. There are no thrills here. You can stay in your wheelchair or ECV in the back. There is a slight incline there. The seats are theater style.

Extra info:

- Time: Approximately 21 minutes
- Guests can stay in their wheelchair or ECV.
- Handheld captioning devices can be used here.
- Guest-activated captioning is available on some video monitors here.
- Assistive listening devices can be used here.

The Timekeeper (open seasonally)
Cautions: Motion sickness
Quick Notes: Multi-media 360° CircleVision Theater showing history across time and space. Audio-animatronics and in-theater effects. No seating here, but rails to lean on. It can be loud and some scenes may scare those who are sensitive.

This is a multi-media show in a 360° CircleVision Theater showing history across time and space. There are in-theater effects and audio-animatronics. There is no seating here, but only rails to lean on. You can stay in your wheelchair or ECV. Remember that these 360° presentations can cause some loss of balance or motion sickness in some folks. If you have a problem, just hold on to the rail and close your eyes or look at the floor.

It can be very loud here. There are scenes that can scare some people.

Extra info:

- Time: The pre-show is about 4 minutes; the show is approximately 16 minutes long.
- Guests can stay in their wheelchair or ECV.
- Guest-activated captioning is available on some video monitors here.
- Assistive listening devices can be used here.
- Reflective captioning is used at this attraction. See a cast member.

Tomorrowland Arcade
Cautions: Fear of guns, loud noises
Quick Notes: Fair-style arcade games including a shooting range. Loud noise.

Some kids and even adults may be drawn to these outdoor fair type arcade games. The area is wheelchair accessible. You may not be able to play all the games in a wheelchair, though. It can get pretty loud here.

Tomorrowland Indy Speedway
Cautions: Neck and back problems, allergies, breathing issues, mobility
Quick Notes: Drive real mini gas-powered racecars on a track with a guide rail. Bumpy ride with low-to-the-ground vehicles, small seats and gas fumes.

This is a very small version of a raceway geared toward little drivers. Real mini gas-powered racecars drive the course, controlled by anyone tall enough to reach the pedal. Though it's on a guide rail, you steer and control the speed of your car. Folks too young to drive often love this.

It's kind of a bumpy ride in a low-to-the-ground vehicle. You must be able to transfer to the car from your wheelchair. The seats are pretty low and small. Some folks will find it uncomfortably tight and hard to get in and out of. There are high seat backs with two seats side by side. The gas fumes can be strong.

The cars can bump one another from behind, giving a big jolt. The cars can roughly move from side to side around the rail if the driver has difficulty steering. You will see a lot of children drivers weaving and ramming the rail from one side to the other. This can cause some jolts and jerks. Top speed is seven miles per hour, though you could get behind a slow driver, making your drive less exciting. It can be a long wait for this ride, as it's very slow loading. Kids will often crash their cars into those waiting in front of them as they enter into the disembarking area.

Though there is a minimum height requirement, littler folks can go on with an adult. The adult can work the pedals while the child steers the car.

The queue can be long and hot.

Extra info:

- Time: Approximately 5 minutes
- The height requirement is 52" (132 cm) or taller.
- You must transfer from your wheelchair to the ride car.
- To drive you have to be able to reach the pedals, steer and see the track adequately.

Tomorrowland Transit Authority
Cautions: Fear of dark, must be able to walk and stand on angled surface, neck and back pain
Quick Notes: Elevated car on a track tours around Tomorrowland and passes through the inside of some attractions. Bumpy, jerky track with sharp turns, times of complete darkness. Must walk on a very steep moving walkway.

Many seem to find this ride relaxing; however, Sarah finds it quite uncomfortable. It's a ride in an elevated car on a track around Tomorrowland. It's a sightseeing tour, even passing through the inside of some of the attractions, giving you a peek inside. For example, you can get a quick look at Buzz Lightyear and Space Mountain, but honestly you don't see much.

You are seated in a bench seat with a back and some light padding. The seats are like those in a diner—two bench seats face each other—with two people facing forward and two people facing backward. If you are prone to motion sickness, be sure to face forward.

You must be able to walk to go on this ride. Some folks may find the entry and exit challenging. Both include moving walkways, which are incredibly steep ramps. You can lean on the railing for support; it moves at the same speed as the walkway. Once up to the ride car loading area, you must board a moving car from the moving walkway. (Both move at the same speed.)

This ride actually goes fairly fast at times, taking some sharp corners at increased speeds. This can be uncomfortable for very sensitive people with neck pain or similar issues. The ride car is actually kind of bumpy and jerky on the track, which can be uncomfortable to people sensitive to that kind of motion.

Some portions of the ride are very dark. There are some fairly long areas of pitch darkness, particularly when passing through Space Mountain. On a sunny day you'll pass from very dark areas to very bright sunlight, but you're moving at a pretty slow pace.

Extra info:

- Time: Approximately 10 minutes
- You must be able to walk to participate in this ride.
- Handheld Captioning devices can be used for parts of this attraction.

Mickey's Toontown Fair

This section of the park seems especially tight and challenging to navigate a wheelchair through. Even the walkways to the restrooms are very tight. The bathrooms themselves are tighter. Additionally, there's very little shade to be found here, and it can feel like you're baking as the sun hits the ground and reflects back up at you.

The Barnstormer at Goofy's Wiseacre Farm

Cautions: Heart problems, back or neck problems, motion sickness, difficulty keeping yourself upright under force, pain issues of any kind

Quick Notes: Child-sized roller coaster that can feel rough, despite its size. It includes moments of being angled sideways, dips, quick turns.

This is a child-sized roller coaster where kids board Goofy's crop-duster for a ride around the cornfields. It's a very brief ride, lasting less than 1 minute. The cars are pretty small, as they are not really designed for adults, but adults can join the kids. Larger adults may find it difficult. The "airplane" cars have bench seats with a lap bar. You have to step over the side of the car and down into it.

The ride can feel rough, and remember it is a roller coaster, though small and toned down. There are still the same basic moves. There are moments of going around bends where you are angled sideways. There are also some dips and quick turns.
The queue is partially shaded.

Extra info:

- Time: Approximately 1 minute
- The height requirement is 35" (89 cm) or taller.
- You must transfer from your wheelchair or ECV to the ride car.
- Service animals are not allowed on this ride.

Mickey's Country House
Cautions: We did not observe any noteworthy obstacles, impediments or challenges, but please judge for yourself as everyone is different and attractions may change.
Quick Notes: Walking tour of Mickey's home

This is a walking tour of Mickey's bedroom, living room, kitchen, game room and garden. It is wheelchair accessible. Children will enjoy seeing Mickey's home with lots of cute details.

You can catch Mickey here, but there are often long waits. He also hangs out in the Judges Tent nearby.

Extra info:

- Guests can stay in their wheelchair or ECV.

Minnie's Country House
Cautions: We did not observe any noteworthy obstacles, impediments or challenges, but please judge for yourself as everyone is different and attractions may change.
Quick Notes: Walking tour of Minnie's home

This is the Minnie Mouse home through which you can take a walking tour. It is wheelchair accessible. There can be long waits to get in. Minnie is not usually there, but she shows up once in a while unannounced.

Extra info:

- Guests can stay in their wheelchair or ECV.

Toontown Hall of Fame Tent

Cautions: We did not observe any noteworthy obstacles, impediments or challenges, but please judge for yourself as everyone is different and attractions may change.

Quick Notes: Souvenir shop and "meet and greet characters" spot

---

This is a souvenir shop and also a "meet and greet characters" spot.

Extra info:

- Guests can stay in their wheelchair or ECV.

Fantasyland Attractions

Cinderella's Golden Carrousel

Cautions: Motion sickness, dizziness

Quick Notes: Carrousel ride with various types of seating

As the name says, you get a carrousel ride. The horses go up and down, and there are some stationary chariots. The stationary chariots are hard wood with backs and some thin padding. You must transfer from your wheelchair to one of the ride seats.

The queue has mostly shaded areas. The ride is 2 minutes, so though the lines get long they move pretty quickly. It is pretty popular, so there can still be a long wait for this ride.

To board this attraction, people in wheelchairs should go to the exit gate, which is at the right side of entrance. Let a cast member know you wish to board.

Extra info:

- Time: Approximately 2 minutes
- You must transfer from your wheelchair or ECV to the ride car.
- Guests with service animals need to check with a cast member to see if your animal will be okay on this ride.

Dumbo the Flying Elephant

Cautions: Motion sickness, dizziness, inner ear problems, fear of heights

Quick Notes: Smoothly spinning ride with elevated cars that allow you to control how high or low you fly

---

This children's attraction is a smoothly moving spinning ride with elevated cars. It allows you to control how high or low you fly. Little ones seem to generally adore this ride. It spins at a pretty good clip, so anyone with a problem irritated by spinning should avoid this.

It's a really popular ride with a very long queue. It's slow loading, so there can be a very long waiting time. First thing in the morning may be a good time to try and avoid the wait.

The queue is mostly shaded. There is a wheelchair entrance right next to the regular entrance. Transferring into the ride car may be challenging. A member of your party must be able to do this for you, as the Disney staff cannot physically help you.

The seats are fairly wide and two adults and a small child could conceivably squeeze in. It would be more comfortable for two, though. The seats are hard benches with backs.

Extra info:

- Time: Approximately 2 minutes
- You must transfer from your wheelchair or ECV to the elephant car. You must be able to walk from the entrance to the ride vehicle and then step into the ride vehicle.
- Service animals are not permitted on this ride.

It's a Small World
Cautions: Flashing lights, neck and back pain (see below)
Quick Notes: Slow-moving, smooth ride that passes costumed dolls from around the world. Boats can bump each other, creating a jerking motion. Flashing lights, spotlights.

This classic Disney ride is a pretty slow, smooth ride with no big surprises. You pass by costumed dolls set in scenes from around the world. Some of them move with the music, some don't. Kids will like the bright colors and doll costumes. The theme song plays over and over again for the full 11-minute cruise. It will be in your head for quite sometime after that!

The boats have hard bench seats with backs. The seats in the front and back of the boat are quite low. For more leg room, request the center rows. Some boats are designed to take wheelchairs. Let a cast member know if that's your preference.

There are some flashing lights, as well as spotlights in various colors. There are miniature moving rides that have lights on them, including a carousel. There are also lights within the many small sets representing the various countries.

On occasion, the boats can get backed up and bump into one another, creating a jerking motion. It's a low rate of speed, and it's usually pretty gentle, but some people may need to take note of this.

Extra info:

- Time: Approximately 11 minutes

- There are some boats that can accommodate wheelchairs. If you are in an ECV you must transfer to a wheelchair to board this ride in a mobile chair.
- For boats without wheelchair accommodations, you must transfer from your wheelchair or ECV to the boat seat.
- Flash photography is not allowed
- Handheld Captioning is available here.

Mad Tea Party
Cautions: Motion sickness, dizziness, weakness
Quick Notes: Ride in a spinning teacup. Centrifugal force created by the spinning motion can make it challenging for those with weakness to stay upright.

This is a children's ride that spins as you sit in your teacup. The base of the ride revolves, and your cup spins on the base. You are able to decide whether to spin wildly or remain gentle by how you turn the wheel in the center of the cup. The platform the teacups are on spins. The cups themselves can stay immobile or spin by using that center wheel. Even those with strong stomachs sometimes can end up queasy on this.

People who are weak or have difficulty maintaining an upright position should be aware that the spinning motion creates centrifugal force. This can make it more challenging to stay upright against the force of the spin. There are no restraints on this attraction.

You must transfer from your wheelchair into the ride cup vehicle through a fairly small opening on the side of the cup. We have heard that you may have to leave your wheelchair at the entrance and walk or be carried to the teacup. The seats are benches with backs. When the ride stops your teacup may not be near the exit point, which can involve a longer walk. It can be uncomfortable for tall people.

The queue area is mostly shady. Lines can get pretty long, as it's a slow loading ride.

Extra info:

- Time: Approximately 2 minutes
- You must transfer from your wheelchair, ECV or scooter to the teacup vehicle.
- Service animals are not allowed on this ride.

The Many Adventures of Winnie the Pooh
Cautions: Back or neck problems, pain issues, fear of dark, fear of storms and lightning (which appears similar to a strobe light), allergies
Quick Notes: Ride in a honey-pot car through Pooh scenes. At one point the car moves up and down to simulate jumping. Some darkness, thunder and lightning, honey fragrance pumped in, and a heffalump blowing a smoke ring as people pass.

Another cute ride that the littlest folks will enjoy, this is a romp in a honey-pot ride car through Pooh scenes. There is one part where your ride car is bouncing with Tigger. The honey-pot car moves up and down to simulate jumping. It can be bumpy as your ride car moves up and down. Disney gives no back and neck warnings about this ride. Most people we've talked to, even those with back and neck problems, do not seem to have a problem. However, those with extreme sensitivity may have an issue with this.

The cars seat four and have hard bench seats with a back and lap bar. The ride is pretty dark with some very dark moments. There is a simulated storm with lightning. The lightning effect looks similar to a strobe light. There is a honey smell pumped in where you leave the ride car and enter the gift shop. Many folks find it hard to detect the fragrance. There is a bit of smoke when a heffalump (a Disney character) blows a smoke ring at the people as they pass by. It's not a lot, and it doesn't happen with every car that passes by. The car travels moderately fast.

Most of the queue area is shaded.

Extra info:

- Time: Approximately 3 minutes
- ECV riders must transfer to a wheelchair to go through the queue.
- You can transfer from your wheelchair to the honey pot vehicle.
- You can wait for a honey-pot vehicle that can accommodate your wheelchair and board on your wheelchair.
- Video Caption-ready monitors are available.
- Flash photography is not allowed.
- Handheld Captioning devices can be used here.

Mickey's PhilharMagic
Cautions: Allergies, loud noise, blast of air blown at guests
Quick Notes: 3-D movie starring Mickey and Donald. Sensory effects include wind gusts blowing at your face, apple pie-scented fragrance blown at you. Some startling 3-D effects, though they don't seem designed to cause fright.

Many folks just love this show, and children will be dazzled. This is the newest of the 3-D's at Disney, and it is presented on one of the largest seamless screens in the world. It stars Mickey Mouse and Donald Duck and is full of many of the Disney animation favorites.

The seats are padded theater-style with arms. There are some special effects including wind gusts repeatedly blowing at your face, and apple pie-scented fragrance is blown at you. The show can seem very loud for some folks. You must wear 3-D glasses, which fit over regular glasses. The theater is pretty dark, as with any movie.

Remember that 3-D effects can sometimes be startling, as they do really seem to come right at you and even close enough to touch. The effects don't seem to be designed to cause fright. Still, some very young children sometimes get scared just by the impact of the 3-D effects.

At one point there is a small blast of air blown at guests around face level. It's not extremely dramatic but it can startle the occasional very sensitive person. This happens when Champagne bottles pop their corks.

The queue is indoors and can overflow to the outdoors. Most of the outdoors area is shaded.

The back row has wheelchair spots between theater seats. You can either stay in your wheelchair or transfer to a theater seat.

Extra info:

- Time: Approximately 10 minutes
- Guests can stay in their wheelchair or ECV.
- Reflective Captioning is available at this location.
- Assistive Listening devices can be used here.

Peter Pan's Flight

Cautions: Fear of heights, fear of the pirate and crocodile from the Peter Pan story, fear of the dark, allergies, pain, mobility. See ride boarding description below.

Quick Notes: Flying is simulated as you ride a sailboat suspended over various scenes. Periods of darkness, minor jolt of ride car in the disembarking area.

You sail aboard a flying pirate ship and follow Peter Pan on a journey into Neverland. This ride is smooth with your ride vehicle suspended in the air as you "fly" over various scenes. The vehicle does go higher and lower, but the angles are not severe. People with fear of heights should take note that you are suspended above scenes looking down. Despite that, it never feels very high to us and shouldn't concern most folks unless the fear is severe.

There are a lot of darker scenes and periods of extreme darkness between scenes. There is one fairly brief point where it's almost pitch black, but then you turn a corner and you have light. During the ride there are twinkling lights. The vehicle has bench seating with a back and lap bar. There is no neck support, but there is a sail that you can put your head on if you need the support. It's whimsical and made to look like a colorful pirate sailboat.

Boarding the ride may be an issue for some people. Those in a wheelchair must step out of the wheelchair onto a moving walkway, walk to the ride vehicle and then into the vehicle. You must be able to step upwards into the moving vehicle and board your seat while walking. The walkway cannot be stopped on this ride.

At the end of the ride there is a minor jolt as the boat brings you into the disembarking area.

The queue is mostly shaded. Lines can be long here with shorter waits possibly first thing in the morning. Many folks complain because this queue has nothing for kids to look at.

This attraction smells particularly musty to us.

Extra info:

- Time: Approximately 4 minutes
- Handheld Captioning devices can be used here.
- You must transfer from your wheelchair to the ride vehicle by stepping onto a moving walkway and up onto a moving ride vehicle. The walkway can't be stopped.
- Service animals are not permitted on this attraction.

Snow White's Scary Adventures

Cautions: Back or neck problems, pain issues, fear of dark, fear of witches, loud noises, fear of skeletons, strobe lights

Quick Notes: Fast-moving rough ride that jerks you around quite a bit, with frequent sudden sharp turns. May be scary for some.

You ride a dwarf mine car through Snow White's adventures. The Evil Queen pursues Snow White through scenes from the animated film. This is really a fast-moving rough ride that jerks you around quite a bit. It moves in ways that will challenge some people, including frequent and sudden sharp turns. Those with pain, back and neck issues should consider avoiding this attraction. We heard from several people who expressed how surprised they were at the rough ride.

We find that this attraction can really scare some people. The very ugly witch and Evil Queen audio-animatronics often pop out menacingly with lots of evil laughter and threats, the ride is often quite dark and it can be very loud with screaming. (Snow White even screams.) There are lots of spooky, almost roaring sounds in the background during some scenes. It does have a happy ending, but those who are sensitive may wish to avoid this ride.

The ride vehicle is a three-row car. It has hard bench seats with seat backs that go to mid-back, and a lap bar, which you must manually pull down. You must transfer from your wheelchair to the ride car. You must step up into the ride car.

A couple of times there are some lights that strobe for brief periods.

Extra info:

- Time: Approximately 3 minutes
- You must transfer from your wheelchair or ECV to the ride car.
- Handheld Captioning is available here.
- See a cast member to determine if your service animal can go on this ride.

Liberty Square Attractions

The Hall of Presidents

Cautions: We did not observe any noteworthy obstacles, impediments or challenges, but please judge for yourself as everyone is different and attractions may change.

Quick Notes: Widescreen 180° film and audio-animatronics are combined to share American history.

People who love history will enjoy this attraction. It's a combination of a widescreen 180° film and audio-animatronics. Forty-two U. S. presidents gather to hear the words of Abraham Lincoln. The audio-animatronics are extremely detailed. This show is housed in a 700-seat theater. There is a film that goes over some U.S. history. The seats are theater style.

Wheelchair guests should go inside through the door to the right of the turnstiles. Wait on the right side of the rotunda. A cast member will bring you inside to be seated before the other guests are allowed in. You can stay in your wheelchair, or park it and transfer to a regular seat. There are no special effects that the seats provide; it's a matter of choosing where you'll be most comfortable.

This starts every half hour.

Extra info:

- Time: Approximately 20 minutes
- Guests can stay in their wheelchair or ECV.
- Assistive listening devices can be used here.
- Reflective Captioning is available here.

The Haunted Mansion

Cautions: Fear of the dark, fear of ghosts, fear of heights, claustrophobia, allergies, flashing lights, fear of spiders, fear of thunder and lightning, lightning effect (which has the appearance of flashing or strobe lights)

Quick Notes: Ride a "doom buggy" through a haunted mansion. Smooth ride with sharp inclines and declines. Long periods of darkness. Pre-show may challenge people with claustrophobia. Some might find this attraction scary.

At the time of this writing this attraction was closed for refurbishment, so there may be changes once it's re-opened that we are unaware of at this time. The following information is written from the perspective of what we have experienced to date.

Although the theme is innately scary, it's not horror-movie gross. I would describe it more as spooky with some humor. Some folks, especially small children and those who fear the dark, may find it very scary.

There are two parts to this attraction. The pre-show is on foot and may be scary to some sensitive people. There's also the possibility of claustrophobia. We'll summarize some of what happens in the pre-show to help those with fears know what to expect. Warning: Anyone who doesn't want to have the surprise spoiled should bypass the following paragraph.

For the pre-show you and a group of people are led into a round room. You are asked to move away from the walls toward the center of the room. The door shuts, and then there is no visible exit door. (It's camouflaged.) Some find this claustrophobic, especially if the room is crowded. The walls begin to have the appearance of stretching to give the illusion that you are shrinking. The ceiling is actually rising along with some pictures that rise and appear to stretch. Then the spooky voice of the house begins to say some scary things, including talk about what happened to other people who dared try this ride you are about to embark on. Suddenly the room goes pitch dark. Then there is lightning and thunder, and a skull appears. The lightning effect is on the ceiling. It looks more like flashing camera lights or strobe lights. After that you are led into the next room, where you are boarded onto your ride car.

You can bypass the entire pre-show by going in the wheelchair entrance. Wheelchair riders cannot participate in the pre-show. If you can't stand in the queue and stand for the pre-show then you must bypass the pre-show and go directly to the ride.

The ride car is a clamshell-shaped vehicle called a "doom buggy" with a high back and a lap bar. Once you are in, the front portion comes up and locks in place. The bar comes down over your legs automatically. Make sure your legs are not crossed or the bar will come down on your legs, which is painful! Some folks may find this car claustrophobic.

There are speakers inside each private car. To board the car you must enter a moving walkway, and you also exit on a moving walkway. If you are transferring from a wheelchair onto the ride car, a cast member will help you. You will move your wheelchair onto the walkway and then board the ride car, which is moving at the same speed as the walkway. They may be able to slow or stop the walkway if necessary. Tell the cast member if you wish them to slow or stop the ride so you can board.

It's a pretty slow moving ride. You can feel the minor roughness of the track, but it's very mild. The entire attraction is really quite dark. In fact, there are long periods in pitch black. There are some steep inclines and declines, and you move backwards downhill. Your ride car gently moves in different directions so that you can continually face the action. It's actually a relatively smooth ride.

> *Tip:* Because the back of the seat is curved like a clam shell, it's hard to rest your neck and head on it. Sarah finds that it's much more comfortable to take along a sweater and use it behind her neck and head for more comfort and support. It's especially helpful when going downhill backwards.

This ride smells especially musty to us. As you exit your ride car, it can move a bit, so be careful getting off of it.

There's a fun effect when a ghost figure is projected so that it looks like it's sitting with you in your ride car as you look into a mirror. This may scare some people.

The queue outside is in full sun. The walkway leading up to the Haunted Mansion is textured like cobblestone and rough for a wheelchair.

If you get to the pre-show and decide you don't want to go through with it, you can exit before it begins. Just let a cast member know and they'll escort you out through a special exit. If you wish to skip the pre-show and go right to the ride portion, just let a cast member know, and they can escort you right to the "doom buggy" ride. If others in your party want to see the pre-show, you can wait for them there instead of boarding the ride immediately. There's also an exit after the pre-show and before the ride portion of the attraction. If you decide you don't want to go on the ride, just get the attention of a cast member and they can escort you out.

Extra info:

- Time: The pre-show is approximately 3 minutes and the ride approximately 7 minutes.
- You must transfer from your wheelchair or ECV to the ride car.
- Handheld Captioning devices can be used here.

Liberty Square Riverboat

Cautions: Motion sickness

Quick Notes: Ride around Tom Sawyer Island in an early American steamship. Very few seats on board. Steam coming off the stacks may bother some people.

This is a gentle boat ride aboard a genuine replica of an early American steamship with a large paddle wheel on its stern, or back, side. You cruise around Tom Sawyer Island. Some find it a pleasant way to relax, especially if the weather is nice. If it's hot out, it will be hot on the boat.

There can be a wait at times. The queue is in a shaded area with some benches nearby. The boat leaves twice an hour on the half hour, and if there are more folks than can get on, it's a pretty long wait. There are some seats on board the boat, but most people will have to stand. You can lean on the rails if you need to. There are three levels on the boat, with steps to get to the other levels. You may feel the steam coming from the stacks if the wind is pushing it towards you. Try and get a spot upwind if this is an issue for you.

Extra info:

- Time: Approximately 20 minutes
- Guests can remain in their wheelchair or ECV.

Frontierland Attractions

Big Thunder Mountain Railroad

Cautions: Heart problems, blood pressure issues, back or neck problems, joint or muscle pain, motion sickness, balance or weakness problems, pain issues of any kind, fear of heights, fear of the dark, on a sunny day there are fast changes between darkness and light as you go in and out of tunnels at high speed

Quick Notes: Roller coaster themed after a runaway mine train reaching 30-35 miles per hour. Sharp turns, plunges, intense curves, short stops, earthquake simulation, falling rocks, bats, darkness.

Considered mild compared to some of the other roller coasters at Disney, this one still gives thrills. This may be a good one to start with if you're uncertain about how you will handle a roller coaster.

It's themed after a runaway mine train rushing through an Old West mining town and also through the mine itself. Speeds reach 30-35 miles per hour over rough tracks. There are sharp turns, plunges, intense curves and short stops. The plunges are not anywhere as high and deep as some of the major coasters. You will not turn upside down at any time. The curves are enough to have you almost sideways, so people with neck, pain or weakness issues should take note.

The train goes through some mining caves where it gets very dark. The ride cars move in and out of dark caves at a high speed. On sunny days this contrast of outdoor light and dark can be a problem for some people. There is a simulated earthquake with rocks falling and some bats. We don't find this to be very scary but some might.

Big Thunder Mountain Railroad

The seats are bench style with backs, some thin padding and a lap bar. You must transfer from your wheelchair or ECV to the ride car. Some people feel that the back of the vehicle may be rougher and offer more of a thrill.

The queue has partial shade. It winds through a partially enclosed area, which can be really hot. The lines can get really long for this attraction.

Extra info:

- Time: Approximately 5 minutes
- The height requirement is 40" (102 cm) or taller.
- You must transfer from your wheelchair or ECV to the ride car.
- Service animals are not allowed on this ride.

Country Bear Jamboree
Cautions: We did not observe any noteworthy obstacles, impediments or challenges, but please judge for yourself as everyone is different and attractions may change.
Quick Notes: Audio-animatronics musical revue with singing, dancing and joke-telling bears and other animals

This is an audio-animatronics musical revue in a darkened theater that generally appeals to young children. It has country music singing, dancing and joke-telling bears and other animals. It is generally appreciated most by very small children. Several reports from teens and adults indicated that they were quite bored. This might be an attraction to skip if you don't have young children with you.

The seats are padded benches with a partial back. (This is a thin section that goes across the upper back of an average person.) There's wheelchair seating in the front row. The cast members will direct you there.

Extra info:

- Time: Approximately 18 minutes
- Guests can remain in their wheelchair or ECV.
- Assistive Listening devices can be used here.
- Reflective Captioning is available here.

Frontierland Shootin' Arcade
Cautions: Loud noises
Quick Notes: Rifle range with pop-up, moving and stationary targets.

Try your rifle marksmanship on pop-up, moving and stationary targets. There are two guns that can be used while staying in your wheelchair. Use the ramp on the left side to get to them.

Extra info:

- Guests can remain in their wheelchair or ECV.

Splash Mountain
Cautions: Heart problems, blood pressure issues, back or neck problems, joint or muscle pain, motion sickness, balance or weakness problems, pain issues of any kind, fear of heights, fear of the dark, claustrophobia, allergies, fear of heights. On sunny days there are changes between darkness and light as you go in and out of tunnels.
Quick Notes: Part calm boat ride, and part water flume thrill ride. Multiple flume drops including a five-story plunge, sharp turns, high speeds, sudden stops and sudden drops. Low seat with little legroom. Ride car frequently hits the side as it travels, creating mild jolts. Periods of darkness, musty smell. Ride cars can hit one another as they approach the disembarking area. Some scenes may be scary for sensitive people.

Splash Mountain®

This is a ride that most people who can handle the physical challenges seem to love. It starts out as a slow and pleasant boat journey through audio-animatronics–filled scenes from Disney's *Song of the South*, and then turns into a water flume thrill ride. It follows Brer Rabbit as he outfoxes Brer Fox and Brer Bear. You will get wet on this attraction!

The queue is outside with some tree cover and some sun. It winds up a staircase. (People in wheelchairs either use FASTPASS and go through the FASTPASS entrance or see a cast member for directions). The queue leads to an indoor section that is made like a cave which is cool inside. There is dim lighting. Some folks find the winding queue portion towards the end claustrophobic.

The ride car is made to look like a hollowed-out log. The seats are hard bench seats with a back and very little legroom. There are handles in front of you to grab onto. You must step over the side of the log, which is approximately two feet high. You then sit down in a low seat that has very little legroom. It may be a challenge for some people to get in and out of this ride car.

As you are riding, the log car frequently hits the sidewall, especially as it's making turns. This creates a mild jolt.

The first part of the ride is very dark as you pass through a swamp by the various scenes. Some parts are pretty dimly lit. That combined with some of the characters and scenes you see may seem scary to young kids or the very sensitive.

The ride has three smaller flume drops, and then the real thrill ride portion comes with a high-speed but smooth five-story drop down a water flume. The second drop is in pitch-black darkness so you don't know how to brace yourself for the ending drop. Those with fear of heights may be challenged at the top of some of these drops.

You can feel jolted at the bottom of the drops as the ride car lands. Still, many people with neck and back problems report that it's a mild jolt, and they do not feel discomfort. With her level of neck pain, Sarah has opted not to try this ride. We feel the jolt is enough to irritate her neck problems. There's a lot of splashing as the ride car goes down the flume and lands. This gives the appearance of a rough landing, but many people seem to think it's not as rough as it looks. You may get wet.

Keep in mind that Disney does include back and neck problems in their warning for this ride. Also keep in mind that you will ride at angles similar to those on roller coasters. The upward angle to the big drop is very steep. Your head and neck are not supported in any way. However, we have heard from several people with neck issues who don't feel any discomfort with this ride. There are sharp turns, high speeds, sudden stops and sudden drops as well.

The very beginning of the ride feels bumpy, like driving over cobblestone. This is fairly brief. At the end of the ride, boats often hit each other, creating an unexpected jolt. Be prepared!

On a sunny day you will go in and out of dark caves into bright light. There is a flash when your photograph is taken.

The ride can get very crowded; this may be a ride to go to first thing in the morning, or during fireworks and parades. The crowds may be lighter at these times.

This ride can smell pretty musty. We've heard reports of people seeing mold on the ride cars.

> *Tip:* If you want to get less wet, you can get a Disney poncho raincoat and wear it onto the ride. They are sold in most stores in the park. Even if you plan to get wet, you'll want to protect your camera with a plastic bag.

> *Tip:* If you are waiting for someone to come off the ride, a good spot to wait is near the restroom area where there is an overhang. You can even go just beyond the restrooms into the small gift shop, which is air conditioned and wheelchair accessible. You will be sure to find the

person you're waiting for, as guests must pass by this area after disembarking ride.

Extra info:

- Time: Approximately 12 minutes
- The height requirement is 40" (102 cm) or taller.
- You must transfer from your wheelchair or ECV to the ride car.
- Service animals are not allowed on this ride.

Tom Sawyer Island

Cautions: Allergies, claustrophobia, mold sensitivities. See description below for further warnings for those with mobility issues.

Quick Notes: Play area reached by a raft ride with trails, narrow caves, tunnels, hills, swinging suspension bridges, stairs, steep inclines, a play fort and rugged trails that will not support wheelchair use. Musty smell in some caves and tunnels.

This is a play area that is reached by raft. We hear that parents with hyperactive children love this area, as their children can blow off a lot of steam here.

ECVs cannot board the raft, but wheelchairs can. ECV users can transfer to a wheelchair. The island itself is not designed for wheelchair users. There are trails with narrow caves, tunnels, hills, swinging suspension bridges, stairs, steep inclines, a play fort and rugged trails that will not support wheelchair use. You may be able to get to the island on a wheelchair, but you must be able to walk to explore the area.

The caves and tunnels may induce claustrophobia in some people. They also can smell moldy and musty. Parents should be aware that kids can go in one side and exit out the other side.

Please note that it's a good idea to avoid this attraction if it looks like it might rain, especially if there is thunder and lightning involved. There's not much cover on the island. To get off the island you'll have to wait for a raft and go back over to the other side.

There isn't a roped queue and at times people will start pushing to get into the boat as it's loading. It can get disorderly.

Extra info:

- You must transfer from your ECV to a wheelchair to ride the raft to the island. You can also just take a round-trip on the raft, and wait for your party at the dock.
- You must be ambulatory to experience the island.

Adventureland Attractions

The Enchanted Tiki Room Under New Management

Cautions: Flashing lights, lightning effect, fear of darkness, fear of thunder and lightning, allergies, smoke/fog effect.

Quick Notes: Audio-animatronic birds host a show. Darkness, scary "volcano goddess," lightning and thunder, flashing lights, fog/smoke effect. Most of the show is up towards the ceilings, so you must look upwards.

Audio-animatronic birds host the show filled with singing and bantering. "Tiki gods" also show up and entertain. One in particular may frighten little ones. There is a scene where a female tiki god gets really angry. It gets dark and the Tiki birds get scared. There's lightning, thunder and flashing lights. Smoke rises, and she appears with glowing eyes. She's pretty creepy. She screams, threatens the birds, sings and screams a bit more. Her part doesn't last very long, and the other tiki gods seem gentle enough.

You will mostly look upwards toward the birds and characters suspended from the ceilings. The place is kept quite dark, and there are moments where it's completely dark. The birds have bright lights on them, so there are brightly lit birds in a very dark room. There are flashing lights and a fog/smoke effect. There is some lightning and thunder that's pretty intense. The lightning effect is brief. There is a "volcano goddess" with glowing eyes that can scare some sensitive people. Smaller children and sensitive adults can find it really scary.

There is a small pre-show outside with a couple of birds bantering. It's in a shaded area where guests stand. There are bench seats with backs.

Extra info:

- Time: This pre-show is approximately 2 minutes and the main show lasts approximately 9 minutes.
- Guests can stay in their wheelchair or ECV.
- Assistive Listening devices can be used here.
- Handheld Captioning devices can be used here.

Jungle Cruise

Cautions: Fear of the dark, fear of snakes, fear of jungle animals

Quick Notes: Boat ride that passes scenes with audio-animatronics and non-animated creatures and settings. You may get wet. Sudden gunshot sound, sudden bursts of water from the river, dark cave.

This is a simple boat ride that passes by various scenes with audio-animatronics as well as non-animated creatures and settings. You will pass through some mist and near waterfalls and water bursts from the river, so you might get damp (but not really soaked like some of the other water rides). You enter a dark cave during this ride. Inside there are some snakes and a tiger, which the very young or sensitive might find a bit scary.

There is a sudden gunshot sound, as well as sudden bursts of water from the river. At one point the guide may start screaming about an ambush; however, nothing really dramatic happens.

The seats are wooden benches with the side of the boat as the seat back. Some boats also have a backless bench running down the center of the craft. There are wheelchair accessible boats, but you may have to wait quite a while for one to come. If you can transfer, you must step across the dock upwards to the boat, and then down into the boat. You must then walk to your seat. The boat itself can do a lot of bobbing while at dockside. You may need to have a member of your party help steady you as you step down to get into the boat and step up to get out of the boat.

Extra info:

- Time: Approximately 10 minutes
- Guests can stay in their wheelchair or ECV.
- Assistive Listening devices can be used here.
- Handheld Captioning devices can be used here.

Magic Carpets of Aladdin
Cautions: Motion sickness, dizziness, fear of heights
Quick Notes: Elevated spinning ride that allows you to control how high or low to fly. You must step up and over a decoration on the vehicle to get into the ride seat. Camels spit water at the riders.

This children's attraction is an outdoor elevated spinning ride that allows the rider in the front seat to control how high or low to fly. The rider in the back seat can control how to pitch the vehicle forward and backward.

It spins at a fairly good clip, so anyone with problems affected by spinning should avoid this. It's a really popular ride with a very long queue. The queue is mostly shaded. The chairs are well-padded bench seats.

The magic carpet vehicles are really whimsical and colorful. There are two rows of bench seats that hold two people in each row. Wheelchair users can either transfer to the ride seat, or wait for a wheelchair accessible carpet car. You must transfer from your ECV to a wheelchair. To transfer right into the carpet you must step up and over a decoration on the vehicle side and into the seat.

There are some spitting camels that spit water at the riders, but it's not enough to get really soaked.

Extra info:

- Time: Approximately 2 minutes
- You must transfer from your wheelchair or ECV to the carpet car or you can transfer to a wheelchair and board a wheelchair accessible carpet car.
- Service animals can't go on this ride.

> ### Pirates of the Caribbean
>
> **Cautions:** Back or neck pain or anything that might be worsened by a jolt, fear of the dark, lightning effect, loud cannon noise, long step down into the boat. Some people may get wet, but most won't. See description below for other fears.
>
> **Quick Notes:** Indoor boat ride with audio-animatronics and pirate scenes. Most of the ride is gentle, but there is one point where the boat accelerates and drops down a short drop with a jolt. You must be able to step down into the boat to get in and up to get out. Darkness and dim lighting, cannons, gunshots and water splashes to simulate cannonballs hitting the water. Some spooky images including skeletons, thunder and lightning, fire simulations. Boats can hit one another while waiting in the disembarking area. Some parents feel that some of the scenes are a bit too graphic for their children.

This ride has been recently updated to reflect the *Pirates of the Caribbean* movie with Johnny Depp. This is an indoor boat ride that travels through scenes of pirate life with audio-animatronics. The newest audio-animatronics additions are remarkably life-like.

Most of the long queue is indoors, winding in an atmosphere like an underground cavern, with dim lighting. Some people find this claustrophobic, especially when it's crowded. There are some gradual inclines as you move along. The outdoor queue is shaded. Since the remodeling of the ride, crowds have picked up here, and it can be a long wait.

ECV users are transferred to a wheelchair to go through the queue. People in wheelchairs must then transfer to the boat seat. You must be able to step down two steps, into the boat and onto your seat. There is a good-sized step down required to get into the boat. It's approximately 12 inches long. A member of your party may need to steady you. The cast members can't do this. Folding wheelchairs will be stowed on the boat with you. The boats have hard bench seating with backs.

Although the majority of this ride is gentle, there is a point at which the boat makes a short and sudden acceleration and then a sudden short, steep drop. Some find the drop to be insignificant, even with pain issues. Sarah found it to be too much of a jolt for her condition. For people with back, neck or other similar issues, it can cause discomfort. The people in the first couple of rows may get wet.

There are times when the boats get backed up, and occasionally one boat will hit the boat in front of it. The collision occurs at a slow rate of speed, and some folks will find it nothing to write home about. However, some may find it uncomfortable.

During the ride, there are some times of darkness, and much of the ride has low lighting. The set is designed to look like you're riding through caverns. There is the sound of cannons shooting and guns being shot.

Some parents feel that the scenes are a bit too graphic for their children. These include a prisoner being dunked in a well, some drunken pirates, some spooky images including the Davy Jones character from the movie, skeletons, thunder and lightning, a woman being auctioned off and a building on fire.

When you get off the boat there is a steep, inclined moving walkway. There is a hand rail for those who need it. There is an elevator at the unload area for those in wheelchairs to use to leave the attraction. Those with GACs can request the elevator as well.

You may get wet from the splashing water effect when the cannons shoot, but usually not soaked.

Extra info:

- Time: Approximately 10 minutes
- You must transfer from your ECV to a wheelchair, then from the wheelchair to the ride boat vehicle. Folded wheelchairs can be taken on the boat.
- Handheld Captioning devices can be used here.

Swiss Family Treehouse

Cautions: Fear of heights, fear of falling. You must be ambulatory. You must climb a large number of stairs.

Quick Notes: Climb 128 steps to tour a treehouse

You will climb approximately 128 steps high up into a tree house. This is a tour of this rendition of how the Swiss Family Robinson would have lived. You don't enter the living quarters—you view them from just outside the area.

Extra info:

- You must be ambulatory to experience this attraction.

Wishes: A Magical Gathering of Disney Dreams

Cautions: Loud noises, possible smoke, heavy crowds in some areas

Quick Notes: Beautiful fireworks display over the park

Location: Throughout the park

At night the sky comes alive with a really beautiful fireworks display over Cinderella's Castle. There is no special viewing area; however, you'll find the largest concentration of people around the castle and down Main Street U.S.A. This can be uncomfortably crowded, and we really suggest you avoid it. There are many other areas of the park where you'll be able to look upwards for a good view of the display.

Trying to leave the park can be very difficult, as the largest crowds congregate right on the main exit path of the park. If you are in a wheelchair or have mobility issues and decide to stay in the park for the show, I'd strongly suggest you wait until the crowd disperses before trying to leave.

Personally we enjoy seeing Wishes from outside the park, from places such as the beach at the Polynesian or Ohana's restaurant inside the Polynesian. Also, California grill in the Contemporary has a great view. Several Disney restaurants turn down the lights and play the accompanying music, which is very pleasant! At this writing they no longer do this at Ohana's, although the view is good from there.

Keep in mind that the fireworks are extremely loud, and there is always the possibility of some smoke settling.

Magic Kingdom is not really the place to go if you're looking for an outstanding dining experience. Most of the food is equivalent to fast food, with the occasional upgraded experience. For us, food at this park is just to refuel.

It's very difficult to maintain a diet on the snacks you find here. The choices are more limited than at the other parks. Even the snack carts seem to offer fewer choices. Low-carbohydrate and low-calorie snacks are very seldom found. It's a challenge to find a healthy snack alternative here as well. For those who wish to keep a special diet, it might be a good idea to bring some snacks of your own.

Full-service Restaurants

Cinderella's Royal Table

Who wouldn't want to check out the restaurant in the castle? The atmosphere inside is fairly simple and less themed as we expected to find. However, for those with little princesses and even princes, the fixed-price breakfast and lunch may be worth the stop to participate in the princess character meals.

Breakfast is all-you-can-eat, with the food brought to your table. It includes fruit, eggs, bacon, sausage, cheese Danish, French toast, potato casserole, granola and low-fat yogurt and caramelized bananas.

For lunch, you will have a variety of appetizers followed by your choice of one entrée: pasta al pomodoro (pasta in sauce with vegetables), salmon, pork tenderloin, focaccia sandwich or beef pie. Children can get a small beef pie, chicken strips, pretzel dogs or pasta with marinara sauce.

Dinner is a set price meal hosted by the fairy godmother, who leads folks in celebration of occasions like birthdays, new marriages and anniversaries. It is usually a bit more subdued than breakfast and lunch. The meal choices include braised lamb shank, grilled pork tenderloin, cheese tortellini with julienne vegetables, spice-rubbed roast chicken, roast prime rib of beef and pan-seared salmon.

Chairs are padded with backs. The restaurant is on the second floor. There is a narrow and winding staircase that takes you to the restaurant, or you can use the elevator.

The Crystal Palace

This is a very busy character dining experience serving breakfast, lunch and dinner. It's designed to be a kind of "classy" experience. There is a cast member who opens the door dressed in a spruced-up uniform, and classical music playing inside. However, we find the interior to be quite casual.

The tables and seats are very close together, and the aisles are often blocked by Disney characters, children and parents taking photos. The atmosphere can be a bit chaotic.

The food is a buffet with a decent selection. The lunch menu includes several salads and vegetables including Mediterranean pasta salad, edamame salad and shrimp/black bean/mango salad. There's also sliced turkey and ham, cheeses, mashed potatoes, stir-fried curry noodles, various pastas, chicken dishes, flank steak and barbecued pork tenderloin. There are several vegetarian dishes as well as some health-oriented choices.

There is a wheelchair ramp to the left of the main entrance. Chairs are metal with backs and a bit of cushioning on the seats.

Liberty Tree Tavern

This is a home-style American theme in a recreation of an 18th-century colonial inn. Dinner is a character buffet. Lunch is a step up from the fast-food restaurants that make up the majority at Magic Kingdom. Lunch appetizers include New England clam chowder, Maryland crab cakes, and "Declaration Salad," which is field greens. Main courses include salmon, penne pasta, cheddar and chicken salad, a vegetable and grain dish, pot roast and a traditional turkey dinner. There are also sandwiches available.

The character dinner buffet features Minnie, Goofy, Pluto and friends. This can be a noisy and even chaotic environment with the characters going from table to table. Parents and children are up in the aisles with the characters, often taking photos. The menu includes tossed mixed greens, smoked pork loin, roasted turkey breast, carved beef, mashed potatoes, herb bread stuffing, macaroni and cheese and seasonal vegetables.

There are wood tables and primarily wood chairs with backs. People in wheelchairs can enter by an outdoor ramp to the left of the lobby entrance.

The Plaza Restaurant

This has a Victorian interior reminiscent of turn-of-the-20th-century America. It's both attractive and pleasant. The menu includes sandwiches such as cheese, grilled chicken, grilled Reuben, hamburger, vegetarian, club and tuna. You will also find soup and salads. Perhaps more interesting are the desserts, including ice cream floats, cones, sundaes and banana splits. Even more exciting for some of us sugar avoiders is the no-sugar-added ice cream available here.

There is indoor and outdoor seating. It can get really tight inside when crowded, and it's pretty popular. It can be difficult for a wheelchair to navigate. The seats indoors are metal with seat cushioning. There is also some booth seating.

Tony's Town Square

This is an Italian-style restaurant with décor inspired by the movie *Lady and the Tramp*. It's a pleasant environment with character artwork on the walls. Appetizers include soup, salad, garlic breadsticks and calamari. For lunch, main courses include meatball submarines, grilled chicken panini, vegetable calzone, pizza, Caesar salad with chicken, a chicken parmigiana hero, grilled salmon and a variety of pasta dishes.

For dinner you can get beef and spinach cannelloni, spaghetti with or without meatballs, eggplant rotini, chicken Florentine, grilled salmon, NY strip steak and seafood diavoli.

Indoor seating has wood chairs with backs combined with booth seating. There is a sun room with metal chairs with backs and padded seats.

Counter Service Restaurants

Casey's Corner

Pure Americana is served here with classic hot dogs, french fries and drinks. There are also corn dog nuggets and chili. This restaurant offers mostly outdoor seating.

The outdoor tables have umbrellas. The seats outside are tiny metal chairs. The backs have a thin metal outline of a heart for support. There is a tiny seat cushion on the tiny seats. The seats are pretty close together, and it can be hard to maneuver a wheelchair here. People in wheelchairs can use the first register on the left.

There are a very small number of seats indoors. The chairs are wood with cushioned seats, and there are some wood benches.

As with many of the outdoor restaurants at Disney, this is a bird favorite. Some of the birds get really aggressive about grabbing food. They'll come right up to you, and there's the occasional swooping bird dive-bombing for your food.

At times there is a piano player there.

Columbia Harbour House

This restaurant has a nautical theme with a cool, air conditioned environment and low lights. The food selection and the atmosphere are a bit more upscale than the typical fast-food place at the Magic Kingdom.

The menu includes fried chicken strips, fried fish, tuna sandwiches, ham with tomatoes, broccoli and cheese sandwiches, vegetarian chili, hummus sandwiches, salad and New England clam chowder.

The seats are wood with backs. There are also picnic tables with benches. There's extra seating upstairs, which can be reached by stairs or an elevator.

People in wheelchairs should use the first register on the left.

Cosmic Ray's Starlight Café

You'll find three different "bays," or counters, with completely different types of food at each station. The problem with this is that if you want anything from the other stations, you have to get into another line and wait again. The lines can be long at times.

The setting has a futuristic motif; however, we find that it's not very heavily themed. There is an animatronic singing character in a large side hall that sings like an old-fashioned piano bar singer. He also makes corny jokes.

The seats and tables are very close together. There are places a wheelchair just can't get to. It's best to find seating on the outskirts. The chairs are hard with backs like an upside-down triangle.

Beware: The no-sugar-added brownie has malitol in it. For some people, that can create stomach distress.

Food includes kosher meals, rotisserie chicken, barbecued ribs, fried chicken strips, Caesar salad with chicken, vegetarian wrap, vegetable soup, chicken soup, grilled chicken sandwiches, pork sandwiches, turkey bacon wraps, hamburgers, hot dogs and vegetarian burgers.

Wheelchairs use the first register on the left at both Blast-Off Burgers and the Starlight Soup-Salad-Sandwich sections. At the Cosmic Chicken section wheelchairs use the first register on the right.

El Pirata Y El Perico Restaurant

This is only open during the highest attendance seasons. It's located across from the Pirates of the Caribbean attraction. When it's closed, there is seating outside and under cover that can offer a quiet resting place where very few people hang out. The menu includes Mexican food such as tacos, nachos and taco salads.

There are metal seats with backs and cushions, with plenty of maneuvering space.

Main Street Bakery

This little shop serves continental and hot breakfasts, gourmet sandwiches and lots of tempting desserts. These include ice cream sundaes, cookies, smoothies, frozen lattes and specialty coffees, cakes and candies. There are usually no-sugar-added alternatives as well as vegetarian choices. They also offer fresh fruit such as cantaloupe or strawberries.

This is another small shop with a queue and interior that are challenging and tight for wheelchairs. It can get very crowded here also. The chairs are metal with backs and cushioned seats.

Pecos Bill Café

Found in Frontierland, this restaurant has a western motif. It also has an appealing "fixin's bar" with items such as fresh sautéed mushrooms and onions. Menu items include cheeseburgers, hot dogs, chicken wraps, salads, barbecued pork sandwiches, chicken salads, chili cheese fries and root beer floats.

The seats are wood with backs and seat cushioning. It can be very tight for wheelchairs to navigate here. Sit on the outskirts to make things easier.

People in wheelchairs can use either of the middle registers.

The Pinocchio Village Haus

This is a building that looks like a Swiss chalet but has mostly Italian food. It's actually very attractive for a counter service location. They serve pizza, fried chicken strips, grilled turkey and bacon panini, Italian sub sandwiches with capicola, ham, salami and cheeses, antipasto salad, macaroni and cheese, and peanut butter and jelly sandwiches.

There is indoor and outdoor seating. Indoor seats are wood with backs. It can be difficult for wheelchairs to maneuver, as it's very tight inside. Outside there are tables with umbrellas and metal chairs with a narrow metal heart frame back and seat cushioning.

People in wheelchairs should use the third register from the left.

Tomorrowland Terrace Noodle Station

The menu here includes chicken noodle bowls with broth, beef and broccoli, vegetarian noodle bowls with tofu and broth, chicken teriyaki, Caesar salad with chicken and fried chicken strips. The interior has hard seats with backs and padded seats.

Disney World Resort Tips

There are many facts and tips for folks with disabilities that can help make your trip smooth and relaxing. We've learned a lot over the many years of staying on Disney World properties.

Hotel choices

Personally, we will only stay at Disney-owned resorts when we go to Orlando. For years we stayed off-property. We thought it would be beyond our reach financially to stay at a Disney resort. When we eventually decided to splurge, we called and found that the pricing was comparable to some of the off-site hotels where we'd stayed.

In general, we have found that there is no comparison to the Disney resort experience. I have to admit that most of the resort rooms are not very large and most are not particularly luxurious, even in the upper-level resorts. What you are paying for is something besides the room that you don't get elsewhere. In the Disney resorts, the themes, amenities, ambiance, generally cheerful and polite service, disability support and perks are just priceless. We would rather stay at the lowest-level Disney resort than at an Orlando off-property better-quality hotel.

In addition to what you experience within each resort, you get many perks. When you use a Disney hotel you are guaranteed entrance to the parks even when they have reached their full capacity. You can charge your meals to your room, send packages back to your resort, participate in early openings and late closings at the parks and enjoy free parking at parks. The Swan & Dolphin hotels offer the same perks even though they are non-Disney resorts. You can use Disney transportation, which is particularly useful if you are using an ECV or wheelchair. Personally I just love that I don't have to drive myself everywhere. That's vacation!

When choosing your hotel, you may want to pick one that is closest to the areas where you will spend the majority of time. For example, we spend a lot of time at Downtown Disney, Epcot and Hollywood

Studios, so we often stay in a Downtown Disney resort to cut down on travel time.

Most of the resorts are quite spread out, so that you will need to either walk or have a wheelchair. The resort designs vary; if you need help determining which would be the best one for you with your particular needs, you can call the Special Reservations line at Disney for advice. Let them know the parks that you plan to visit, and what your particular needs are, and they can help you determine which resorts may work best for you. Call: (407) 939-7807 and press #1 or (407) 939-7670 (TTY).

Disney categorizes their on-property resorts into three levels: value, moderate and deluxe.

Value resorts include:

- Pop Century Resort
- All-Star Movies Resort
- All-Star Music Resort
- All-Star Sports Resort

The value resorts have the lowest rates. The rooms have outside sidewalks with outdoor room entry. We would describe their themes as targeted toward children. The amenities are a blast for kids. However, we have found that we received a much lower level of service and assistance than at the moderate or deluxe level resorts.

Keep in mind that the higher the level of the resort, the better the quality of the amenities. Regardless, if we could not get reservations anywhere else on property, we would still choose a value resort over leaving the property. We would choose the newest of the value resorts, which is the Pop Century Resort. Still, the moderate and deluxe resorts offer more service, which is very important to us.

> *Tip:* If you are looking for a hot tub to relax in during your stay, check to see if the particular resort you are interested in has one. A hot tub can provide some great pain relief. Also, you may wish to call the resort directly just before your trip to make sure the hot tub is in working condition. If not, you may wish to see if you can change to another resort.

The value resorts each have a good-sized food court serving breakfast, lunch, dinner and snacks. They also have Disney stores on their premises selling Disney goods, snack foods, toiletries, and over-the-counter medications such as aspirin. There is no valet parking in these resorts. You'll find the rooms to be quite simple and on the small side at just 260 square feet.

Moderate resorts include:

- Caribbean Beach Resort
- Coronado Springs Resort
- Port Orleans Resort – French Quarter
- Port Orleans Resort – Riverside

These resorts are a good step up from the value resorts in amenities, service and style. Most of the rooms are around 314 square feet. They have outside sidewalks with outdoor room entry. The grounds are more themed and landscaped than the value resorts, and the rooms reflect a higher quality than the value resorts, though I wouldn't call them spacious.

The resorts each have a store, food court, and a lounge serving alcoholic beverages and some snacks. Port Orleans Riverside, Caribbean Beach and Coronado Springs each have a full-service restaurant. Each resort has a main pool, which is very themed, and several quiet pools. You'll also find things like arcades, bicycles and boats for rent and lovely walking paths. Port Orleans has horse and carriage rides in the evenings, and fishing in the mornings. Coronado Springs has a health club where you can get massages.

> *Tip:* If you make use of a massage therapist at any of the Disney resorts and spas, you may wish to ask for someone who has been out of school for at least a couple of years. Sarah tried the spa at Coronado Springs and paid $160 plus a tip for an 80-minute massage. The massage therapist turned out to be fresh out of massage school, and it was not a very satisfying experience. Later we heard that Disney has a company that supplies them with massage therapists. Many of the therapists are newly out of school and inexperienced. Sarah feels that for her it is not be worth the cost unless the therapist is very experienced. If an experienced therapist is not available she'll skip it.

Only Coronado Springs has valet parking. These resorts are extremely spread out, and it can be a lengthy walk to the car if your room is not near a parking lot. You can request to be near your car, but then you may be quite a distance from the resorts dining, pool and other amenities.

Of the moderates our personal favorites are Port Orleans Riverside and Port Orleans French Quarter. We find the condition as well as the themes, amenities and service to be more to our liking in these resorts.

At Port Orleans we particularly love the open-sided boats that take you on a pleasant ride to Downtown Disney. We go there often, so it's very convenient and far more pleasant than any other mode of transportation. These boats are wheelchair accessible.

Both Port Orleans Riverside and the French Quarter properties are huge, but the main buildings and main pools are close together. This makes it easier to get from one place to another if you are using the resort amenities. We always request a room that is closest to the main building and pool to minimize walking.

The main building at Coronado Springs, on the other hand, is quite far from the main pool. The main building contains the restaurants, snack bar, bar and front desk. If you have walking limitations, this resort is a huge challenge. There are no room locations that put you close to the main building and the pool. You will walk a lot no matter where you stay at this resort. There is a small snack/food bar at the Coronado Springs main pool, but there are not many healthy menu choices.

We found overall that we received better service and support in some of the other Disney resorts. Keep in mind that this particular resort is also a convention center. The food here is much more expensive than at the other moderates. However, the quality of the food court is significantly better than at the other resorts, offering far more choices. Also, on the upside for adult travelers, there may be more adults and fewer children here at times. Many people really enjoy the theme and ambiance of this resort.

While the Caribbean Resort is attractive, we find that it does not offer the same level of ambiance and amenities as the other three moderate resorts. Still, it's a great choice for many people who are drawn to that particular theme.

Disney's Animal Kingdom Lodge

Deluxe resorts include:

- Animal Kingdom Lodge
- Beach Club Resort
- BoardWalk Inn
- Contemporary Resort
- Grand Floridian Resort & Spa
- Polynesian Resort
- Wilderness Lodge
- Yacht Club Resort

If we can go all-out with our budget, we choose a deluxe resort. We find that we consistently get very good service in these locations. This makes for a pleasant time, and it can be very helpful when dealing with special needs. We find that it's just easier to get service, special housekeeping requests and any other assistance we need.

We really enjoy the atmosphere and themes of most of these locations. All of the deluxe resorts offer more upscale amenities. Some of them really make you feel like you're in another land, such as Animal Kingdom Lodge, Wilderness Lodge and Polynesian Village. For us, the more heavily themed a resort is, the more we like it. Some of these deluxe resorts go all out. Animal Kingdom Lodge puts you in the middle of Africa with live animals and incredible décor. Polynesian Village is lush and tropical. Wilderness Lodge is like being in a national park in the middle of nature.

The rooms are all interior rooms with inside hallways. Valet parking is available at all these resorts for a fee. You can also self-park, but some of the lots leave you with a very long walk. Don't forget that if you have a disabled sign for your car you can have free valet parking. As with the moderate resorts, these resorts feature one larger themed pool and other quiet pools. The Grand Floridian has a spa.

You'll find many more food choices in these resorts. They each have a 24–hour, counter-service restaurant. They each have at least one full-service restaurant, and many of them are pretty extraordinary. You'll also find some buffets, family restaurants and bars.

Room sizes vary in these resorts and some of the resorts actually have larger rooms available. Here are the approximate base room sizes:

Deluxe Resort	Size by Square Feet
Animal Kingdom Lodge	344
Beach Club Resort	400
BoardWalk Inn	385
Contemporary Resort	394
Grand Floridian Resort & Spa	403
Polynesian Resort	407
Wilderness Lodge	344
Yacht Club Resort	400

Although the Polynesian resort has the largest rooms, and we find it to be very beautifully themed, we tend to stay elsewhere. This is because it's the only deluxe resort that doesn't have a whirlpool. If this is important to you, pick another resort.

On the other hand, the pool at the Polynesian has a zero-entry on one side, which means that you can go into the water the same way as if you were at the beach. The entrance slopes gradually so that you can actually ride a wheelchair right into the water. This feature, in addition to the larger rooms, may make this resort a good choice for wheelchair users. The resort has a water wheelchair that you can use. Just ask the lifeguard at the pool.

Other resorts with a zero-entry pool are the Animal Kingdom Lodge and the Grand Floridian. Both of these resorts have whirlpools as well.

The Contemporary, Wilderness Lodge, Grand Floridian and the Polynesian are all in the vicinity of the Magic Kingdom. All but the Wilderness Lodge have access to the monorail. Still, it's only a short bus or boat ride to get to the monorail. You can also use the buses, and all but Animal Kingdom Lodge have boat service. The Wilderness Lodge has a remote feel to it that's unique. Many people find this resort quite peaceful and beautiful. For some, this more than makes up for the extra time it takes to commute. It is one of our favorite resorts.

In the Epcot area you'll find the Swan, Dolphin, Beach Club, Yacht Club and Boardwalk resorts. Two of these resorts are actually joined together—the Yacht Club and the Beach Club. These resorts have a common pool called Stormalong Bay, which is over 3 acres large. This is a huge pool/water park that has a lazy river, water slide, multiple whirlpools and a sandy bottom. Both adults and children seem to consistently love this pool. It's a great place for adults to relax and for kids to blow off some steam.

Many people love the location of these two resorts. They are within walking distance to Epcot. If you have mobility or if you're riding an ECV you can enter the International Gateway in the World Showcase within minutes. This is especially great after the IllumiNations Show, which is the big fireworks display that happens just before the park closes. You can avoid all the crowds running for the buses, cars and boats, and just take a relatively short walk back to your room. You can take a boat to and from MGM or Epcot as well. From the resorts, you can also take a boat across to the Boardwalk as well as to Downtown Disney to enjoy shopping, dining and entertainment.

On the other end of the spectrum is Animal Kingdom Lodge. This is an amazing place that we find particularly beautiful, especially at night. Even if you're not staying there, it's worth a visit! However, it's in the Animal Kingdom area, making it less convenient to the Magic Kingdom, Epcot and Hollywood Studios area activities. We find that it's worth the extra commute, though. It's another of our favorite resorts.

A few of these resorts do have parking that is extremely far away from your room. For example, at the Boardwalk resort, parking is a long distance from the hotel. You can drop off the disabled person at the entrance and then self-park, or you can use the valet parking.

Other hotels: In addition to the Disney property resorts, there are non-Disney–owned hotels. The Swan and Dolphin are on the Disney grounds. We've found these hotels to be well run and pleasant but not very themed. We would definitely stay in these two resorts again, but we prefer a more heavily themed experience.

There are other hotels that are close to Disney and publicized as Disney resorts. They have many of the same perks available, but they are not actually run by Disney. Our clear preference is to stay on Disney grounds. Disney runs their own resorts with certain standards and practices that make for a great guest experience. We did try one of these off-site hotels in the Disney Marketplace/Downtown Disney area, and it didn't come close to the Disney resorts on any level. Staying in a Disney resort is part of what makes our vacations a true pleasure, and we've decided that it's not worth it to go elsewhere,

> *Tip:* Occasionally we have encountered a reservation agent who did not give us the service we would have hoped for. It's been rare, but it has happened. We suggest that you hang up and try again. It's very unlikely you will get the same person, and chances are the next person will be able to bring you that outstanding Disney customer service. You can call right away or give it some time. It's up to you, but it's unlikely that you'll get the same agent.

Rooms for Guests with Disabilities

All rooms at resorts on the Disney property have doors that are big enough for a wheelchair to pass through. There are also a number of rooms in each resort designed for guests with various disabilities. However, if you are in a wheelchair but don't need any other special aids, a regular room should be just fine. In fact, if you don't need any of the extras in the disabled rooms, we strongly suggest you stick with a regular room. It's best to leave it for someone who really needs it, as there's a limited number of these rooms. These rooms don't really offer you anything extra unless you really have a need for special equipment and accessibility.

Even though all of the rooms are wheelchair accessible, it may be difficult to maneuver a wheelchair within the room. On a recent visit, the room at Wilderness Lodge was so tight that we went down to the front desk to see if we could get a larger room designed for wheelchairs. We were told that even the handicapped rooms were no larger than the room we were in. They suggested we store the chair outside the room, which we did.

For those who must stay in their wheelchairs, you may wish to get a room with one king-size bed instead of two smaller beds. We've been told that this will give you a bit more room to navigate in. You may also wish to consider staying in a resort with a larger room, such as the Contemporary or the Grand Floridian. When you call to make your reservations the cast member can identify the largest resort rooms for you.

When you choose a disabled-equipped room, keep in mind that they are not all the same. You will be assigned a room that will meet your special needs. When you call to make your reservation, they will check on availability for a room with the type of room amenities that you need. These rooms are usually scattered throughout each resort in a variety of locations.

These rooms may include bed accessories, such as beds with open frames, bed railings or rubber bed pads. They also have some beds with lower height. For bathroom support there are rooms with amenities like portable commodes, a bathroom tub with a transfer bench, widened bathroom doors, roll-in showers for wheelchair users, shower benches, wheelchair accessible vanities, bathroom rails and hand-held shower heads.

People with vision and hearing disabilities can request communication support amenities like a bed shaker alarm, a text typewriter (TTY), door knock and telephone alerts, telephone amplifier, strobe-light fire alarm and closed-caption televisions.

If you wish to request one of these rooms, call Special Reservations at (407) 939-7807 and press #1 or (407) 939-7670 (TTY). When you reserve rooms through this office, they will actually place a code on your file to block off a room for you. They will not guarantee a particular location, but they will guarantee the type of room you need.

For those who are sight impaired, the resorts can be easier to become familiar with than the parks. Some of the resorts, such as Wilderness Lodge and Animal Kingdom Lodge, have primarily inside hallways and revolve around a main lobby. Some of the other resorts have a pretty simple design with wide outside walkways. Others are more complex. Particularly if you feel you may be spending time on your own, you may wish to call Special Requests to discuss which resorts will be easiest to navigate. You may wish to request a room that is near the main lobby, the pool and/or the food court.

Special Room Requests

When you call to reserve your room you can make special requests. In our experience, Disney tries to accommodate you, but they won't guarantee that your request will be met. You can make requests that are important to your condition, and requests that just reflect your preferences. It's a good idea to ask for the most important things first. Before you call, it's wise to make a list of your requests and prioritize them. Actually, the fewer the requests you have, the better your chance of getting them met.

Some examples of things people may request include being placed in a particular building or section of a building, being near the restaurants and/or the main pool, and no fragrance in the room before you come. Sometimes they are able to give you what you are hoping for, but not always.

A problem we have run into is that they can lose the special request notes. We don't know how or why, but this has happened to us on several occasions. Although we call several times before our arrival date to confirm our requests are in the system, they have sometimes had no record of them when we arrived. If your requests are simple, that usually is not a problem. They should be able to accommodate you.

For more challenging requests, here's what we do to improve our chances of having our requests granted. First we make our room reservation at the regular number: (407) 939-7630. Then we call the Special Requests number at (407) 939-7807 and press #1 or (407) 939-7670 (TTY). A very nice Disney cast member explained to us that they will put a special code in your file. This way the operations department who assigns your specific room will receive your request sooner than normal. Typically the operations department doesn't get your room request until five days before your arrival. With this special code, they may receive it sooner and can put aside a room for you earlier. By the way, medical requests take priority over non-medical room preferences.

We go even further. Our requests are usually pretty specific and sometimes unusual, depending on the resort. After making our reservation, we call the hotel directly and ask for that hotel's operations department. These are the people who handle the room assignments. Sometimes the operator will just send you to the front desk or general reservations instead. These folks can't help. If that happens we request to be transferred to operations, or we just call again. We persist until we get someone in operations that can help. Honestly, it's been getting more difficult to reach a real room assignment person, but at this writing we've been able to do it with some persistence. If you can't reach operations, skip the next two paragraphs and call the resort directly 4-5 days before your trip.

We find that the people in operations are not usually called directly by the guests. As a result, some have that great Disney customer service attitude, and some just seem a bit annoyed that you called them. Once we reach someone, we ask them to see if someone will confirm that our requests are there with our record.

On occasion we have found a terrific cast member who was willing to go even further by blocking off a specific room for us in advance. However, most of them won't do that. It really depends on the person you get in operations. When you find someone helpful, it's a wonderful thing! At the very least you can confirm that they have your special requests on file.

We then always call again 4-5 days before our trip, and again the day before. We confirm that our requests are there and we ask if they will block off an appropriate room if they haven't done it already. If they've already done it, we call to confirm that our room is still blocked off for us. I realize this may sound like a lot of calling, but we have found that this process makes our check-in far smoother and our trips to Disney much more pleasant.

On the day of our arrival and on the way to Disney, we will often call the front desk from the car. We let them know we are on our way and ask them to check on the room status to see if they have secured what Sarah needs. If not, we ask them to do so. We request an expedited room clean-up if the room is not made up already. Also, we try to get to the hotel as early as possible. We feel this gives the front desk more selection if we must change our room for any reason.

When we first go see our room, if there is anything wrong with it, we call the front desk. They will either try to make things right with the room, or if that's not possible, move us to another room. If your request is reasonable or necessary, we recommend that you be persistent but polite. If you are not happy with the assistance you are getting, request a manager.

Requesting Special Room Locations

When you call to make your reservation, you can request a particular location. Again, there is no guarantee, but they will try to accommodate you if they can. Let them know that your request is being made because of a physical condition.

To give you an idea of what your location special requests can be, we'll share our preferences. We ask to be as close to the hotel amenities as possible. Others may prefer to be close to their car or a bus stop. In many of the resorts the hotel dining, store and pool may be far from the parking lot. Since we use the hotel dining and pool frequently, we tend to request a location that puts us as close as possible to those locations. We also prefer to be on a first floor when we are staying in one of the moderate hotels such as Port Orleans. This is far more convenient for wheelchair use. Another thing we try to do is to get a room in a quiet location if possible. If you're in a heavily trafficked area it's very likely that you'll be woken up late at night or early in the morning by outside noise.

In the resorts that have indoor elevators, we do usually request either a first-floor room or an upper room close to the elevators. If you have difficulty walking, that may be helpful for you. However, some elevators are pretty noisy and you may wish to request a room that's a couple of doors away from the elevator. Keep in mind that some of the rooms near the elevators can be quite far from the hotel amenities. It's kind of a juggling act. Based on the layout of the resort you are in, you may need to prioritize what will be the most important to you. Discuss this with the Disney cast member when you make your reservation. They can give you an idea of the resort layout and help you make your request more specific.

Sometimes the resort will accommodate you with your choice, but during very busy times you may not get the location of your dreams.

Pool Planning

© Disney

Wheelchair in pool at Disney's Grand Floridian Resort & Spa

We love hanging out at the resort pool. When the weather permits, we arrange days just for lounging at the pool. The pools can get very crowded even during slower seasons. The seats can be claimed very quickly in the morning. Sarah is really particular about her lounging spots. She needs shade and to be close to a rest room. On the morning of our pool days, we head right over to the pool before breakfast and claim our seats. We put our towels down—the resort provides them for guests at the pool—and leave a couple of personal items on our chairs that are not of great value. We then go over to breakfast, returning afterwards to our pool lounges.

Many of the resorts have one or more "quiet pools," which some folks prefer. These are usually smaller than the main pool and don't have a lifeguard on duty. These also don't have other amenities such as a hot tub or drink and snack bar. They are often far less crowded, and may be situated closer to your room.

The pools are all heated in the cooler weather. Despite that, it's really too cool in the winter for many Floridians who are shocked by any temperature that's not blazing hot. Those from colder climates seem to be comfortable with the water temperature.

There are a few pools that have zero-entry, which allows you to ride a wheelchair right into the water. These resorts include the Grand Floridian, Polynesian and Animal Kingdom Lodge. The resorts should have a water wheelchair available for guests. Ask a lifeguard at the pool for assistance with this.

Late Check-out

If you have the time, you can request late check-out from the resort. They will often give you a check-out time of 1 PM instead of 11 AM. You can call 1-2 days before your departure to make this request. If they say no, call again. Things change fast at Disney, and we've often gotten late check-out by calling several times.

Late check-out enables us to take a dip in the pool, go back to our room, pack and then leave. We often head to Downtown Disney for lunch after check-out. Instead of just getting up, leaving and heading back to reality, it gives us one more day to enjoy Disney.

If you have rented an ECV from an outside company, you will have to return it to the baggage area for the company to pick it up. Some companies will allow you a late pick-up time. We usually try to get a late check-out of the resort, so we always request a pick-up time for Sarah's ECV that corresponds with the approximate time we think we will actually be leaving.

Canceling Your Room

Room cancellations must be done at least 5 days before you arrival date. If you cancel after that, you will lose your first night's deposit. We have had to cancel several trips because of Sarah's health issues. If you need to cancel within 5 days of your trip, you may wish to consider postponing instead. Disney may allow you to postpone your arrival date, even within the 5 days, without being penalized.

Package Delivery

A nice perk for us when we stay at a Disney property is that you can have your packages delivered to your resort. This way you can shop to your heart's content without having to lug around packages. Of course you can't be leaving that day or the next day. The packages are delivered to the resort store, where you pick them up, usually by the next day.

Allergies & Chemical Sensitivities

When making our reservations and while staying in the room we have made a variety of special requests. Disney will take special requests for allergy cleaning. Let them know what this would include for you. Personally, we request that they don't use pesticides, heavy chemical cleansers or air fresheners. They will even do a particularly complete dusting job for people with dust allergies.

Sometimes we have had our requests honored, and occasionally not. It depends on a lot of variables including the communication ability, customer service skills and time pressures of the reservations and housekeeping departments in your resort. To increase our chances that they will follow through, we call the hotel directly a day or two in advance, and then again while we are on our way to Disney.

Once we are checked in, we have often opted to refuse any housekeeping during our stay. This way we are sure no one will spray anything in the room. Additionally, Sarah brings several pieces of medical equipment to the resort, which she leaves in the room. We feel the equipment is safer if we don't have anyone in there unattended. Still, we have had housekeeping services many times with our equipment in the room, and there's never been a problem.

If we don't want housekeeping, we call the housekeeping department from our room phone, and let them know that we do not want our room cleaned. We then always leave up the "Do Not Disturb" sign. We call housekeeping and request things as we need them, such as extra towels or drinking glasses. They are simply delivered to the room. We either call when we know we will be in the room to take the delivery, or we do it late in the day when housekeeping is no longer cleaning. Be sure to remove the "Do Not Disturb" sign after you call for a delivery so they can deliver your items.

Generally we have found that the rooms do not have any strong lingering fragrances such as floral room fresheners. Of course, this is really subjective because in the world of allergies and chemical sensitivities everyone is different. On one occasion when we first went to our room after checking in, we noticed a strong fragrance coming out of the air conditioning unit. We called maintenance. They came quickly and changed the filter. It took maybe 20 minutes for the smell to completely dissipate. We were told by the maintenance person that they had sprayed the filter with a fragrance at a previous guest's request. Fortunately the fragrance was easy to remedy and disappeared quickly.

One resort, Wilderness Lodge, uses the smell of smoke in its lobby. There is a real gas fireplace inside the lobby that frequently has wood burning in it.

Sarah brings her own pillow with her own pillowcase, as we use fragrance-free detergent on our linens. People with allergies may wish to bring their own sheets.

Pesticides: Disney does use pesticides at the resorts, though you seldom see it being applied. We've seen it once, maybe 15 years ago, being applied outdoors early in the morning. Remember that this is Florida and bugs can be a problem. It's a fact of life for Florida living. Really the only thing you can control for sure as a guest is whether they use it in your room after you check in.

For more details on pesticides in the resorts, please see the Allergies & Chemical Sensitivities at Disney section in the Disney World Overview chapter.

Non-smoking rooms: As of June 1, 2007, smoking is banned in all Disney-owned hotel rooms. It is no longer necessary to request a non-smoking room. We were told that Disney has completely cleaning out all of the rooms where smoking was allowed so that they no longer smell of smoke. It's our understanding that they replaced things that could hold smoke odor such as curtains and carpets. If housekeeping detects the smell of smoke in a room, Disney will charge the guest for the special cleaning of that room required to remove the smoke odor.

If there is a smell such as smoke in your room, maintenance may offer to ozone the room for you. Ozone is a gas that can destroy odors. We actually own two ozone air purification machines. These machines do vary significantly. Some can really destroy odors in a room in a short time, but many machines won't make a significant difference in a couple of hours. Keep in mind that if your belongings are in the room while they run the machine, they will probably smell like ozone.

If you allow them to use ozone in your room as a solution to a smell, remember that you should not be in the room while it's running. Once the room is aired out it should be fine for most people. There are some very sensitive folks who are allergic to ozone. For our home use, we find that it helps us minimize mold and allergens. However, it's usually not a great instant fix for something as strong as a room permeated with cigarette smoke.

Service Animals

If you are brining a service animal to your resort, be certain to let the cast member know when you make your reservation.

Resort Perk - Extra Magic Hours

When you stay at a Disney resort, you can participate in this perk. Every day one park opens an hour early or stays open up to three hours longer in the evenings. Since this is available only for resort guests, the parks are much quieter and the lines are much shorter during those extra hours. Be sure to have your resort ID with you. (Your door key should work.) You also need to have a park ticket for that day.

Keep in mind that on the days that extra magic hours are offered at a park, that park tends to be more crowded during the regular park hours. You'll see a larger share of the resort guests in addition to the non-resort guests. To avoid crowds, you may wish to go to the park during the Extra Magic Hours, but go to a different park during the regular hours.

To check when and where the extra magic hours are, go to www.disneyworld.com or call (407) 824-2222.

Valet Parking

Some of the resorts offer valet parking to guests. If you have a valid Handicapped Parking Permit, they will give you free valet parking. You probably still will want to tip the valet runners, though.

Resort Dining

Almost all of the resorts have a quick-service restaurant, while the moderate and deluxe resorts also have at least one better full-service restaurant. Some of the full-service restaurants are great dining experiences. At many of them you will need reservations for dinner. You can make those at the same time you make your dining reservations for the parks.

Most of the resort fast-food restaurants have decent quality food. Some of it is actually quite good. Most resorts have a food court with a fairly wide variety. We normally bring certain food items to breakfast such as low-carb, low-calorie bagels. There is usually a toaster accessible to the guests, along with a microwave.

We usually have breakfast at our resort before going to the parks. It can be a huge challenge to get breakfast at some of the parks. On the days we stay by the pool, we have lunch there also. We'll often have our lunch put in a bag, and we'll eat by the pool. It's convenient and very relaxing!

In some of the resorts, wheelchairs cannot fit in the queues for food. If that's the case, approach a cast member and ask for help. If there is no one available on the floor, you can ask the cashier for help. They will order your food and bring it to you when it's ready.

You can get kosher meals at the resorts. It's a good idea to verify this at your particular resort when you make your reservations. Some resorts may require your request in advance.

If you have some health needs, you can bring your own food, condiments or snacks. Most rooms have refrigerators, except at the value resorts. However, even at the value resorts, you can request one of their rental units, which are currently $10 per night. Let them know if the rental is for medical purposes, because they can drop the rental fee. Mention that you have to refrigerate food because of a medically necessary diet or that you need to store medication in the refrigerator. Ask for the fee to be waived.

By the way, the majority of the refrigerators in the resorts are those small dorm-room types. They do not have a freezer section. There are ice machines in all the resorts.

Many of the resort restaurants now carry Splenda®, though not all.

Mugs: At the food courts you will find resort mugs for sale. Once you purchase this mug you get unlimited drink refills, but only at your resort, and usually just at that food court. This usually includes coffee, tea, soda, juice and hot chocolate. Depending on how long your visit is and how much you will be drinking, this can save you a lot of money.

Gift Shops

Every resort has a Disney gift shop. In addition to Disney keepsakes, they also have snacks and some things you would find in a drug store. Although most of the snacks are not in the healthy eating category, you can usually find things like nuts or pretzels. They also carry fun foods like donuts, chips and cookies. You can also get some over-the-counter medications, toothbrushes, peroxide, some feminine hygiene products and other necessities.

What Else to Bring

If you are bringing any kind of medical equipment you may wish to bring an extension cord. Another thing Sarah brings is a special pillow that's helpful for her neck. She also brings her own pillowcase for allergy avoidance. She needs several pillows to prop her up as she sleeps for help with pain issues. We usually call housekeeping right away and order extra pillows. There have been times during busy seasons where they could not supply her with the number of pillows she needed. We now bring extra pillows with us.

For those using electrical devices related to sleep such as a C-PAP, most of the Disney resort hotels have an outlet behind the night table by the bed. However, you may wish to check this out before you come, or just bring an extension cord to be on the safe side.

Resort Rehabilitation

On a couple of occasions we've arrived to find that the hot tub was not functioning or was being remodeled. On another occasion the roof on the refreshment building next to the pool was being repaired with intensely loud noise going all day. We've experienced rooms near us being painted with noxious sprays and roof reparations. We learned the hard way that it's a good idea to check in advance for resort repairs and rehabilitation projects.

Call your hotel operations department directly, shortly before your trip. Ask if there will be any rehabilitation going on during your stay. Ask if all facilities are in working order including the pool and hot tub if you plan to use them. If there is something going on we will either try to change resorts, or request a room far from the work.

If you get there and find that something major is not available for use, you can try requesting a transfer to another resort. Once when the pool was not available we requested that we be allowed to use the pool at another resort for the day. Though we were at a moderate resort, we requested the use of the pool at Wilderness Lodge. This is a deluxe resort. We didn't feel the pools at the other moderates compared to the one at which we were staying. They allowed us to do this.

Wheelchair Tip

Most of the resorts do have some doors that will open with the press of a button for wheelchair riders. While you are at other Disney locations you will encounter doors that are not automatic. In fact, your room door will not be automatic. If you expect to be alone at any point, and you are able to get in and out of your wheelchair, bring a door stop or have a Disney hotel representative get you one. You can call maintenance or the front desk at your resort and explain that you need a doorstop.

If you are not able to use the doorstop on your own, you will need to wait for someone to pass by and request that they hold the door open for you. People tend to be very nice and very helpful at Disney, including other guests.

Helpful Websites

www.Diz-Abled.com	Official website of Walt Disney World® with Disabilities.
www.passporterboards.com	Info & boards with *active disabilities board.*
www.wfun.com	Photos of the resorts, parks.
www.wdwinfo.com	Lots of info, photos, and forums including an *active disabilities board.*
http://pscalculator.net	A site with everything you need to know about dining reservations. You can calculate the exact date 180 days prior to your visit falls on. This is the date when Disney allows you to start making dining reservations.
www.wdisneyw.co.uk	Online Disney guide with message boards from the UK.
www.allearsnet.com	Excellent site for all kinds of Disney info.
www.allearsnet.com/pl/diabetes.htm	This section of the previous site is for those with type 1 *diabetes* at Disney World
www.magicalmountain.net	Disney news, discussion forums, park info.
www.magictrips.com	Disney articles, discussion forums, park info.
www.mickeynews.com	Latest Disney news in detail.
www.themouseforless.com	All about how to save money at Disney World.
www.mouseplanet.com	News, info, concert dates, park updates, discussion boards.
www.mousesavers.com	Lots of ways to save money.
www.intercot.com	Disney news, info, tips/rumors, discussion boards.
www.laughingplace.com	News, park info, discussion boards.
www.miceage.com	News & discussion boards.
www.mouseinfo.com	News & discussion boards.
www.mydisneyworld.com	Chat boards, news, facts.
www.tikiman2001.homestead.com	Polynesian hotel info.
www.cassworld.ca	Full of photos, trip reports, even photos of Disney bathrooms.
www.disneysurvivalguide.com	You can purchase a book with games and activities for waiting in Disney World attraction queues.
www.tourguidemike.com	Membership service designed to help you avoid long lines at Disney.

Phone Number References

Special Room Requests Reservations	(407) 939-7807 and press #1 or (407) 939-7670 (TTY).
Guests with Disabilities	(407) 824-5217
Behind the Scenes Tours	(407) 939-8687
Dining Reservations	(407) WDW- DINE or (407) 939-3463
Transportation Information	(407) 939-7433
Park Hours	(407) 824-4321
Main Parks & Disney Switchboard	(407) 824-2222
Boating & Tennis	(407) 939-7529

Contact Us

We appreciate your picking up this book. We hope that it's a huge help to you, and that you have a fantastic trip! We would love to hear from you about your Disney experiences.

Do you have any tips, opinions, suggestions or stories that you would like to share with other Disney World travelers? Email us with your information, and we may include it in future editions of this book. Let us know if you prefer to be referenced by your full name, or just your initials, city and state. Please be aware that by sending a message, we reserve the right to print its contents in our current and future books and on our website. Please feel free to email us here:

info@Diz-Abled.com

Remember to visit us on our website for updates and more!

Visit us at:

www.Diz-Abled.com

We look forward to meeting you there!

Printed in the United States
99851LV00003B/123/A